CRITICAL EXCESS

CRITICAL EXCESS

*Overreading in Derrida, Deleuze, Levinas,
Žižek and Cavell*

Colin Davis

STANFORD UNIVERSITY PRESS

STANFORD, CALIFORNIA

Stanford University Press
Stanford, California

Printed in the United States of America on acid-free, archival-quality paper

Library of Congress Cataloging-in-Publication Data

Davis, Colin, 1960–
    Critical excess : overreading in Derrida, Deleuze, Levinas, Žižek and Cavell / Colin Davis.
        p.   cm.
    Includes bibliographical references and index.
    ISBN 978-0-8047-6306-6 (cloth : alk. paper)
    ISBN 978-0-8047-6307-3 (pbk : alk. paper)
    1. Criticism.   2. Literature—Philosophy.   3. Literature—History and criticism—Theory, etc.   I. Title.
PN81.D374   2010
801'.95—dc22

                                                    2009029772

Contents

Acknowledgments

An earlier draft of parts of Chapter 4 originally appeared in *Studia Phaenomenologica*. I would like to thank the following for help, advice and encouragement: Eddie Hughes, who invited me to give the paper which turned out to be the earliest part of the book; Andrew Bowie, for organising and chairing a seminar in which later parts were presented; Christina Howells, who read some of the material in draft; and Jane Hiddleston, who has been a source of support which I could not even begin to quantify. Some of the material in this book was given its first public airing in a course entitled "Philosophy, Literature and Film" at the Ecole Normale Supérieure—Lettres et Sciences Humaines (Lyon) in 2007. I am grateful to Frédéric Regard for inviting me to give the course and for many subsequent illuminating discussions, and to the students who participated in the course. I would also like to thank John Bodnar for the invitation to give a Branigin Lecture at the Institute for Advanced Study at Indiana University, Bloomington, in November 2008. The title and some of the material from that lecture, "In Praise of Overreading," are used in the final chapter of this book. Ivona Hedin was magnificent in handling the practical arrangements for the lecture; and I thank Sonya Stephens very warmly for her generous introduction on that occasion, and for much else besides. Finally, I would like to express my gratitude to the two anonymous readers of an earlier draft of this book for their helpful and constructive comments.

Preface

"Hermeneutics teaches us . . . to discover and to avoid misunderstandings and misrepresentations, for these have caused much evil in the world" (Chladenius 1985: 64). With these words the eighteenth-century thinker Johann Martin Chladenius succinctly and—one might have thought—uncontroversially summarised the mission of hermeneutics. Its role is to help us understand things properly, or at least to prevent us from getting them wrong. Hermeneutics begins with the realisation that meaning is obscure, not immediately accessible, and possibly also multiple or ambiguous; it aims to counter an unregulated semantic free-for-all by delimiting the field of acceptable interpretations.

This book is about practices of reading which appear, on the contrary, to refuse the hermeneutic regulation of interpretation. What I call *overreading* entails a willingness to test or to exceed the constraints which restrict the possibilities of meaning released by a work. Specifically, the book is about five overreaders—Jacques Derrida, Gilles Deleuze, Emmanuel Levinas, Slavoj Žižek and Stanley Cavell—who in their different ways push the interpretation of literature and cinema beyond the limits of what we might readily expect or accept that a text or film might mean.[1] What is gained in this process, and what is lost? Does it have rules, principles and protocols which can be formulated and applied by others, or would any fixed guidelines betray the radical impulse that made overreading so fascinating, exciting, irritating and frustrating in the first place? Does the overreaders' brilliance as interpreters leave any reason to retain the conviction that some readings are better than others, more or less enlightening, valuable, or true? These are the questions which resonate throughout the book.

What is at stake here can be illustrated by an exchange about the limits of interpretation between Umberto Eco, Richard Rorty and Jonathan Culler published in the book *Interpretation and Overinterpretation* (1992).[2] The exchange begins with a series of lectures by Eco on the relations between texts and readers. Eco proposes what appear to be unobjectionable conditions for interpretation to occur: "If there is something to be interpreted, the interpretation must speak of something which must be found somewhere, and in some way respected" (Eco 1992: 43; see also Eco 1990: 7). So first of all there must be something which is "out there" in the world, available to be interpreted; we must then find it, and respect it, in the sense that our interpretation must be appropriate to it and not arbitrarily imposed on it. Eco provides limits to the range of possible interpretations, but does not unduly restrain it. His use of "something," "somewhere" and "in some way" refrains from pinning down the object of interpretation and the means of interpreting it to specific identities and rules. In this account there is some freedom in interpretation, some scope for imagination and dispute, even if the range of possible meanings is not entirely open. Eco hints here at what he elaborates in the rest of his lectures: a sensible hermeneutic which allows for multiple readings but does not endorse interpretive anarchy. How could anyone possibly object to this in theory or justify departing from it in practice?

And yet, Eco's views do not command universal assent; indeed if they did, this study of critical excess would have no reason to exist. In the exchange following Eco's lectures, the philosopher Richard Rorty and the literary theorist Jonathan Culler immediately take him to task, albeit for quite different reasons. Rorty suggests that Eco's view requires there to be something "in" the text, some meaning and internal coherence, which pre-exists and moulds its subsequent deciphering. However, Rorty insists that "the coherence of the text is not something it has before it is described" (Rorty 1992: 97). It is not possible to separate the text and its meaning from our interpretation and use of it. The notion of overinterpretation is redundant, because it falsely implies that we have a reliable distinction between what is in the text and what is merely supplied by a wilful interpreter, and therefore that we have a measure for ascertaining which interpretation(s) may be correct. In the absence of such a distinction there is no essential difference between reading and overreading, there are just more or less interesting and useful acts of reading.

Culler, on the other hand, accepts that there may be such a practice as overinterpretation, and he sets out to defend it. Moderate interpretation, guided by widely accepted principles and yielding widely accepted results, articulates a consensus which is of little interest. Culler insists that "interpretation is interesting only when it is extreme" (Culler 1992: 110). Extreme interpretation may of course be as dull and ineffective as its moderate counterpart; but if successful it pushes thinking as far as it can go, puts pressure on its objects in order to uncover things which might have remained hidden, and gives fresh insight into language, literature and ourselves. Whereas for Rorty there is no such thing as overinterpretation, for Culler the notion remains valuable because it is through overinterpretation that new questions are asked, new answers discovered and new paradigms created. Eco describes as an "excess of wonder" (Eco 1992: 50) the inclination to treat as significant what might simply be fortuitous; Culler argues that this excess is "a quality to be cultivated rather than shunned" (Culler 1992: 123). Without it we will only incessantly rediscover what we already know. And today's overinterpretation may turn out to be tomorrow's consensus.

This book examines some of the most brilliant and challenging philosophical readers or overreaders of literature and film. The thinkers who feature here bring an exciting vitality to the study of the arts. For many of today's critics, Derridean deconstruction served as a lesson in how to read, even if it was as bitterly repudiated by some as it was eagerly embraced by others. Deleuze wrote powerful studies of Proust, Sacher Masoch and Kafka (the latter with Félix Guattari), as well as articles on numerous other literary authors. Žižek has revitalised the study of popular culture by arguing for its Lacanian resonance. Following Heidegger (whose work is discussed in Chapter 1), these thinkers rank poets and artists alongside or even ahead of philosophers; and filmmakers may enjoy a similar status. Deleuze insists that the essence of cinema is thought (Deleuze 1985: 219), and Cavell argues that film "exists in a state of philosophy" (Cavell 1981: 13). Deleuze wrote two hugely influential volumes on cinema; Žižek has written extensively about popular film as well as the work of directors such as Krzysztof Kieślowski and David Lynch; and Cavell has inspired a new direction in the interpretation of film through the philosophical seriousness with which he reads Hollywood comedy and melodrama.

These approaches may, though, be as bewildering as they are inspiring in that they characteristically depend upon what might appear to be bizarre, disorientating interpretive leaps. Does Nietzsche's scribbled note "I have forgotten my umbrella" really instruct us about the nature of textuality, as Derrida suggests (Derrida 1978: 103–19)? Can Hitchcock really tell you "everything you always wanted to know about Lacan," as we are informed in the title of a book edited by Žižek (Žižek 1992b)? Does the blanket hung up in a motel room in Frank Capra's romantic comedy *It Happened One Night* (1934) invoke the Kantian divide between the knowable phenomenal world and the unknowable things in themselves, as Cavell argues (Cavell 1981: 71–109)?[3] The force of these readings depends upon their dual ability to shock and to persuade. The philosophical interpreters court outrageousness whilst also seeking to create a context which will lend plausibility to their claims.

Each of the thinkers discussed in this book wants to follow a trail of reading as far as it can possibly go in order to reach the most unexpected conclusions. Like Heidegger, they want to accompany literature or film "into the extreme" (Heidegger 1959: 173).[4] But are they good readers? Do they actually tell us anything we might agree is true, or even usefully false, about the works they discuss? In wanting to go as far as possible, do they go *too* far? The key preoccupation of *Critical Excess* is the possibility, the thrill, and perhaps the danger, of overreading. At what point does reading become overreading, and does the distinction help or matter? The judicious respect for the text urged by theorists of interpretation such as Hans-Georg Gadamer and Umberto Eco seems to be cast aside by the thinkers who are examined in detail here. They suggest instead that the best way to respect a text is ruthlessly and brazenly to seek out its occluded potential to signify. The results can be exhilarating and unnerving. But the thinkers in question make no apology for taking the risk of overreading. Their practice depends upon the faith or hope that more is to be gained than lost in pushing meaning beyond the boundaries of common sense.

Despite coming from very different intellectual positions, Derrida, Deleuze, Žižek and Cavell are included in this study because they have all made reading a central part of what they do as thinkers, and they have played an important role in the development of literary and film studies. Levinas serves as a discordant voice. Far from embracing literature as an ally in the work of philosophy, he re-ignites the ancient quarrel between philosophy and literature in strongly Platonic terms. In his account, art promotes a shadow-world of illusion and error, which it is the philosopher's role to combat.[5] In his commentaries on sacred texts, Levinas is often brilliant, inventive and witty; but when it comes to secular works he resists the instruction of literature just as resolutely as others seek to attend to it. Levinas reminds us that philosophy's distrust of the arts has not simply disappeared; and he brings to light what may be implicit in the work of the other thinkers who are discussed here: the ancient quarrel is by no means settled, and the philosophical seriousness which some thinkers now seem eager to accord to literature and film may in fact mask a continuing rivalry.

The exchange discussed above between Eco, Rorty and Culler sketches very effectively the terms of debate about literary meaning which revolves around their conflicting positions: overreading is wrong because it distorts what is actually in the work (Eco); overreading is good because it gives new life to our continuing discussion (Culler); and there is no such thing as overreading (Rorty). This book asks whether there is any way out of this argumentative deadlock. In writing it I have become increasingly convinced that the overreaders I discuss offer a way forward of sorts for the debate about the meaning of art through their practices if not by their arguments. They do not offer decisive ways to resolve the problem of how or whether to police the limits of meaning. If they move the agenda onward it is by inciting us, usually implicitly, not to worry about those limits. The rest of this book examines this claim, first by looking at the key contributions of Plato and Heidegger to defining and redefining the troubled relationship between philosophy and the arts, and then by examining in turn the critical practices of my five overreaders. The final chapter draws together some of their shared characteristics in what I call the hermeneutics of overreading.

This book grew out of my previous study *Scenes of Love and Murder: Renoir, Film and Philosophy* (2009). There, I tried to undertake a philosophical engagement with some of the French director Jean Renoir's great films of the 1930s. To understand what such an engagement might entail, the first chapter of the book examined very rapidly the contributions of Deleuze, Žižek and Cavell to the philosophical interpretation of film. The focus on Renoir did not allow me to develop very far either the general question of the relation of philosophy to the arts or what has become for me the increasingly alluring topic of overreading. The current project attempts to go at least a little further in addressing those issues. I should confess that in the treatment of overreading there is a conflicted interest on my part: I want to follow (in order to enjoy) the daring, exhilarating moves taken by the various overreaders; at the same time I don't want to abandon the skepticism towards them which characterises me as, and condemns me to be, a more pedestrian critic. Derrida says that there is no deconstruction without *jouissance*, and indeed that deconstruction has the effect of liberating *jouissance* (Derrida 1992: 56). I suppose that writing this book is an endeavour to have a share in the *jouissance* of excess without giving up on the more modest pleasures afforded by following in the wake of others' brilliance.

CRITICAL EXCESS

CHAPTER ONE

The Ancient Quarrel:
Philosophy and Literature

"Both poetry and thinking need each other, when it's a matter of going into the extreme, each in its own way in each other's neighbourhood. Poetry and thinking will determine where that neighbourhood has its place, certainly in different ways, but so that they find themselves in the same domain" (Heidegger 1959: 173). Here, Heidegger describes the need of literature and philosophy, or more precisely what he prefers to call poetry and thinking, for one another. Each remains separate; there is no overcoming of the differences between them. And yet they are companions in the journey into extreme places, each drawing strength from the other's specific resources. Literature is not the "other" of philosophy, nor the illustration or the testing ground of its theses, nor a well-earned relaxation after a hard day's philosophising. Literature and philosophy have equal but different, distinct but interdependent, roles to play if we are to release ourselves from ingrained habits of thought, to find again valid ways of dwelling in what, following Hölderlin, Heidegger calls a destitute time (from "Bread and Wine," Hölderlin 1965: 298; quoted Heidegger 1971: 89).

Some readers will have no difficulty agreeing with the claims made in the previous paragraph whilst others may find them blatantly nonsensical. Many philosophers still have little time for literature, and would regard Heidegger's way of writing about poetry as extravagant, portentous, prophetic rather than properly philosophical, or just vacuous. Other philosophers take literature very seriously indeed, finding in it vital sustenance for their own activity. They learn more, it seems, from a book of poems than from the publications of their professional colleagues. In some quarters at least, it is now uncontroversial, banal even, to insist that literature, music or film are places where thought happens. The most brilliant minds garner the intellectual meat from the obscure recesses of Shakespeare, Celan or Hitchcock. Does this mean, though, that the ancient enmity between philosophy and the arts has been overcome? Or, despite all their protests to the contrary, do the philosophers in fact discover only what they already thought, rather than encountering anything genuinely new, in the works they purport to revere with Heideggerian earnestness?

These questions underlie the discussion of Derrida, Deleuze, Levinas, Žižek and Cavell in the following chapters. The current chapter prepares the ground for that discussion by considering what is at stake in the encounter between philosophy and literature. Why does the ancient quarrel *matter* and what is achieved by its resolution? Understanding this entails first of all going back to Plato to see why he outlawed the poets from his ideal republic, and then leaping across the centuries to Heidegger, the key thinker whom some consider to have completed what the Romantics began by achieving the philosophical rehabilitation of poetry.

Plato and the Poets

Let's begin at the beginning, or at least quite close to it. In Book 10 of Plato's *Republic*, Socrates reiterates his conviction that poets should not be tolerated in the ideal city:

Let us, then, conclude our return to the topic of poetry and our apology, and affirm that we really had good grounds then for dismissing her from our city, since such was her character. For reason constrained us. And let us further say to her, lest she condemn us for harshness and rusticity, that there is from of old a quarrel between philosophy and poetry. (607b)[1]

This quarrel, which Socrates also calls the "ancient enmity" (607c) between philosophers and poets, is described as already being "from of old" in Plato's time; yet there is also something inaugural and performative about the *Republic*. It names the quarrel and outlaws the poets at the same time. Socrates is not, though, advocating that the poets should be executed or violently punished. If a great poet arrives in the city, "we should fall down and worship him as a holy and wondrous and delightful creature"; we should "[pour] myrrh down over his head and [crown] him with fillets of wool" (398a), and then we should ensure that he leaves and goes somewhere else. He should be revered, and politely accompanied to the city gates. He may be bad, but he is not evil.

A number of questions immediately present themselves. Why does Plato want to banish the poets? Does he offer arguments which are coherent and consistent? Is his hostility integral to his philosophical system, or is it an unnecessary or temporary aberration? And how does his rejection of poetry fit with what, from our perspective, look like the eminently literary qualities of his own writing? Plato in fact offers several different arguments for hostility towards the poets. However, in the twenty-four centuries since the *Republic* was written, few—even amongst his fervent admirers—have been persuaded that Plato was right, and many have been bemused that such a brilliant philosopher was so blinkered when it came to the arts. Nevertheless, the banishment of the poets in the *Republic*, even if it is not Plato's only or last word on the subject, is directly linked to themes developed elsewhere in his dialogues. In Plato's account poetry is dangerous because it purports to know things of which it is ignorant, and thereby it confuses us in our search for truth.

Some of Plato's misgivings about poetry are adumbrated in the early, short dialogue *Ion*. Socrates' interlocutor in the dialogue is the rhapsodist Ion, a man who makes his living by reciting poetry. Ion specialises in the work of Homer, whom Socrates describes as "the best and most divine of all [poets]" (530b). Reflecting on the nature of poetry, Socrates argues that epic poets are "possessed" (534a) and "inspired" (534b); lyric poets are "not in their senses" when they compose (534a). A poet is, he says, "a light and winged thing, and holy, and never able to compose until he has become inspired, and is beside himself and reason is no longer in him" (534b). Poets do not speak of truths which they have conceived themselves; instead, "it is the god himself who speaks, and through them becomes articulate to us" (534d). If the poet is the interpreter of the gods, the rhapsodist is the interpreter of the interpreter. Socrates then goes on to question what the rhapsodist actually *knows*. Ion concedes that even though, quoting Homer, he speaks of driving a chariot, he does not know the art of the chari- oteer; even though he speaks of healing the sick, he does not know the art of the physician; even though he speaks of catching fish, he does not know the art of fishing. In fact he more or less confesses that he knows nothing. Gamely, though, and apparently unaware of the fun that Socrates is hav- ing at his expense, he insists that the art of the rhapsodist and the art of the military general are inseparable; because his knowledge of Homer is unmatched, he can regard himself as the ablest general among the Greeks. Socrates is not discourteous towards Ion. Indeed he agrees in the closing exchange to call the rhapsodist divine rather than, as we might suspect he is considering, dismissing him as a charlatan who passes himself off as an expert in everything whilst in fact knowing nothing.

In *Ion* Socrates' polite mockery is directed at the rhapsodist, not the poet himself; it is not difficult to see, though, how his comments could quickly be turned into an attack on poetry. The poets are "inspired," "pos- sessed" and "not in their senses" because they are the mouthpieces of the gods; but it is also only a short step from here to say that they are irrational, estranged from clear thought and communication. And the claim that the rhapsodist knows nothing of the arts of which he speaks can easily be extended to the poet whose works the rhapsodist recites. If Ion does not know what it is to be a charioteer or a physician, then neither did Homer. When Socrates turns on the poets, it is in part because they speak without knowing, and thereby make themselves the allies of rumour, falsehood and illusion. In the *Apology*, for example, Socrates compares poets to seers and prophets who do not understand the meaning of their own words. Moreover, they nurture the illusion that they in fact know everything: "I also observed that the very fact that they were poets made them think that they had a perfect understanding of all other subjects, of which they were totally ignorant" (22c). Knowing nothing, they speak as if all wisdom were at their command.

In Books 2 and 3 of the *Republic* Socrates describes the dangers and potential social utility of poetry. Poets tell false stories about the gods and as such they may be morally corrupting. Some stories, even if true, should not be told to the young; at best they should be buried in silence, or revealed only to a very small audience bound to a pledge of secrecy (378a). The right stories, told in the right way, may nevertheless be used by nurses and mothers to help shape the souls of the young, giving them decorous lessons in virtue. So poetry is allowed an important role in education, even if it can be dangerous when it is not properly censored.

Book 10 of the *Republic* resumes the discussion of poetry, and to some extent appears to shift position. Whereas earlier in the work, poetry appeared to be the paradigm of the arts, Book 10 sets up painting as the paradigmatic art, with the painter demeaned because he is the imitator of an imitator: God creates the ideal form of a couch; the carpenter copies that form when making a material object; the artist copies the copy rather than the thing itself and thereby creates images and illusions instead of engendering true knowledge. The attack on poetry is now problematically derived from this account of visual art. Commentators have observed further differences between Book 10 and other parts of the *Republic*. The key term *mimesis* appears to be used in a different sense from earlier in the work: in Book 3 it referred to the imitation of actions, whereas in Book 10 it is used in reference to pictorial representation.[2] The earlier tolerance for the right kind of poetry and the acceptance of its role in education are now replaced by an outright ban; only hymns to the gods and the praise of good men will be tolerated in the ideal city (see 607a). These differences have prompted some to suggest that Book 10 is not an organic, necessary part of the work and may even have been a separate piece of writing which was added later.[3] It is as if some of Plato's descendants were reluctant to believe that his attack on the poets could belong integrally to his system of thought.

It may be, though, that Socrates is not so much contradicting his earlier view as radicalising it. The poet is deemed to be an imitator who does not have real knowledge. He does not genuinely know, for example, about how to be a general or how to make a pair of shoes. Instead, he charms his audience, appealing to its irrational side and fostering its desire for pleasure rather than its rational faculties. So the poet is on the wrong side in the struggle between emotion and reason, between knowledge of the real world and illusion. Poetry is an art of the floating world rather than a pathway to unchanging truths. In Book 10, three distinct arguments are deployed to support the poet's exclusion from the city: like the visual artist, the poet does not have true knowledge of what he depicts, so he promotes a world of illusion; poetry appeals to the lower, desiring part of the soul and by strengthening it may destroy the higher, rational part; and finally, in what Socrates calls his "chief accusation" (605c), which develops the previous point, poetry is morally corrupting, because it encourages us to give in to what is bad and weak rather than to choose the harder path, which leads to the good and the true. A particularly disturbing aspect of the poet's dangerous influence is that, by causing us to be moved by the suffering of others, poetry makes us behave like *women*. Rather than bearing our sorrows calmly, which is the conduct of a man, we praise the poets who move us most (see 605d–e). Reason is male and good, and the domain of philosophy; emotion is female and corrupting, and the domain of poetry. To be overly affected by poetry is to be unmanned.

It is small wonder that Socrates wants rid of the poets; and yet their banishment is not entirely irrevocable. Having described the ancient enmity between poetry and philosophy, Socrates invites the poets to defend themselves: "But nevertheless let it be declared that, if the mimetic and dulcet poetry can show any reason for her existence in a well-governed state, we would gladly admit her, since we ourselves are very conscious of her spell. But all the same it would be impious to betray what we believe to be the truth" (607c). Socrates is torn between love for the truth and an appreciation of the charms of poetry. His ambivalence suggests, perhaps, that the enmity between philosophy and poetry is not definitive, and that poetry may after all be rehabilitated. Socrates appeals to lovers of poetry who might argue its cause in prose: "And we shall listen benevolently, for it will be clear gain for us if it can be shown that she bestows not only pleasure but benefit" (607d–e). Having made what appeared to be a virulent, unanswerable and uncompromising case against poetry, Socrates concedes that he may not have spoken the last word on the matter. Indeed, the later dialogue *Phaedrus* seems to mark a distinct change in Socrates' position. There, Socrates conceives of philosophy as an inspired activity, and therefore closer to poetry than it previously appeared. When he ranks lives in order of excellence, he places at the top "a seeker after wisdom or beauty, a follower of the Muses and a lover" (248d). The poet and lover are now, perhaps, no longer the philosopher's enemies; they may even be his equals.[4]

The question remains: what exactly is Plato doing when he banishes the poets from his ideal city? In two related books, *Love's Knowledge* and

The Fragility of Goodness, the philosopher and classical scholar Martha Nussbaum provides an instructive context for understanding Plato's rivalry with the poets. Dissatisfied with the compartmentalisation of different disciplines, Nussbaum became convinced that literature and moral philosophy are allies rather than enemies. Their concerns are the same even if their languages and styles are different. In fact Nussbaum goes further than this: she regards the style of literature as an integral part of its ethical significance. Style is not merely a decoration, but part of the very texture of ethical engagement. This belief lies behind her account of the quarrel between Plato and the poets. As she explains the situation, before Plato the Greeks did not distinguish between philosophy and literature in the manner that we do now. The epic and tragic poets were understood to be ethical thinkers and teachers, to whom people turned for guidance about how to live. Tragic poetry in particular was committed to what Nussbaum calls "a certain, albeit very general view of human life, a view from which one might dissent," which she undertakes to summarise:

The elements of this view include at least the following: that happenings beyond the agent's control are of real importance not only for his or her feelings of happiness or contentment, but also for whether he or she manages to live a fully good life, a life inclusive of various forms of laudable action. That, therefore, what happens to people by chance can be of enormous importance to the ethical quality of their lives; that, therefore, good people are right to care deeply about such chance events. (Nussbaum 1990: 17)

This view of human life, implicit in the plots, rhythms and language of tragedy, was not shared by Plato, and his rejection of it underlies his wholesale rejection of poetry:

If one believes, with Socrates, that the good person cannot be harmed, that the only thing of real importance is one's own virtue, then one will not think that stories of reversal have deep ethical significance, and one will not want to write as if they did, or to show as worthy heroes people who believe that they do. Like Plato's *Republic*, we will omit the tears of Achilles at Patroclus's death, if we wish to teach that the good person is self-sufficient. Nor will one want to have works around that make their connection with the audience through the emotions—since all of them seem to rest on the belief (a false belief, from this point of view) that such external happenings do have significance. In short, one's beliefs about the ethical truth shape one's view of literary forms, seen as ethical statements. (Nussbaum 1990: 17–18)

The important point here is that the ancient quarrel is not just between philosophers and poets, but between competing ethical positions and the literary forms which are suited to them. In the Platonic-Socratic view, chance events can have no moral impact on a human being's moral worth; in the tragic view, chance events do matter ethically: as moral beings, we are subject to accident and good or ill fortune. Oedipus did not intend to kill his father and sleep with his mother, but he is radically altered in his moral stature for having done so. So the quarrel is as much *within* philosophy, between competing versions of the good, as it is between philosophy and literature. This is illustrated by Aristotle, who is Nussbaum's chief philosophical authority in *Love's Knowledge* and *The Fragility of Goodness*. Plato banishes the poets because they confuse the rational subject in the search for truth; Aristotle, on the other hand, defends the claim of tragedy to tell the truth. Moreover, Aristotle is a philosopher, not a writer of tragedy, and as such he provides Nussbaum with a model of a possible collusion between philosophy and literature, with both disciplines sharing the same values, pursuing them in different styles but to related ends.[5] *Alliance* becomes a key term in Nussbaum's conception of the relation between philosophy and literature. It replaces the Platonic enmity with the possibility of fruitful exchange.[6]

Nussbaum's analysis of the ancient quarrel also provides an account of the "literary" nature of Plato's own writing. Iris Murdoch summarises a prevailing view of Plato's literary merit when she calls him "a great artist" (Murdoch 1977: 87), and Nussbaum also calls him "a literary artist of genius" (Nussbaum 2001: 393). This might be regarded—as it is for example by Murdoch—as a paradox or contradiction: Plato banished the poets, but was himself a creative writer of the first order. For Nussbaum, though, there is no paradox here. Plato's distrust of the poets hinged essentially on a disagreement about which literary forms were appropriate for expressing the true nature of things:

The subject [of the "ancient quarrel"] was human life and how to live it. And the quarrel was a quarrel about literary form as well as about ethical content, about literary forms understood as committed to certain ethical priorities, certain choices and evaluations, rather than others. Forms of writing were not seen as vessels into which different contents could be indifferently poured; form was itself a statement, a content. (Nussbaum 1990: 15)

On this account, Plato was not altogether rejecting literature as we now understand it; rather, he was inventing a new literary form, the dialogue, which could convey his ethical commitment to the power of reason and debate. The dialogue is a kind of theatre which aimed to replace the tragic theatre of Plato's Athens. Instead of appealing to the emotions and subjecting the human good to the whims of particularity and chance, it presents calm debate and rational reflection in search of what is stable and eternally true. It speaks to our reason rather than to our desire or our fear. Plato does not repudiate literature; he re-invents it: "In Plato's anti-tragic theater, we see the origin of a distinctive philosophical style, a style that opposes itself to the merely literary and expresses the philosopher's commitment to intellect as a source of truth. By writing philosophy as drama, Plato calls on every reader to engage actively in the search for truth. By writing it as anti-tragic drama, he warns the reader that only certain elements of him are appropriate to this search" (Nussbaum 2001: 134). In this way, Plato's style and the peculiar literary form which he invents are bound up with his conception of human rationality.

In Nussbaum's account of the ancient quarrel, there is no inherent enmity between the philosopher and the poet. There is rather a rivalry between the world view implicit in certain types of poetry—epic poetry and tragedy—and Plato's moral and epistemological commitment to search for rational, stable truths. The problem with poets is not that they don't think; rather it is that they do think, but they think the wrong kind of things. Their truths, their literary forms, are too much those of the transient world for Plato's liking. They are too dependent on the obscure workings of luck and contingency. For Plato, poetry in its prevalent forms is a dangerous distraction from the proper understanding of what really matters. It entices us to misperceive the world.

If poets are to be banished because they say the wrong kind of things, there are two obvious ways forward which do not involve the total abandonment of poetry. One is Plato's: to invent a new, more placid poetry, that of the philosophical dialogue. The other is to find a poet who will say, or can be made to say, the right kind of things. More than two millennia after Plato, Heidegger resolved Plato's dilemma in his own way. He found Hölderlin.

Heidegger and the Truth of Poetry

Heidegger's meditations on the relation between art and philoso-phy have been greeted by some in hyperbolic terms. Giorgio Agamben, for example, refers to Heidegger's contribution as "the third and deci-sive event" (Agamben 1999: 53) in the history of the divorce between the art and thought, the first two being Plato's *Republic* and Hegel's *Lectures on Aesthetics* (delivered 1820–29). Plato banned the poets because they do not reveal the truth; whilst acknowledging that art had truth-disclosing power, Hegel nevertheless suggested that in its highest function it was a thing of the past. According to Hegel, "art is not, either in content or in form, the supreme and absolute mode of bringing the mind's genuine in-terests into consciousness" (Hegel 1993: 11). Philosophy has now taken over the pre-eminent role. Even if his reasons are quite different from Plato's, Hegel re-affirms the divorce between philosophy and art. It would be for Heidegger to effect their ultimate reconciliation.

In Heidegger's work prior to the 1930s, notably *Being and Time* (1927), art was barely mentioned or discussed in any detail. "The Origin of the Work of Art," first presented as lectures in 1935 and 1936, indicates that his thought was undergoing a re-orientation which made the nature of art, and especially of poetry, paramount amongst the philosophical questions which he believed to be worth considering. From now on, thinking (which is his preferred term for what others might call "doing philosophy") would be strictly inseparable from reading and writing about poetry. At the heart of "The Origin of the Work of Art" is the key claim which bluntly signals the distance travelled since Plato's *Republic*: *"Art then is the becoming and happening of truth"* (Heidegger 1971: 69; emphasis in original). For Plato, art propagated illusion and falsehood; for Heidegger, it is the medium through which truth comes to us. Heidegger follows Book 10 of the *Re-public* by beginning with visual art and applying some of the insights gained from it to poetry; but Heidegger departs radically from Plato's ar-gument. Whereas Plato's poets replicated the painters' estrangement from truth, Heidegger's poets distil the truth of art in its purest form: *"All art, as the letting happen of the advent of the truth of what is, is, as such, es-sentially poetry"* (Heidegger 1971: 70; emphasis in original).[7] Poetry founds truth in a triple sense: as bestowing, as grounding, and as beginning (Heidegger 1971: 72). The poets, it would seem, have fully taken over the role that Plato might have thought was reserved for gods and philosophers.

In the Epilogue to the published version of "The Origin of the Work of Art" Heidegger acknowledges the importance for modern thinkers of Hegel's reflections on art in his *Lectures on Aesthetics*. In particular, Heidegger muses over Hegel's claim that "art is, and remains for us, on the side of its highest vocation, a thing of the past" (Hegel 1993: 13; quoted in Heidegger 1971: 78). For Hegel, writing at the beginning of the nineteenth century, the age of art was over. This did not mean that no further art works could or should be produced; rather, it reflects a view that art is no longer the means by which absolute spirit reveals itself. That role is deemed to have passed back to philosophy. Heidegger suggests that the truth of Hegel's judgement has not yet been decided, and much of the rest of his career was spent in insisting, *contra* Hegel, that art still serves as the place where truth happens. Whereas the Hegelian philosopher should now assume the pre-eminent role in the revelation of the absolute, his Heideggerian counterpart sets himself alongside the poet as separate but equal in the endeavour to hearken to the event of truth.

Heidegger is undoubtedly a major figure, perhaps *the* major figure, in the re-evaluation of the philosophical seriousness of art which underpins the work of the thinkers discussed later in this book. Heidegger's work does not emerge from a vacuum, however, and his approach to poetry would be unthinkable without a long history of post-Platonic reflection upon art, in which, as well as Hegel's *Lectures on Aesthetics*, Kant's *Critique of Judgement* (1790) and the work of the early German Romantics are of particular importance. In his *Aesthetics and Subjectivity* Andrew Bowie argues that a radical transformation occurred in the relationship between art and philosophy between the end of the eighteenth and the end of the nineteenth century, and that much recent philosophy and literary theory are still influenced by that transformation (Bowie 2003: 1).[8] A key factor here is something that Plato resisted, even if he sometimes entertained it as a possibility, namely the linking of art to truth. This entails the acknowledgement that the poet's role is allied to the philosopher's, rather than being in competition with it. Hegel's view of the "end of art" suggested that such a link had existed in the past, but that it is now broken so that the philosopher can assume the leading role in the revelation of the absolute. For the Romantics, the link might be restored in the future. Moreover, the great Romantic aspiration to fuse all the disparate regions of knowledge in one grand synthesis gave a role of supreme importance to art. In his *Critical Fragments* (1797) Friedrich Schlegel foresees that "all art should become science and all science art; poetry and philosophy should be made one" (Schlegel 1988: 191). In his *System of Transcendental Idealism* (1800) Schelling argues that only art sets forth in objective forms the intuitions that philosophy cannot represent directly; and for this reason "art occupies the highest place for the philosopher" (Schelling 1988a: 228).

Two points about the Romantic aspiration are significant in the current context. First, the demand for a future union of poetry and philosophy concedes that they are presently separated: to write poetry is not to do philosophy, even if it should be and one day might be. Indeed, Schelling argues that from Homer onwards there has been a process which has led to "the total polarization of poets and philosophers" (Schelling 1988b: 241). Second, even if art has "the highest place," as Schelling argues, philosophy retains a distinctive role which may turn out to be at least as important as that of poetry. Schelling is speaking here as a philosopher, not a poet: "art occupies the highest place *for the philosopher*." It is the philosopher who accords to art the highest place, and who decides wherein its nature consists and why it is pre-eminent. Art can set forward what philosophy cannot represent, but philosophy can describe what art cannot put into concepts: "Only philosophy can open up again, for thought, the sources of art which are largely dried up. It is only through philosophy that we can hope to manage to give a meaning which only a god can give . . . because it expresses in ideas, in an eternal way, what a true artistic temperament intuits in the concrete, and through which authentic judgement is determined" (Schelling 1978: 397). Poetry may be ideally fused with philosophy, but it is contingently separate. Art may occupy the highest place, but without philosophy its sources are dried up and its truths unexpressed. The bitterness may have gone out of the ancient quarrel, but philosophy still implicitly vies for supremacy with its poetic rival.

Like Schelling, Heidegger does not collapse the distinction between poetry and thought even if each of the two activities has some of the other's qualities and even if they collaborate in the same fundamental task, which is to endeavour to hear the voice of Being. There may be a reunion of poetry and thought, but they are not unified: "All philosophical thinking, and precisely the most rigorous and most prosaic, is in itself poetic, and yet is never poetic art. Likewise, a poet's work—like Hölderlin's hymns—can be thoughtful in the highest degree, and yet it is never philosophy" (Heidegger 1961: 329; quoted Hoeller 2000: 13). Thought may be poetic, but it is not poetry; poetry may be thoughtful, but it is not thought. The poet and the thinker stand on separate peaks, at equal heights and in close proximity to one another, but distinct in their capabilities and roles.

The list of poets whose work Heidegger discusses in detail is in fact far from extensive, and it consists exclusively of authors writing in German. There are Georg Trakl, Rainer Maria Rilke, Stefan George, and especially Friedrich Hölderlin, whom one critic suggests he comes close to deifying.[9] Hölderlin (1770–1843) left behind a body of difficult and often unfinished work. The last half of his life was blighted by mental illness, and his poetry was largely overlooked through the nineteenth century. The early twentieth century saw a revival of interest in him and the preparation of the first complete edition of his work. In a series of essays and lectures from the 1930s onwards, Heidegger reflected in detail on some of his poems. His importance for Heidegger is that he is *"the poet's poet"* (Heidegger 2000: 52; emphasis in original), whose poetic mission is to make poems solely about the essence of poetry.[10] He provides Heidegger with the means to counter the Hegelian view that art's world-revealing role is over. He also shows him how to break with a Greek model of what art should be and to appreciate instead the specific nature and achievements of modern art.[11] For Plato, poetic frenzy might be a sign of the estrangement from thought; for Heidegger, on the contrary, Hölderlin's madness could be taken as what Megill calls "evidence of the depth of his vision as a seer" (Megill 1985: 173). He is the unsurpassable precursor of modern poetry, because he reveals better than anyone else what poetry is for in a destitute age. The historical essence of poetry, which Heidegger finds in Hölderlin's poetry, is the determination of a new time: "It is the time of the gods who have fled *and* of the god who is coming. It is the *time of need* because it stands in a double lack and a double not: in the no-longer of the gods who have fled and in the not-yet of the god who is coming" (Heidegger 2000: 64; emphasis in original).

Heidegger's discussions of poetry are very varied in approach. Sometimes he takes whole poems and discusses them in great detail; sometimes he interrogates individual lines or phrases without reference to the context of the poems in which they appear. He uses biography, etymology, details of grammar and punctuation, textual variants or alternative readings. He invokes these as it suits him and insofar as they fit his overall purpose. His readings do not need to conform to normal standards of academic study because, he insists, they "do not claim to be contributions to research in the history of literature or to aesthetics. They spring from a necessity of thought" (Heidegger 2000: 21). As Paul de Man points out, Heidegger rejects the scholarly editor's preferred reading if it does not suit his interpretation, ignores passages from poems which contradict what he wants to argue, takes words and lines out of context, bases an entire study on a text of dubious authenticity and ignores matters of poetic technique (De Man 1983: 249–50). Nevertheless, de Man concedes that what he calls "Heidegger's heresies against the most elementary rules of text analysis" (De Man 1983: 250) are manifestly deliberate. Heidegger is not interested in elaborating a consistent critical method; nor does he seek approval for his interpretations as "correct" in any conventional philological or literary critical sense. The "truth" that happens in the poem is not a proposition that can be re-formulated and then offered to others for their assent or dissent; it is what the thinker *hears* on encountering the poem. It is not the thinker's concern if others do not also hear it.

Moreover, the poem itself is an act of hearing, as it responds to the primal address of language, which is also the address of Being. Heidegger's understanding of language lies behind his insistence on the related tasks of poetry and thought. He has no time for the view of language as a human expression through which we represent the world to ourselves. Rather, as he puts it, "*language speaks [die Sprache spricht]*" (Heidegger 1959: 12; emphasis in original). We are the instruments of language, not its masters. Both the poet and the thinker understand this, and they endeavour to listen to the commanding summons of language.

In " . . . Poetically Man Dwells . . . ," first given as a lecture in 1951, Heidegger characterises the related but different postures of listening adopted by the poet and the thinker:

Language beckons us, at first and then again at the end, toward a thing's nature. But that is not to say, ever, that in any word-meaning picked up at will language supplies us, straight away and definitively, with the transparent nature of the matter as if it were an object ready for use. But the responding in which man authentically listens to the appeal of language is that which speaks in the language of poetry. The more poetic a poet is—the freer (that is, the more open and ready for the unforeseen) his saying—the greater is the purity with which he submits what he says to an ever more painstaking listening, and the further what he says is from the mere propositional statement that is dealt with solely in regard to its correctness or incorrectness. (Heidegger 1971: 214)

Poets are poets insofar as they listen attentively to the appeal of language. The thinker, as reader of poetry, in turn listens to the poem in the endeavour to hear as purely as possible what the poem recalls. There is an implicit allusion to and reversal of Plato here. Book 10 of the *Republic* describes how the artist is at the furthest remove from the truth because he merely copies what others create or know. In Heidegger's scheme, the poet is closest to the heart of things because he is most attentive to language; the thinker is at a further remove because he attends to the poem rather than directly to what the poet hears. The poet hears language and the thinker hears the poem; each is attempting to dwell in language, but the poet's access to it may be more direct. Heidegger's approach to poetry relies on the related beliefs that the poem may contain insight of which its author was unaware, and that by careful attentiveness its concealed wisdom may be teased out. In these assumptions lies the source of both post-Heideggerian hermeneutics and deconstruction. With reference to Gadamer and Derrida, the next chapter discusses how modern hermeneutics and deconstruction draw on Heidegger's insight into poetry but take it in very different directions.

The immediacy of the poem's access to language does not reduce the thinker to a merely ancillary role. Schelling reserved for the philosopher the capacity to say conceptually what art intuits concretely; similarly for Heidegger, the role of the thinker may be secondary, yet it is no less indispensable. The poem attends to language and speaks of the essence of poetry, but it is the thinker's role to make this explicit to us and to tell us of the essence which the poet himself cannot directly name. The essay "Language in the Poem" on the poet Trakl (first published in 1953) is particularly interesting for its philosophical determination of the poet's activity. The essay begins with a reflection on the dialogue between poetry and thought, and it introduces what will prove to be a crucial distinction between the terms *Gedicht* and *Dichtung*. *Gedicht*, which normally might be translated merely as "poem," is used here to refer to a kind of poetic source from which emerges the actual poem or poetic act, the *Dichtung*. In this dense and deeply complex introduction, Heidegger makes two key, related claims. First he says that "every great poet composes [*dichtet*] out of one single Poem [*Gedicht*]"; second, he insists that "the Poem [*Gedicht*] of a poet remains unspoken" (Heidegger 1959: 37). Every actual, existing poem which a great poet writes circles around the single Poem which cannot be spoken or written. We might immediately ask: how does Heidegger know this? The blunt answer is that we are not invited to ask such questions. Heidegger's pronouncements are not subject to argument, demonstration or disproof. We can take them or leave them.

The scheme which distinguishes between Poem (*Gedicht*), poetry (*Dichten*, the activity of making poetry), the poem or poetic act (*Dictung*) and thinking (*Denken*) reproduces the implicitly anti-Platonic hierarchy to which reference has already been made. At the source stands the Poem, to which poetry comes closest, and which thinking approaches only through the mediation of the poem. Yet the fact that the Poem is unspoken gives authority and necessity to thought. Although poetry is closer to the Poem than thought, it is never fully adequate to it, requiring the assistance of the thinker to articulate what it cannot itself say: "For this reason, every individual poem [*Dichtung*] needs an elucidation [*Erläuterung*]" (Heidegger 1959: 38). The word *Erläuterung* is also used by Heidegger to describe his essays on Hölderlin. It suggests a "making clear," or "stating out loud," implying that it makes audible something that is present but silent in the poem itself. In his preface to the second edition of *Elucidations of Hölderlin's Poetry* (published in German as volume 4 of his complete works), Heidegger indicates what he means by *Erläuterung*: "For the sake of preserving what has been put into the poem, the elucidation [*Erläuterung*] of the poem must strive to make itself superfluous. The last, but also the most difficult step of every interpretation, consists in its disappearing, along with its elucidations, before the pure presence of the poem" (Heidegger 2000: 22). The elucidation, then, is meant as a modest intervention. It makes perceptible what was unspoken in the poem, and then aims to withdraw so that we can experience the pure presence of the poem. The poem has priority, yet it is not quite sufficient in itself. There is a tension here between the assertion that what matters is only the poem itself and the suggestion that the poem needs its elucidator because it cannot speak for itself.

In "Language in the Poem," by making the unspoken Poem (*Gedicht*) into the true referent of the poet's actual poem (*Dichtung*) Heidegger both elevates poetry above thinking and creates a situation in which poetry relies on thought to point to a core of meaning which the individual work itself cannot state. The primacy of the Poem over particular poetic works also justifies his approach in this essay, as he quotes from different poems without paying attention to their detailed contexts. He does not need to refer his extracts to particular poems because, his introductory comments establish, their *true* context is not the poem, but the Poem, to which all individual poetic acts are tributary. Moreover, although the Poem may be unspoken, it is not entirely unavailable to speech. The poet speaks of it as best he can, and Heidegger's whole essay endeavours to bring it into the thinker's language. His resourceful probing of the resonance of poetic utterances opens up the meanings of the works, but also traces them back to a single, self-identical source. Whilst telling us that the language of the poem is essentially open and ambiguous, he also insists that there is an ultimate unity behind its manifold meanings: "The many meanings of the poetic saying do not dissipate into an undetermined multiplicity of senses. The many-meaninged tone of Trakl's Poem [*Gedicht*] comes from a gathering [*Versammlung*], that is, from a Monotone [*Einklang*], which, in itself, remains always unsayable" (Heidegger 1959: 75). The Poem is single, monotonous; its meanings are gathered together in an unsayable unity, about which there is nevertheless a great deal to be said. This is the precise point at which Derrida, who is in many respects a very Heideggerian reader of poetry, departs from his precursor. As will be discussed in the next chapter, Derrida's "disseminal reading [*lecture disséminale*]" entails the resistance to any notion that the multiple senses to be found in the poetic utterance could ever be gathered together, even in some ideal, unspoken Poem. Heidegger's patient exploration of manifold meanings points back to a single source, even if that source can never be simply named; Derrida's practice, on the contrary, spreads outwards in ever-widening circles, without even the regulating fantasy of some ultimate reunion of sense.

The suspicion arises here that Heidegger claims the final word for himself as thinker even when he accords priority or equality to the poet. The poet can never quite utter the Poem which it is his one purpose to say; the thinker may get closer to succeeding. Sometimes, Heidegger suggests that we should merely listen to the poem, opening ourselves up to its profound call. If elucidation is called for, then it should be discreet, reverential and ready to disappear as soon as its work is done so that we can stand again in the pure presence of the poem. Sometimes, though, Heidegger also suggests that the poem fundamentally *requires* interpretation; it is incomplete without the interpreter's intervention, which is thus neither dispensable nor incidental. It needs elucidation because otherwise the unspoken Poem remains beyond our hearing (Heidegger 1959: 38). Indeed, Heidegger finds that this requirement is part of the lesson of poetry itself. Hölderlin's poem "Homecoming" ends with the lines:

Cares like these, whether he likes it or not, a singer
Must bear in his soul, and often, but the others not.
(Hölderlin 1965: 302; quoted in Heidegger 2000: 31)

In Heidegger's reading, the abrupt "not" which ends the poem does not mark the indifference of others to the poet's cares. An interpreting audience is necessary for the preservation and understanding of the poetic word:

By heeding the spoken word and thinking of it, so that it may be properly interpreted and preserved, they [the others] help the poet. . . . But because the word, once it is spoken, slips out of the protection of the caring poet, he alone cannot easily hold fast in all its truth the spoken knowledge of the reserving find and of the reserving nearness. That is why the poet turns to others, so that their remembrance may help in understanding the poetic word, so that in understanding each may have come to pass a homecoming appropriate for him. (Heidegger 2000: 49)

Without the audience the poetic word may not be fully understood. Heidegger finds confirmation of this reading in two lines from Hölderlin's "The Poet's Vocation" with which he concludes his discussion of "Homecoming":

And a poet gladly joins with others,
So that they may understand how to help.
(Hölderlin 1965: 262; quoted in Heidegger 2000: 49)

In "Hölderlin and the Essence of Poetry" Heidegger enlists a variant of the poem "Voice of the People" to draw similar conclusions:

. . . yet there is also a need of
One to interpret the holy sayings.
(Hölderlin 1965: 266; quoted in Heidegger 2000: 64)

It no doubt helps Heidegger in the formulation of his views to find such comments in Hölderlin's poetry, but even without Hölderlin's collusion this need for the thinker's interpretive intervention is essential to Heidegger's conception of the bond between poetry and thought. From the opening of "The Origin of the Work of Art" onwards, Heidegger consistently stresses that the work has priority over the artist; it is the work which makes the artist, not the artist who makes the work. So the poem makes the poet. Because it is language which speaks not the human subject—even if the human subject in question is the most gifted, the most poetic of poets—the poet is at best a brilliant mediator rather than a genuine originator. The poet is not the master of his own activity; on his own, he does not understand his creation. Commenting on Hölderlin's claim that "hints are/From time immemorial, the language of the gods"(from the poem "Rousseau," Hölderlin 1965: 238), Heidegger describes the poet's role: "The poet's saying is the intercepting of these hints, in order to pass them on to his people" (Heidegger 2000: 63). The poet receives something which is not his, and passes it on to others. By "his people" here, we might understand: the true addressees of the messages of the gods, those uniquely capable of comprehending them, that is, thinking readers such as—and above all—Heidegger. The poet himself is not the author of the poem, in the sense that his activity consists in intercepting and transmitting something of which he is not the source; and nor is the poet the addressee of his poem, since he is not able to preserve it and to understand it on his own. In a sense, then, the poem needs the thinker more than it needs the poet: "But often his [Hölderlin's] voice falls silent and exhausts itself. It is not at all capable of saying by itself what is authentic—it has need of those who interpret it" (Heidegger 2000: 63).

Left to itself, the poetic voice cannot say what is authentic. The thinker may be at a further remove from the Poem than the poet, but it turns out that he is its most proper addressee, the agent without whom its dark sayings will go unheard and uncomprehended. Heidegger reverses Plato's hostility towards the poets and places them instead in a position of high reverence. At the same time, Heidegger reverses Plato in a less obvious way. In Plato's dialogues, the demeaning of the poets does not negate some sense, made explicit in *Phaedrus*, that they may be the philosopher's equals; in Heidegger, the highest explicit respect for poetry is shadowed by the implication that the poets on their own, even Hölderlin, are inadequate to their task. One of the themes of this book emerges here. For modern thinkers such as Heidegger and those discussed in later chapters, the ancient rivalry seems now to have been settled; and yet it persists in the form of a tacit re-assertion of the priority of the thinker over the poet. Another, related theme which will return throughout the book is discussed in the next section of this chapter. How far do the thinkers genuinely learn anything from the works they discuss, or are they imposing their ideas on them, all protestations notwithstanding? Is it possible to distinguish between reading, misreading and overreading?

Reading and Overreading

In an epilogue to *Elucidations of Hölderlin's Poetry*, the editor of the German edition on which the English translation is based records a curious exchange of letters. In his paper "Hölderlin's Hymn 'As When on a Holiday . . . ,'" Heidegger makes the following statement: "The text [of Hölderlin's poem] which shall serve here as the basis for the present lecture, and which has been repeatedly checked against the original manuscripts, rests upon the following attempt at an interpretation" (Heidegger 2000: 74). In 1953 a doctoral student named Detlev Lüders wrote to Heidegger querying this sentence. Heidegger seems to be claiming that the text of the poem, which is the basis of the lecture, is in fact grounded in his interpretation rather than the other way around. Surely an interpretation should be based on a text, not a text based on an interpretation. Heidegger wrote back immediately, entirely conceding the point in his opening sentence: "You are right. The cited sentence is impossible in its present version. If there should be a new version I will strike it" (Heidegger 2000: 237). As he continues, though, it seems that Heidegger is a little less wholehearted in accepting that he was in error. Merely to reverse the sentence, so that it would read, "The following attempt at an interpretation is based upon the text," makes it trivial and superfluous; and anyway, Heidegger insists, "The question, what a 'text' is, how one should read it and *when* it is completely established as a text, of course still remains" (Heidegger 2000: 237; emphasis in original). He acknowledges that recent scholarship has shown a quotation he used to be incomplete and sketchy at best, but he asks whether this necessarily makes his interpretation untrue, or even whether the editor's reading is correct. Having begun with a blunt confession that the student was right, he ends with a question which implies that his correspondent may be wrong after all: "Is there a text in itself?" (Heidegger 2000: 237). Two more editions of *Elucidations of Hölderlin's Poetry* appeared in Heidegger's lifetime, and in neither does Heidegger make good on his undertaking to delete the offending sentence. We have no way of knowing whether he forgot or whether he decided after all that he wanted to retain the suggestion that the interpretation has priority over the text.

What is at issue here is the extent to which the thinker more or less wilfully appropriates the poem for his own purposes rather than attending earnestly to its distant, barely audible otherness. Although he wants "to let the poem sing out of its own peace" (Heidegger 1959: 39), Heidegger is fully aware that the commentary might in fact disturb what it is the poem has to say. He refers to "the risk of intruding foreign thoughts" or introducing "something foreign" into Hölderlin's poems (Heidegger 1971: 216; Heidegger 2000: 173). Although he leaves the question open ("This question must be left for further consideration," Heidegger 2000: 173), he also claims that Hölderlin and he are essentially saying the same thing, one "poetically" and the other "thoughtfully" (Heidegger 2000: 65). Hölderlin speaks differently from Heidegger; nevertheless, the thinker claims, "we are thinking that same thing that Hölderlin is saying poetically" (Heidegger 1971: 216). In the preface to the second edition of *Elucidations of Hölderlin's Poetry* Heidegger compares his practice of elucidation to snowfall on a bell, quoting a passage from one of Hölderlin's unfinished poems:[12]

Put out of tune
By humble things, as by snow,
Was the bell, with which
The hour is rung
For the evening meal. (Heidegger 2000: 22)

Just as the snow will be knocked off the bell when it begins to ring, the elucidation "must strive to make itself superfluous" (Heidegger 2000: 22), falling away so that the poem can ring out unhindered. Heidegger observes but does not linger over the poem's claim that the bell is *put out of tune* by the snow. Something about it has been altered, even if it still fulfils its function of marking the hour for the evening meal. As we have already seen, an element in Heidegger's thinking implies that the poem simply *cannot* ring out on its own without the intervention of the interpreting thinker, even if the commentary is one of the "humble things" to which the fragment refers; the poem requires its reader to make clear or say out loud (*erläutern*) the appeal which it conveys, to interpret and preserve its call so that it may be heard properly. It may be that the passage quoted by Heidegger here lays out what the thinker knows but is not always willing to concede, namely that his intervention *necessarily* changes the poem to which he responds.

How far Heidegger genuinely needs Hölderlin or learns from him has been a matter of critical disagreement. Werner Brock argues that often Heidegger and Hölderlin are "merged into one" so that it is idle or senseless to ask what is Hölderlin's and what Heidegger's (Brock 1949: 194–95). Focussing on shifts in Heidegger's work, Julian Young indicates that in his earliest essays on Hölderlin, Heidegger tended to treat him as a thinker who more or less shared his own thoughts, but that subsequently he became more receptive to Hölderlin's poetry, allowing himself to be educated by the poet and to understand his specifically *poetic* achievement (Young 2001: 105). Robert Bernasconi considers the possibility that Heidegger sometimes imposes his own singular voice on the works he reads: "Whenever Heidegger rendered a text barely recognizable, the temptation is to suggest that he was engaged less in a dialogue than in a monologue" (Bernasconi 1993: 137). Allan Megill concurs that Hölderlin may be more of a pretext than a text; through "selective quotation" and "highly strained interpretation," Heidegger "constructs a fictional Hölderlin who is a radical intensification of certain aspect of the actual historical figure" (Megill 1985: 174).

In his article "Heidegger's Exegeses of Hölderlin" Paul de Man is dubious about the extent of Heidegger's debt to Hölderlin. De Man claims that there is no real exchange between Heidegger and the poet, so that—for all his interpretive brilliance—Heidegger imposes a reading on Hölderlin which is exactly the opposite of what the poet actually says (De Man 1983: 254–55). In a detailed argument, de Man picks on a line from the poem "As When on a Holiday . . . ," which Heidegger repeatedly quotes in his commentary on the poem: "And what I saw, may the holy be my word [*Und was ich sah, das Heilige sei mein Wort*]" (Hölderlin 1965: 316). At the end of his commentary, Heidegger concludes that "Hölderlin's word conveys the holy" (Heidegger 2000: 98). De Man points out, though, that the poem uses the subjunctive "be," "sei" in German: the poet does not say that the holy *is* his word; he expresses the aspiration that it *might* express the holy coupled with the knowledge that it *cannot*: "for as soon as the word is uttered, it destroys the immediate and discovers that instead of stating Being, it can only state mediation" (De Man 1983: 259). At this level it is difficult to tell how far de Man is disagreeing over a reading of the poem or over fundamental beliefs about language: for de Man the word mediates and estranges, whereas for Heidegger it speaks of the holy. To use de Man's own terms, for both him and Heidegger the blindness and the insight of their readings are bound up with one another, inseparable from one another because blindness is the condition of insight and insight brings with it its own blindness.

If error is both inevitable and creative, overreading may cease to be a danger and become a strength: it may be only when an interpreter gives up the anxiety of being wrong that anything worth saying will actually be said. On the one hand Heidegger suggests that we should listen to the poem and let it speak for itself (see for example Heidegger 2000: 209); on the other hand he concedes that some more or less intrusive intervention—the snowfall on the bell—is necessary if it is to be heard at all. In "The Essence of Language" Heidegger describes the twin dangers of reading too much into the poem and not going far enough in taking the risks of thought:

The danger exists that we overstrain [*überanstrengen*] such a poem, that is, we think too much into it [*zuviel hineindenken*] and block ourselves off from being moved by the poetic. But to tell the truth there is the even greater danger—unwillingly admitted today—that we think too little and struggle against the thought that the authentic experience with language can only be the thinking experience, the more so as the high poetry [*Dichten*] of every great poem [*Dichtung*] always soars in a thinking. (Heidegger 1959: 173)

Whilst acknowledging the risks which are involved, Heidegger suggests that overstraining the poem is in fact the only way of reading it properly. By attending unwarily to its uncanny call, we respond authentically to the thought of the poem, which, in Heidegger's resolution of the ancient quarrel between philosophy and poetry, is its inner truth. What Heidegger calls "overstraining the poem" is what I am calling here overreading. It is always open to the charge that it distorts or falsifies what it purports to describe, or that it privileges the act of interpretation over due fidelity to what we are supposed to be interpreting. Nevertheless, Heidegger's position is resolute and clear. Between overreading and reading too little he chooses the former. Moreover, since reading and thinking are for him strictly coextensive, to overread is to think more boldly, to push thought further along the way to truth by forcing the poem to disclose its half-unspoken wisdom.

For Heidegger, it matters little in the end whether his interpretive acts might be thought to be misguided or wrong according to normal scholarly criteria. He offers no regulative principle by which correctness or incorrectness could be judged, other than the thinker's and his audience's own sense of appropriateness. Stanley Cavell, who is more like Heidegger than their very different styles and vocabulary might lead us to think, suggests that the point comes where arguments in favour of an interpretation are exhausted and are superseded by what he calls "a bunch of assertions" (Cavell 1984: 162).[13] Heidegger, likewise, effectively says, "This is how it seems to me, this is how I make sense of it." No amount of detailed refutation could damage his readings, because they do not appeal to correctness in any conventionally assessable, verifiable understanding of the term. What matters for Heidegger is the philosophical yield of his readings, not their critical persuasiveness.

This rapid excursus through Plato and Heidegger raises a set of questions which will be the themes of the rest of this book. What do the philosophers learn, what do they have to gain, from their encounters with the arts? Has the ancient quarrel between philosophy and poetry really been settled, or does the rivalry nevertheless continue under less overtly agonistic forms? How far is it possible or interesting to submit the philosophers' work to normal academic standards in order to test their coherence or falsehood? At this level of philosophical brilliance and importance, does it matter whether, in any ordinary sense, they are right or not? What can we learn from their bold, inspiring, outrageous and sometimes implausible encounters with literature and film? The shadow of Heidegger looms very large in the next chapter, which discusses the place of literature and literary hermeneutics in the work of a thinker who is sometimes regarded as a "French Heideggerian": Jacques Derrida.[14] As we shall see, though, Derrida may be indebted to many, but he is disciple to none. His practice as a reader of poetry recalls Heidegger's whilst remaining distinctively his own.

CHAPTER TWO

Derrida, Hermeneutics and Deconstruction

Derrida Reading/Reading Derrida

Jacques Derrida was one of the most admired and reviled thinkers of the latter part of the twentieth century. To some he corroded the foundations of reason, collapsed all values into an anarchical free play, and endorsed an intellectual stance according to which anything could mean anything, so that in effect everything meant nothing. To others he represented a necessary, beneficial challenge to encrusted, latently (and sometimes overtly) violent traditions of thought, giving us the tools to re-think our place in the world, and paving the way for an ethical embrace of the future without simply casting off what was worth preserving of the past. Even admirers do not agree whether Derrida was at his best when he was at his most conventional, rigorously reading the great philosophers of the past, or when he was at his most wild, completely eschewing recognisable scholarly forms of writing.[1] In some cases neither enemies nor supporters had actually *read* a great deal of his work with any care.[2] Even so, the fact that his work gave rise to such contradictory responses dramatically raises the problem of interpretation. What is the truth about Derrida? Would it be possible, interesting, or even desirable to settle the dispute over the meaning of his work?

This question *about* Derrida is also one of the key questions posed *by* Derrida in his long, patient encounters with numerous writers, thinkers and texts. Whatever else he may have been (hero or villain, anti-Christ or saviour, charlatan or genius), he was before all else a *reader*.[3] Almost always, he starts from the position of someone who reads the work of others, developing his views through critical engagement with the texts of his predecessors and contemporaries, amongst whom figure what are normally called both philosophers and literary authors. This chapter begins by considering what it means for Derrida to be a reader of literature, when basic terms such as "reader" and "literature" need to be treated with caution. Then, the chapter looks at what may be regarded as the key encounter or non-encounter between Derrida and Gadamer, in which part of what is at stake is the scope and viability of interpretation. The final section continues the story of this (non-)encounter by examining one of Derrida's late texts, *Béliers. Le Dialogue ininterrompu: entre deux infinis, le poème* (2003). Here, in a tribute to Gadamer delivered after his death, Derrida engages again (perhaps) with the German hermeneutic philosopher and discusses one of their shared interests, the work of the poet Paul Celan. Derrida's book serves to bring out why hermeneutics and deconstruction should and cannot speak to one another, each missing the other when looking for common ground, unable even to agree where the text ends and its interpretation begins.

The most cursory survey of Derrida's writing shows that, to say the least, he is interested in literature, and particularly in a modernist strand of difficult writing including authors such as Mallarmé, Artaud, Joyce, Kafka, Jabès, Blanchot, Celan, Genet, Ponge and Sollers. In his thesis defence of 1980, he states that his interest in "that writing which is called literary" precedes and is more constant than his interest in philosophy (Derrida 1983: 37; quoted in Attridge 1992: 2). So Derrida is a reader of literature. Hillis Miller goes so far as to describe him as, amongst so much else, "one of the great literary critics of the twentieth century" (Miller 2001: 58). On the other hand, Rodolphe Gasché suggests that Derrida's interest in literature "has in his thinking never led to anything remotely resembling literary criticism or to a valorization of what literary critics agree to call literature" (Gasché 1986: 256).[4] Is Derrida a great critic, or someone who never practised anything like literary criticism? In fact, even to describe him as a reader of literature requires qualification, since neither reading nor literature is accepted by him as a secure, self-evident category. He consistently rejects questions of the type "What is . . . ?" (what is literature, what is reading?) on the grounds that the form of the question takes for granted an ontological perspective insofar as it calls for an answer in terms of essences. For Derrida, none of the categories or terms available to us should be taken for granted. In particular, the question "What is literature?" is badly posed because literature does not have an unchanging nature.[5] Rather than the name for a fixed entity, the term "literature" becomes for Derrida, in Simon Critchley's words, "the placeholder for the experience of a singularity that cannot be assimilated into any overarching explanatory conceptual schema, but which permanently disrupts the possible unity of such a schema" (Critchley 2008: 2). What interests Derrida in texts normally referred to as literary is a residue, a remainder or excess which unsettles stable meaning and interpretive control. This is not unique to texts conventionally considered to be literary. Although Derrida certainly does not collapse the distinction between literature and philosophy (as it is sometimes claimed),[6] he nevertheless suggests that, if sufficient critical pressure is applied, a disruptive semantic excess can be tracked in every kind of writing, whether it be Plato, Kant and Husserl or Mallarmé, Joyce and Genet.

Reading is no more stable a category than literature. Derrida is on the whole respectful towards literary critics and scholars, but he has little interest in or time for their work because they overlook what interests him most in texts. In his view both formalist and thematic critics of all varieties attempt in their different ways to pin the work down, to restrain it by identifying its formal features or encoded messages. Contrary to such approaches Derrida's deconstruction is not a critical method amongst others, despite the attempts of some critics to turn it into one; rather, it is an attempt to traverse the *event* of the text in its utter singularity, to stand exposed—and obliged to respond—to its untameable strangeness. Derrida is uncomfortable saying he writes "about" texts, since to do so would imply some degree of interpretive mastery and the identifiable separateness of a critical metalanguage; he prefers to say he writes "towards" them, or "in the face of the event of another's text" (Derrida 1992: 62). He uses the term *countersignature* to characterise the relationship between his writing and the texts to which it responds:

There is as it were a duel of singularities, a duel of writing and reading, in the course of which a countersignature comes both to confirm, repeat and respect the signature of the other, of the "original" work, and to *lead it off* elsewhere, so running the risk of *betraying* it, having to betray it in a certain way so as to respect it, through the invention of another signature just as singular. Thus redefined, the concept of countersignature gathers up the whole paradox: you have to give yourself over singularly to singularity, but singularity does then have to share itself out and so compromise itself, *promise to compromise itself.* (Derrida 1992: 69; emphasis in original)

The relation between text and commentary entails repetition of something that cannot be simply repeated; it involves respect and betrayal, self-surrender and self-affirmation, an absolute demand and the inevitability of compromise. Derrida immediately adds that the word *duel*, by which he characterised the stand-off between reading and writing, was used "a bit hastily" and may not be appropriate (Derrida 1992: 69). His critical language is compromised, not quite up to its task; the old words need replacing, but no new ones seem able to do their job any better. Derrida airs the possibility of "new distinctions [which] ought to give up on the purity and linearity of frontiers. They should have a form that is both rigorous and capable of taking account of the essential possibility of contamination between all these oppositions, those we encountered above and, here, the one between literature and criticism or reading or literary interpretation" (Derrida 1992: 52). But he does not go on to propose such new distinctions. The old terms are not quite right, but new ones are teasingly elusive.

In Derrida's writing there is, then, no theory of literature or reading; if anything, there is a theory of why there cannot be any such theory. "Literature" names something which cannot be contained by rules and principles. It is wayward and uncontrollable, and this is why it demands the attention of the reader. In *Signéponge* Derrida's attempt to characterise the relationship between poem and thing in Ponge's poetry also describes the relationship between commentary and poem, in which the commentary responds to the imperative of the written text. In the following quotation, what Derrida says about *the thing* is equally valid for *the poem*:

The thing [*La chose*] would therefore be the other, the other-thing which gives me an order or addresses a demand to me which is impossible, intransigent, insatiable, without exchange and without transaction, without any possible contract. Without a word, without speaking *to me*, it addresses itself to me alone in my irreplaceable singularity, in my solitude as well. I owe to the thing an absolute respect which comes from no general law: the law of the thing is also singularity and difference. I am tied to it by an infinite debt, an endless duty. I will never be free of it. So the thing is not an object, it cannot become one. (Derrida 1988: 19; emphasis in original)

The poem-thing is absolutely other, it addresses me without speaking to me, it is mute but its silence issues an imperious command, it offers and withholds itself at the same time, it commands us to listen to what does not speak and to submit ourselves to what is never entirely present. Derrida's talk of the text as *law*, imposing debts, duties and responsibilities, places his encounters with literature in the context of ethics. Attentiveness to the texts of others is, for Derrida, tantamount to an ethical obligation. In fact Derrida's ethics is bound to his reading of literature, insofar as both entail the endeavour to preserve and respond to a singularity which speaks from a position of total otherness.[7] Derrida's stance thereby runs directly counter to the view that his version of deconstruction is irresponsible and relativistic, endorsing critical practices in which one can say anything at all. For Derrida, the text imposes a law of absolute fidelity; his anxiety as reader comes from the knowledge that his reading can never be fully faithful. The remainder will always remain.

It is curious that Derrida is so extremely cautious about nearly all commonplace terms and concepts, including (as we have seen) words such as literature and reading, yet he asserts quite dogmatically that for him the text has the force of law. It is as if its otherness is so extreme that it is beyond the reach of deconstruction; it poses searching questions of its readers, but is not itself subject to question. One might say that, rather than treating texts too lightly, Derrida takes them too seriously, uncharacteristically missing the opportunity to interrogate the duty and responsibility they are said to impose on us. Everything is open to doubt here, except the commanding, unspoken law of the Other.

Derrida, then, insists on unstinting attentiveness to the unique specificity of the text, in the endeavour to tease out as much of its semantic capability as possible on any given occasion. The situation is further complicated by the problem of delimiting the frontiers of the text. Eco's rejection of overinterpretation discussed in the Preface relies on the sense that there is something *in* the text which readers should not falsify by imposing on it associations which are entirely their own. But by what criteria do we decide what is genuinely present in the text and what is added by the reader? For Derrida, this question is much more difficult than for opponents of overinterpretation. He is no more in favour of falsifying the text than they are, even if he knows that some element of betrayal is inevitable; but he is less confident about how to draw the line between the inside and the outside of the text. So he can have no assurance about what should be excluded from an acceptable reading, and indeed about what would make a reading acceptable or unacceptable in the first place. This is not just a contingent difficulty which more and better hermeneutic theory might clear away, since it derives from his conception of textuality in general. The text will never be cleansed of its traces and residues, which are also its resistance to interpretive exhaustion. Derrida might agree that we should not arbitrarily impose on texts associations which are not really there, but no established rule can ever settle once and for all what the work truly contains.

The problems of interpretation which this raises, and their consequence for the status of Derrida's own writing, are elegantly illustrated by "J'ai oublié mon parapluie" (I have forgotten my umbrella), the section which closes the discussion of Nietzsche in *Eperons* (1978). This text is certainly playful; indeed it has a postscript dated the first of April, suggesting the whole thing may be an April Fool's joke. But the joke is also entirely serious. Derrida notes that the sentence "I have forgotten my umbrella," contained in quotation marks, has been found in Nietzsche's papers and published. Derrida wonders whether it was a quotation, something Nietzsche had heard somewhere, or something he intended to elaborate on. In any case, there is no way of knowing for certain what he meant by it, or even whether he meant anything by it. Perhaps it wasn't even written by Nietzsche. The phrase is entirely legible, we all know what it means, and yet it remains secretive. It is open to interpretation, for example in psychoanalytical terms, and yet no interpretation will ever be certain to have finally settled its meaning.

To this point Derrida's musings seem reasonable enough, and we might be led to think merely that Nietzsche's editors were over-zealous or naïve to publish the phrase at all. But Derrida then makes two moves which dramatically raise the stakes of his discussion. First, he suggests that *all* of Nietzsche's writing may be like "I have forgotten my umbrella":

apparently readable, but also parodic, undecidable, providing us with no secure context or code for its deciphering, and therefore unreadable at the same time as it gives itself to be read. Then, Derrida takes this suggestion still further: what if his *own* text were also like "I have forgotten my umbrella"? His essay on Nietzsche might be governed by a code which only he knew, or which he himself did not properly understand; even if he told it to us we would never know whether or not to believe him. There might be more, or less, going on in the text than we could ever suspect. So the text would remain "indefinitely open, cryptic and parodic, that is to say closed, open and closed at the same time or in turn" (Derrida 1978: 117). In the course of a few pages Derrida has gone from illustrating the problems of interpreting one of Nietzsche's apparently trivial posthumous fragments to suggesting the inherent secretiveness of Nietzsche's and his own writing, and by implication everyone else's as well.[8]

Derrida consistently resists the charge that his practice of reading is entirely rule-free, allowing the reader to say anything at all and giving equal validity to all interpretations. There are and must be *protocols*, Derrida insists, though he says relatively little about what the necessary protocols might consist in.[9] His stance in this resembles Kant's in relation to the antinomy of aesthetic judgement. According to Kant's antinomy, judgements of taste must be based on concepts, because we expect to reach consensus about them through discussion; yet they seem not to be based on concepts, because they are entirely individual. Kant resolves the antinomy by arguing that there are concepts, but that they are indeterminate (Kant 1974: 196–200). Derrida's protocols of interpretation seem to be equally ungraspable. His insistence that one cannot say simply anything suggests that there are rules for interpretation;[10] but his reticence about what the rules might be suggests that their usefulness as a hermeneutic brake is not substantial. So there are rules, but we don't know what they are. Whether or not we ever will know what they are, even once we have cleared away the clutter and garbage of a misbegotten tradition, remains an open question.

Derrida is nevertheless clear that whatever rules do or do not apply, they will never allow an exhaustive, definitive and complete reading of a text. This exhaustive reading is, he implies, the dream of hermeneutics. In Derrida's writing, following a tendency in French criticism and thought more generally, the word *hermeneutics* is often used to refer to the fallacy of a stable meaning accessible through interpretation. In *Eperons,* for example, he refers to "the hermeneutic project postulating the true sense of a text" (Derrida 1978: 86), and he attempts to steal Nietzsche away from "any hermeneutic question assured of its horizon" (Derrida 1978: 107). As Gary Madison puts it, Derrida refers to hermeneutics as if it "presupposes that a text has a definite, in-itself sort of meaning that it would be the business of interpretation to *reproduce* in as accurate a form as possible, this meaning being the author's intended meaning" (Madison 1991a: 122; emphasis in original). Deconstruction opposes what it portrays as this hermeneutic naivety with its more sophisticated awareness of semantic indeterminacy. It is not difficult to demonstrate that this entails an appalling caricature of hermeneutics as it was developed in the late twentieth century, most importantly by the German philosopher Hans-Georg Gadamer. Gadamer categorically insists that understanding is "not merely a reproductive, but always also a productive relation" (Gadamer 1986: 301), and he repeatedly argues against identifying the meaning of a work with its author's intended meaning. In fact, as some commentators have shown, Gadamerian hermeneutics and Derridean deconstruction have a great deal in common: the acknowledgement of a major debt to Heidegger, a belief that meaning is a matter of language, an interest in interpretation and in particular the interpretation of works of literature, a rejection of the "single correct reading," a sensitivity to ambiguity, and a concern to preserve and to attend to the text's distant otherness. Could it be that a rapprochement might be possible between hermeneutics and deconstruction, despite the simplifying versions they sometimes give of each other? This possibility was tested, and in the view of some commentators frustrated, in an encounter between Gadamer and Derrida which took place in Paris in 1981.

Gadamer/Derrida, Hermeneutics/Deconstruction

The symposium titled "Text and Interpretation" held at the Goethe Institute in Paris in April 1981 provided the first occasion for Derrida and Gadamer to debate their ideas with one another in public.[11] To open what was hoped might be a productive dialogue between two thinkers representing important contemporary trends in philosophy, Gadamer presented a wide-ranging paper outlining his views on literature and interpretation. Derrida, though, seemed less willing to enter into the spirit of the event. His paper on Heidegger's reading of Nietzsche did not explicitly refer to Gadamer at all; and although it touched upon one of the points of disagreement between them (the validity of Heidegger's critique of Nietzsche), it did not address the theoretical questions of textual interpretation discussed by Gadamer. The sense that the debate was somehow failing to occur was reinforced by an improvised exchange between Derrida and Gadamer, which was recorded, transcribed and subsequently published. Derrida asked three questions of Gadamer which seemed to be largely tangential to the German philosopher's argument. In his reply Gadamer complained of being misunderstood and reiterated some of his earlier points.

The debate, as the symposium organiser later conceded, was "improbable" from the beginning;[12] and those who were present as well as those who have subsequently read the published papers almost unanimously agree with Richard Bernstein when he says that "a serious intellectual encounter never really happened" (Bernstein 2002: 276). Critics describe the event in disappointed, even bitter terms. Gary Madison describes Derrida's response to Gadamer as "manifest nonsense" (Madison 1991b: 194, 196). Donald Marshall calls it "feeble" and "embarrassing" (Marshall 1991: 206); Derrida "evaded the danger that he might learn something from talking with Gadamer," and he will now "go about his merry way, jetting here and there and ignoring the whole thing" (Marshall 1991: 207). Although some critics have stressed that there were misunderstandings on both sides of the debate, on the whole Derrida is portrayed as more responsible than Gadamer for the failure of the symposium to achieve a productive exchange between deconstruction and hermeneutics. Derrida gives no sign of even a passing knowledge of Gadamer's work, and he does not refer directly to any of the German philosopher's voluminous writings. So Derrida seems to be trying to prove what some take to be his point, namely that no encounter can take place, by petulantly refusing to engage in dialogue. Since analyses of the exchange are nearly always partisan, taking the side of one or other of the protagonists, those who favour Gadamer can use Derrida's non-engagement as evidence of the frivolity of deconstruction as compared to the philosophical seriousness of hermeneutics. Actually, though, I want to suggest in what follows that Derrida's response to Gadamer is both pertinent and telling, even if in some aspects it is demonstrably based on misunderstanding. Moreover, the exchange between Derrida and Gadamer entails a dense interplay of astute comment, misreading, appropriation and defensiveness. It illustrates the difficulty of establishing an encounter rather than a simple refusal to engage in dialogue on the part of either philosopher.

In his opening paper, "Text and Interpretation," Gadamer explicitly welcomes the occasion for an encounter with French philosophy and in particular with Derrida (Gadamer 1991a: 24). He outlines some aspects of his thought which might be compatible with deconstruction, such as the insistence that the meaning of a work of art cannot be exhausted and the emphasis on the impenetrability of the otherness of the other. But he also describes some areas which might offer leverage for a deconstructive critique, such as his accounts of irony, textuality and the communality of meaning. His concluding discussion of a line from a poem by Eduard Mörike is a kind of gift to potential critics, since it offers a possible testing ground for how his hermeneutic approach might differ from a deconstructive reading. The poem "Auf eine Lampe" (On a Lamp) ends with the line: "Was aber schön ist, selig scheint es in ihm selbst" (What is beautiful, however, shines blissfully/seems blissful in itself). The interpretive crux here is the German word *scheint*, which might mean either *shines* or *seems*. In discussing this line from Mörike's poem, Gadamer is intervening in and trying to resolve a famous disagreement between Heidegger and the critic Emil Staiger. In a lecture and subsequent exchange of letters with Heidegger, Staiger read *scheint* as *seems* whereas Heidegger insisted that it should be read as *shines*.[13] Gadamer sets out to determine which is the correct reading, because, he says, every double possibility of understanding is "an offence" (Gadamer 1991a: 50). The problem can be resolved with the help of the hermeneutic principle that the larger context should decide the issue. In his following discussion Gadamer shows that for conceptual, historical, generic, thematic and rhythmic reasons, *scheint* in this context must mean *shines*: the poem tells us that in the work of art the beautiful shines out. With the problem thus definitively resolved, Gadamer concludes: "The interpreter, who gives his reasons, disappears—and the text speaks" (Gadamer 1991a: 51). The aim of the interpreter is to efface himself by bringing forth arguments which allow the text's meaning to emerge.

Gadamer exposes himself here, I think deliberately, by providing plenty of grist for a deconstructive mill. He foregrounds a number of moves with which it would be relatively easy to take issue: the attempt to eradicate ambiguity rather than to explore its resonance, the implication that all the broader contexts can be adequately pinned down and reconciled with one another, the concluding suggestion that the interpreter can stand aside and merely listen attentively as the poem speaks. One might even say that, in order perhaps to provoke discussion, Gadamer simplifies his own hermeneutic position, as he asserts the poem's meaning much more decisively than his theoretical work, notably *Truth and Method* (1960), actually allows or requires. Gadamer seems to be challenging his audience to counter his reasoned, reasonable interpretation with something more wildly poststructuralist. Without trying to envisage exactly what that might entail, one might begin by asking why Gadamer is so keen to remove ambiguity from Mörike's poem. The problem of how to read *scheint* might be taken as a key to the poem's appeal. Through its double meaning, the poem simultaneously says two things which exclude one other: in the work of art beauty shines out genuinely *and/or* it is a mere appearance.[14] What this means might be a starting point for interpretation rather than its conclusion. A poststructuralist might prefer to explore the poem's self-contradiction rather than accept Gadamer's judicious resolution of its ambiguity.

However, in his reply Derrida did not pick up on the more obvious points which Gadamer offered for debate. Instead, to Gadamer's apparent bemusement, he chose to focus on the question of good will, to which "Text and Interpretation" had referred only casually. Derrida's "Three Questions to Hans-Georg Gadamer" is characterised by some as a non-response *not* because he doesn't respond to Gadamer's paper, but because he doesn't respond to those aspects of it which seemed most overtly to call for a response. But anyone who is surprised by this has little understanding of how Derrida typically works. His approach often entails seizing on something which seems marginal and then showing it to be a part of a tightly knit web of ideas and associations. An apparently inconsequential detail might provide a means of throwing new light on the text to which it belongs. So Derrida poses three questions to Gadamer, all to do with good will. Taken together these questions, and Gadamer's response to Derrida's response, show a great deal about what is at stake in the encounter or non-encounter between the two thinkers.

1. Derrida preludes his first question by referring back to Gadamer's paper, which had mentioned the importance of good will in interpretation. Gadamer had said that the same fundamental condition obtains for written conversation and oral exchange: "Both partners must have the good will to try to understand one another" (Gadamer 1991a: 33). Derrida begins by implying that no one could possibly disagree with this, even though his rather circuitous formulation implies that there might after all be some grounds for questioning it: "How could anyone not be tempted to acknowledge how extremely evident this maxim is?" (Derrida 1991a: 52). The commitment to the desire for consensus in understanding is, he says, an axiom of ethics; it regulates disagreement and misunderstanding and confers dignity in the Kantian sense. This leads to Derrida's first question: if the axiom is unconditional, doesn't it make of the will a "last resort" or "ultimate determination" (Derrida 1991a: 52)? Referring again to Kant and then to Heidegger, Derrida suggests that this way of thinking belongs to a particular epoch, "namely, that of a metaphysics of the will" (Derrida 1991a: 53). Derrida's move here is to find an axiom that it so fundamental that no one would think to doubt it, not even himself; he then suggests that this point, which is absolutely beyond question, may nevertheless be worth interrogating, precisely because the presuppositions it hides are so fundamentally embedded in our habits of thinking. Perhaps they are hiding something that could usefully be disinterred.

Gadamer replies politely to the questions addressed to him, but he immediately puts the blame on Derrida for any misunderstanding and claims for himself the intellectual high ground:

Mr Derrida's questions prove irrefutably that my remarks on text and interpretation, to the extent they had Derrida's well-known position in mind, did not accomplish their objective. I am finding it difficult to understand these questions that have been addressed to me. But I will make an effort, as anyone would do who wants to understand another person or be understood by the other. (Gadamer 1991b: 55)

Gadamer here reproduces a familiar objection to Derrida and deconstruction. In "The Deconstructive Angel" (first published in 1977), M.

H. Abrams had argued that practitioners of deconstruction contradicted their theoretical belief in the indeterminacy of language, because they had determinate things to say which they wished to communicate to their audience.[15] In echoing this view, there is a hint of impatience in Gadamer's response. He wants to engage in a dialogue, but Derrida is spoiling it by being so difficult to understand. Yet Gadamer's position here also entails a degree of defensive smoke-screening. He says he had "Derrida's well-known position in mind," but gives no indication of what this position is, on what topic, and where it might be that Derrida elaborates it. In fact, Gadamer shows no more knowledge of Derrida's texts than Derrida does of Gadamer's.[16] So Derrida's "well-known position," whatever it is, is vaguely defined, unlocateable, and possibly not actually held by him. Gadamer claims to know what it is Derrida thinks, even though he shows knowledge of none of the French philosopher's texts and admits that he does not understand him when he speaks. Locked in a version of the hermeneutic circle, he says he wants to make the effort to understand, whilst suggesting that he has in fact already understood everything he needs to know.

In what follows Gadamer makes little real attempt to understand Derrida's point. Instead, he insists that he has been misunderstood, and flatly denies the pertinence of Derrida's question. It was, he suggests, a mistake on Derrida's part to refer to the Kantian concept of good will, since what Gadamer clearly had in mind was the quite different Platonic notion, which is "completely unrelated" to the Kantian version (Gadamer 1991b: 55). He "absolutely cannot see" that this has anything to do with metaphysics, and it has "nothing at all to do with ethics" (Gadamer 1991b: 55). He seems exasperated that Derrida should associate questions of metaphysics and ethics with a simple aside about good will. And to prove his point, he appeals to Derrida's desire to be understood:

Even immoral beings try to understand one another. I cannot believe that Derrida would actually disagree with me about this. Whoever opens his mouth wants to be understood; otherwise, one would neither speak nor write. And finally, I have an exceptionally good piece of evidence for this: Derrida directs questions to me and therefore he must assume that I am willing to understand them. (Gadamer 1991b: 55)

Gadamer can't believe that Derrida would disagree with him, and indeed he doesn't. But by resorting to common-sense axioms which no reasonable person could question ("Whoever opens his mouth wants to be understood"), he misses Derrida's point, which is to question whatever is so self-evident that it seems unquestionable, to find the hidden presumptions which are lurking inside it. If good will is necessary for understanding, it is singularly lacking *on both sides* in this mutual misunderstanding about what is meant by good will.

2. In his second question Derrida continues to probe the status of good will as the axiomatic underpinning of interpretation and understanding. Derrida asks what would happen to the notion of good will if psychoanalytic hermeneutics were integrated into a general hermeneutics. This, according to Derrida, "is just what Professor Gadamer was proposing to do last evening" (Derrida 1991a: 53). Psychoanalysis problematises the primacy of the will by conceiving all human experience as inflected by the hidden workings of the unconscious, so it might radically transform a theory of understanding based upon the presumption of good will. In reply, Gadamer asserts bluntly that Derrida has misunderstood him:

Now also I do not believe I have been understood if one attributes to me a desire to integrate a psychoanalytic hermeneutics—that is, the process by which an analyst helps a patient to understand him or herself and to get over his or her complexes—into a general hermeneutics, and to extend the classical-naïve forms of understanding over into psychoanalysis. My aim was quite the reverse: to show that psychoanalytic interpretation goes in a totally different direction. (Gadamer 1991b: 55–56)

Gadamer's limitation of psychoanalytic hermeneutics to what takes place between an analyst and an analysand surely simplifies Derrida's point, since Derrida is presumably referring to the way psychoanalysis has transformed the way we think about human actions, experiences and meanings more broadly. But this misunderstanding returns Derrida's misunderstanding of Gadamer's aims. Gadamer is certainly right that Derrida misrepresents what he had said in "Text and Interpretation." In his discussion of psychoanalysis and what Paul Ricoeur calls the "hermeneutics of suspicion," Gadamer argues that "it is a mistake to privilege these forms of distorted intelligibility, of neurotic derangement, as the normal case in textual interpretation" (Gadamer 1991a: 40). Rather than integrating psychoanalytic and general hermeneutics, Gadamer wants to keep them separate. Psycho-analysis should be regarded as a special case which does not have decisive consequences for the general theory of interpretation.

So in this instance Gadamer is without doubt justified in claiming that Derrida has got him wrong. Derrida seems to be ascribing to Gadamer what is in fact more like his own project. This does not mean, though, that Derrida's question is without pertinence. Can Gadamer's Platonic notion of good will really survive the test of psychoanalysis without being transformed? Can "normal" interpretation really be kept separate from the psychoanalytic hermeneutics of suspicion? Gadamer concedes that for Ricoeur there is no radical break between the two forms of interpretation; but by concentrating on Derrida's misrepresentation of his intentions, Gadamer avoids confronting the real challenge of his question.

3. Derrida's third question concerns, he says, the underlying structure of good will. He asks whether the precondition of what Gadamer calls *Verstehen* (understanding the other), "far from being the continuity of *rapport* (as it was described yesterday evening) is not rather the interruption of *rapport*, a certain *rapport* of interruption, the suspending of all mediation" (Derrida 1991a: 53). Derrida is raising the problem of alterity in hermeneutics; and lurking behind his question there is, I suspect, Emmanuel Levinas's description of the relation with the other as a "relation without relation [*rapport sans rapport*]" (Levinas 1961: 329). In "Text and Interpretation" Gadamer had asked how "the communality of meaning ... and the impenetrability of the otherness of the other mediate each other" (Gadamer 1991a: 27). Otherness is impenetrable, but it can nevertheless be *mediated* in the shared-ness of shared meanings. Derrida implies, rather, that the otherness of the other remains intact despite the attempt to understand and to appropriate it, allowing of no mediation which would bring it back to a common world. Interpretation would thus be about preserving difference rather than about overcoming it through consensus and correct understanding.

In his reply, Gadamer treats Derrida's question as if it were primarily of a practical nature. What he calls "the solidarities that bind human beings together and make them partners in a dialogue" by no means assure understanding and agreement: "Of course we encounter limits again and again: we speak past each other and are even at cross-purposes with ourselves. But in my opinion we could not do this at all if we had not travelled a long way together, perhaps without even acknowledging it to ourselves. All human solidarity, all social stability, presupposes this" (Gadamer 1991b: 57). Gadamer accepts that in practice understanding may not be achieved; but he reiterates the insistence that its underlying condition is the communality of shared experience rather than, as Derrida suggests, the utter otherness of the other. Nevertheless, in a series of articles following this exchange, Gadamer returns to this problem, acknowledging its pertinence even if he does not concede Derrida's point. Referring to "Derrida's qualms about my venture in thought," he considers the possibility that hermeneutics assimilates otherness even as it endeavours to preserve it: "Is there not in hermeneutics—for all its efforts to recognize otherness as otherness, the other as other, the work of art as a blow, the breach as breach, the unintelligible as unintelligible—too much conceded to reciprocal understanding and mutual agreement?" (Gadamer 1991c: 97). Later, he again refers to Derrida's objection that "understanding always turns into appropriation and so involves a covering-up of otherness" (Gadamer 1991c: 119). On both occasions Gadamer recognises the relevance of Levinas to Derrida's point: "One can learn from Levinas how serious this objection is" (Gadamer 1991c: 97); "Levinas, too, values this argument highly, so it is definitely an observation that one cannot dismiss" (Gadamer 1991c: 119). Whilst accepting the seriousness of the point, however, Gadamer does not yield his position, nor does he offer any fresh arguments to support it.

Contrary to how they are sometimes characterised, Derrida's questions to Gadamer are astute and far-reaching, even if, notably in the case of the second one, they are not grounded in a proper understanding of Gadamer's thought. Gadamer's replies reiterate the need for good will in order to understand the other, yet he either misses the thrust of Derrida's points or merely reasserts his position. Moreover, he seems to have been more worried by the exchange than Derrida, since he continues to reflect on it in a series of subsequent articles: "Letter to Dallmayr" (1985), "*Destruktion* and Deconstruction" (1985) and "Hermeneutics and Logocentrism" (1987) (all reprinted in *Dialogue and Deconstruction*). Although in these articles Gadamer returns to some of the issues raised in his exchange with Derrida, in none of them does he show any greater direct knowledge of Derrida's texts than Derrida showed of Gadamer's. He also disconcertingly continues to imply that he knows what Derrida thinks, or would think, without providing any supporting evidence. As we have already seen, in his "Reply to Jacques Derrida" he refers to "Derrida's well-known position" (Gadamer 1991b: 55), without saying what that position is, where it is formulated or how it came to be well-known. He also claims to "understand very well" why Derrida invokes Nietzsche (Gadamer 1991b: 57); and he tells us what "doubtless Derrida thinks," adding with crude irony: "and I am hoping he will excuse me if I try to understand him" (Gadamer 1991b: 57). In the later articles he continues to attribute views to Derrida, suggesting that he knows Derrida's views and effectively speaking in his place without quoting any of his actual texts. At one point Gadamer enunciates a clear guideline which he endeavours to apply in relation to Derrida: "One must seek to understand the other, and that means that one has to believe that one could be in the wrong" (Gadamer 1991c: 119). Gadamer describes this endeavour as "a virtue" and "a nonnegotiable moral achievement" (Gadamer 1991c: 120). It implies a responsiveness and responsibility to the other, the readiness to accept that one's position may be incorrect, and in consequence the willingness to change oneself and one's views. But does Gadamer actually live up to his own axiom and entertain the possibility that he may be wrong? He takes Derrida's voice away from him and speaks in his place; and he repeats views he has already expressed without significantly shifting them. If some were disappointed at Derrida's apparent reluctance to engage in dialogue with Gadamer, I am not convinced that Gadamer is any more receptive to the challenge of the deconstructive other, even if his manner is more conciliatory.

The differences between Gadamer and Derrida reproduce some elements of the debate around overinterpretation between Eco, Rorty and Culler discussed in the Preface. In effect, an excessive critic is set off against a reasonable one. Gadamer's hermeneutics, like Eco's conception of interpretation, is intuitively persuasive: it is open but not anarchistic; it respects tradition but is not overwhelmed by it; it allows interpretive freedom but not nihilism; it is not narrowly prescriptive but neither does it endorse limitless free play. The exchange between Gadamer and Derrida over the status of otherness illustrates the gulf between an overreader and a critic more concerned with achieving consensus. For Gadamer, the otherness of the other may be impenetrable, but it is nevertheless not an absolute block to the possibility of understanding; for Derrida, it is precisely because the other is *totally* other that it makes a demand for understanding which is both irresistible and impossible to meet.

Those who have studied the stand-off between hermeneutics and deconstruction tend to express regret that Derrida and Gadamer did not engage more openly with one another's positions; yet commentators tend also to reproduce the non-encounter in their own writings. Derrida is portrayed as too frivolous and even nihilistic, denying the possibility of truth and thereby encouraging a hermeneutic free-for-all; or Gadamer is depicted as a "closet essentialist,"[17] too dependent on prejudice and the authority of tradition. These accounts call for defences and counter-accusations: Derrida may indeed be playful, but play for him is never merely trivial; Gadamer does respect tradition, but he understands it as something which must be acknowledged rather than blindly obeyed. Gadamer's argument is proved right by the very fact that Derrida wants to be understood; or alternatively Derrida and Gadamer's failure to dialogue with one another proves Derrida's point about the inaccessibility of the other. As Robert Bernasconi sums up the debate, "misunderstandings plague the encounter between Gadamer and Derrida," and "the fault is not one-sided" (Bernasconi 1991: 236, 237). Just as good will seemed to be lacking in the exchange about good will, the attempt to understand the nature of understanding was littered with misunderstandings.

Derrida Reading Gadamer Reading

In 1981 and subsequent decades, the opportunity for an exchange between Gadamer and Derrida seemed to have been irrevocably missed despite some further public appearances together. Gadamer's death in 2002 (at the age of 102) surely signalled the end of the matter. Yet Derrida was not someone to let death get in the way of a discussion. In 2003 he gave a lecture in memory of Gadamer in Heidelberg, published the same year under the title *Béliers. Le Dialogue ininterrompu: entre deux infinis, le poème*. The debate, it seemed, was back on, with Derrida claiming to have got more from Gadamer, and still to be capable of learning more from him, than had previously been apparent. Derrida's renewed engagement with the now-dead Gadamer entails, once again, an intricate texture of respect, appropriation and difference; but now Derrida tries to turn the very missing of the encounter into a fresh and vital intellectual resource.

Béliers consists of a short introduction followed by five numbered sections. In the introduction Derrida expresses his admiration and friendship for Gadamer, and sadness at his death. He also muses on the melancholia which marked their relationship, and refers to their first meeting in 1981: "Our discussion had to begin with a strange interruption, something other than a misunderstanding, a sort of prohibition, the inhibition of a suspense. . . . At that time I remained astounded. I spoke very little to him, and what I did say was only indirectly addressed to him. But I was sure that a strange and intense sharing had begun. A partnership perhaps" (Derrida 2003a: 10). Derrida's reflections here may seem anecdotal and inconsequential, but actually he discreetly introduces some of the persistent themes of his later thought and some of the topics that will be explored in the main part of the lecture and book. Friendship, mourning and death are issues he discusses at length in other contexts;[18] and *Béliers* will return in particular to the issue of melancholia and the interruption which is at the origin of discussion. Moreover, Derrida makes a decisive move by conceding the apparent failure of the 1981 encounter, but re-narrating that failure as the starting point of something shared, which he here uncharacteristically calls, following Gadamer, a dialogue. So this apparently low-key, personal opening raises some of the issues which Derrida will go on to discuss. By looking at the five following sections of *Béliers* in turn, I want to suggest that the book is much more tightly and coherently structured than it seems at first, and that Derrida constructs within it the possibility of engaging seriously with Gadamer whilst differing from him significantly.

1. The first section sets some of the terms of a dialogue with Gadamer. To begin, Derrida says he is pleased to use Gadamer's word *dialogue* because it allows Gadamer to speak through him. Just using the word gives to Gadamer a voice, which Derrida will preserve in his text by going on to quote from various of Gadamer's essays. He then refers again to the 1981 encounter. As in the introduction, he claims that the apparent failure

of the discussion was in fact its success, describing it as "that encounter which was in my opinion all the more fortunate, if not successful, for having been, in the eyes of many, missed"; he goes on: "It succeeded so well in being missed that it left behind an active, provoking trace, promising more future than would have been the case with a harmonious, consensual dialogue" (Derrida 2003a: 14). This is both a tribute to Gadamer and a fundamental departure from his views. Dialogue succeeds in its failure because it retains its power to provoke, not because it tends to agreement or understanding. This approach characterises the treatment of Gadamer in the rest of *Béliers*. Derrida does not expound Gadamer's works in order to achieve a settled understanding of them; rather, as he quotes from them, he uses them to stimulate his readings. In his own term, he is "countersigning" them. In the rest of this first section he begins to weave a web of themes: the uncanny, in the Freudian sense of that which is both familiar and strange, the untranslateability of poetry, melancholia and singularity. He quotes his third question from the 1981 encounter and insists on the importance of the *interruption* between self and other, suggesting that it is the inaugural condition of dialogue rather than an event which curtails it.

2. Derrida begins the second section by quoting the final line of the poem by Paul Celan which he will spend most of *Béliers* discussing: "Die Welt ist fort, ich muss dich tragen" (The world is gone, I must carry you) (Derrida 2003a: 25).[19] He explains that the decision to talk about Celan is an act of homage to Gadamer, since Celan was one of their shared interests. Both Gadamer and Derrida had published short books on Celan: *Who Am I and Who Are You?* (1973) in Gadamer's case, and *Schibboleth pour Paul Celan* (1986) in Derrida's. Talking *about* Celan is, then, a way of talking *to* Gadamer, in a reading which Derrida describes as "an interpretation which is anxious, shaken or shaking, perhaps anything other than an interpretation" (Derrida 2003a: 26).

Derrida explains his decision to begin with the final line of the poem he is going to discuss with reference to Gadamer, and in particular to a comment from *Who Am I and Who Are You?*, which consists of interpretations of a sequence of poems by Celan first published in 1965 as *Atemkristall* (Breath-crystal). Derrida's attention is held by the commentary on a five-line poem:

WEGE IM SCHATTEN-GEBRÄCH
deiner Hand.

Aus der Vier-Finger Furche
wühl ich mir den
versteinerten Segen

(PATHS IN THE SHADOW-ROCK
of your hand.

Out of the four-finger-furrow
I grub for myself the
petrified blessing)
(Celan 1983: 18; Gadamer 1997: 95)

Gadamer's commentary is only three paragraphs long, and in his discussion of it Derrida quotes almost all of the first and final paragraphs. Gadamer's opening words justify his decision to begin with the poem's last line, which in turn will be copied by Derrida as he lingers over the final line of his chosen poem: "Following hermeneutical principle, I begin with the emphatic concluding verse. For it contains the core of this short poem" (Gadamer 1997: 95). Derrida quotes, and to some extent elaborates on Gadamer's reading. Gadamer describes the desire for a blessing from a benefactory hand; yet the blessing, "sought after with the grubbing and despairing fervour of an indigent" (Gadamer 1997: 95), can only be petrified. Derrida stays close to Gadamer's text by quoting from it extensively; even so, he also *intervenes* in the text he is quoting. Introducing a sentence from Gadamer's first paragraph, Derrida marks a development in Gadamer's reading: "He then risks a audacious step. Through this vision, he proposes to read a reversing or subversive scene of reading" (Derrida 2003a: 33). Here, Derrida claims that the "audacious step" is Gadamer's. However, in Gadamer's text, it is the *poem* which acts boldly, not the commentator: "Accordingly, the benefacting hand is inverted boldly into the hand where palm-reading can reveal a message of beneficent hope" (Gadamer 1997: 95).

Derrida's misattribution of the "audacious step" reveals an important divergence between himself and Gadamer. For Derrida, the commentator must be bold to bring out the boldness of the text; Gadamer, on the contrary, sees no such daring in what he is doing. The boldness is the poem's, not his. Derrida dramatises the commentator's intervention, whereas Gadamer plays it down as he endeavours to let the poem speak. This divergence is indicated again later in Derrida's account of Gadamer's commentary when he refers to his "risky questions [*interrogations risquées*]" about the poem (Derrida 2003a: 36). In the context of Derrida's text, the adjective *risky* seems to carry a positive charge, and it also picks up an element of Gadamer's vocabulary. Gadamer describes his attempt to interpret Celan's poems as "risky" (Gadamer 1997: 134); he refers to "the risk borne by interpretation" (Gadamer 1997: 136) and "the risk that one sometimes misunderstands" (Gadamer 1997: 144). Yet Gadamer's risk is quite different from Derrida's. It is the risk of *error*. He is prepared to stick his neck out, and he knows he might get it wrong; Derrida suggests, on the contrary, that it is only by sticking one's neck out that the commentator stands any chance of teasing out the poem's potential to signify. Discreetly but surely, Derrida is making Gadamer sound a little more like himself—the bold deconstructor rather than the cautious hermeneut.

So Derrida intervenes in Gadamer's text even as he quotes it directly. This is most evident in his treatment of the conclusion to Gadamer's commentary. In the last of his three paragraphs Gadamer poses a number of questions about the poem which remain unresolved in his reading of it. This is of the utmost significance to Derrida: "Allow me, in order to underline the firm decision to leave the undecidable undecided, to quote this whole paragraph which concludes without concluding" (Derrida 2003a: 36). In his final paragraph, Gadamer says that, regarding for example who the "You" of the poem is, "the poem does not decide" (Gadamer 1997: 96). Quoting this, along with the rest of the paragraph, Derrida silently adds emphasis: "the poem *will decide nothing* on the question of knowing who is the 'You' here" (Derrida 2003a: 37). Derrida is normally scrupulous at indicating whether emphasis is in the original or added by him. In this instance, though, he does not state that the emphasis is his. By making the emphasis look as if it is Gadamer's, he suggests that Gadamer is drawing more attention to the poem's indecision than is in fact the case. This respect for the poem's openness is what Derrida most admires in Gadamer's commentary: "More than the indecision itself, I admire the respect shown by Gadamer regarding the indecision. It seems to interrupt

or to suspend the deciphering of reading but in truth it assures its future"
(Derrida 2003a: 37). Derrida can now endorse Gadamer's designation of
dialogue as an infinite process and assimilate it to his own position; for
both thinkers, it seems, the poem contains something "unforeseeable, un-
translatable, almost unreadable," a "trace" which will survive the attempts
of all readers to decipher it (Derrida 2003a: 39).

By focussing on one paragraph and stressing one phrase within it,
Derrida gives the impression that Gadamer's approach is closer to his own
than is in fact the case. Gadamer certainly insists that interpretation is ongoing and endless, and that any attempt to establish the unambiguous and
definitive meaning of a Celan poem would be fatally misguided. Unlike
E. D. Hirsch, for example, in his version of hermeneutics Gadamer does
not attempt to provide firm guidelines for arriving at correct interpretation. He strives to achieve a philosophical understanding of the process
of understanding rather than a hermeneutic method which might regu-
late reading. Nevertheless, *correctness* remains a persistent ideal, even if he
knows that it may not be reached. His foreword to *Who Am I and Who
Are You?* describes the fraught endeavour to make sense of Celan's poems:

One must ponder, guess, restore—until finally one will have deciphered, will read
and hear—perhaps even correctly. Without such careful deciphering no one can
believe that he or she is capable of saying or knowing anything about the message
of these verses, let alone the language in which they are written. In bearing witness
here to an extended acquaintanceship, this reader believes he has found "sense" in
these dark characters—not always an unambiguous sense, not always a "complete"
sense. In many cases, he has deciphered merely a few passages and offered some
vague conjectures about how to mend the gaps of his understanding (not of the
text). (Gadamer 1997: 63)

So something like correct understanding may be achieved, even if it cannot be guaranteed. In Gadamer's readings, Celan's poems are conceived
as coherent and precise, even if their meaning is not always fully grasped.
They have a "unity of meaning" (Gadamer 1997: 128); even their ambiguity and indeterminacy have a sense which can be established with some
confidence. Gadamer bases his commentaries on the claim that "I believe
I have more or less understood these poems" (Gadamer 1997: 128). "More
or less" leaves room for debate, error or uncertainty; but even so, there is
something in Celan's poems to be understood, and Gadamer thinks he has
found it.

Derrida quotes Gadamer carefully, but also selectively, picking out elements which speak to his own interests whilst saying little about what might contradict them. If Gadamer begins with the final line of the poem because it reveals the "core" of the work, Derrida follows Gadamer's lead in order to put on display the elusiveness of any such core. This second section of *Béliers* is important because it establishes an exchange of sorts. Gadamer is allowed to speak from beyond the grave, but also subtly manoeuvred so that his approach is more conducive to Derrida's. In most of the rest of the book Gadamer is not as explicitly present as he is in sections one and two, though the approach to poetry which Derrida claims to have derived from Gadamer will inform his reading of another poem by Celan. In the tense mixture of respect and infidelity which characterises his relations with all the thinkers he most admires, Derrida will both follow Gadamer's lead and advocate interpretive moves that Gadamer would not have countenanced.

3. In section three Derrida finally begins the reading of the Celan poem that will occupy the rest of the book. Referring to Gadamer's *Who Am I and Who Are You?*, Derrida writes that "it is as if I were allowing myself timidly [*timidement*] to slip a postscript into it" (Derrida 2003a: 43–44). His ambivalence towards and appropriation of Gadamer is indicated in this phrase. To add a postscript to Gadamer's work looks modest, in that it accepts a secondary, dependent position; but following the logic of supplementarity that Derrida had brilliantly analysed years earlier in *De la grammatologie* (1967), it also suggests that the work is unfinished in itself, and that it can be completed only by the addition of something external to it. The word *timidly* also belongs to a string of references which are highly ambivalent. Later Derrida refers to "what I will have the *temerity* to put forward now" (Derrida 2003a: 45; my emphasis), recalling the "audacious step" attributed to Gadamer in his reading of Celan. And later again, Derrida curtails his formal analysis of the poem on the grounds that it is "not very risky" (Derrida 2003a: 54), picking up his and Gadamer's references to the risk of interpretation. So Derrida is timid but also rash, putting himself in Gadamer's lineage but also implying, perhaps, that it is Gadamer who is the timid one.

This suspicion is strengthened by Derrida's references to hermeneutics in this section. Derrida follows some of the concerns of Gadamer's

Who Am I and Who Are You?, particularly when examining the temporality and use of pronouns in the Celan poem he discusses; at the same time, he is categorical about the limitations of hermeneutics. He describes formal and thematic approaches as indispensable, but contrasts them with his own "disseminal reading-writing [*lecture-écriture disséminale*]" which turns towards "a remainder or an irreducible excess" in the poem (Derrida 2003a: 47). Hermeneutics, he claims, cannot account for this residue: "The excess of this remainder eludes any gathering together in a hermeneutics. That hermeneutics is made necessary by it, it is also made possible by it, as here it makes possible, amongst other things, the trace of the poetic work, its abandonment or its survival, beyond any particular signatory and any determinate reader" (Derrida 2003a: 47–48). Derrida seems still to be using the term *hermeneutics* as he did in *Eperons* to refer to the fallacious endeavour to establish a work's proper meaning. Even though in the previous section of *Béliers* he had stressed the openness of Gadamer's interpretation, he still thinks of hermeneutics as the attempt to foreclose meaning. He portrays his approach as being more comprehensive because it incorporates the search for meaning, but also attempts to account for what makes hermeneutics possible and necessary, whilst also impeding its final success. So, after a brilliant, detailed analysis of some formal and semantic aspects of Celan's poem, Derrida brings this stage of his reading to an end because, as already quoted, it is not risky enough. Hermeneutics may be interminable, but it is also strangely limited and blinkered:

This response [the hermeneutic response], this responsibility, can be pursued infinitely, in an uninterrupted way, it goes from meaning to meaning, from truth to truth, without any calculable law other than the one assigned by the letter and the formal organization of the poem. But although it is overseen by the same law, for ever subjected to it as it is responsible, the experience which I call disseminal undergoes and assumes, through the hermeneutic moment itself, the trial of an interruption, of a caesura or ellipsis, a breach. Such an opening belongs neither to meaning, nor to the phenomenon, nor to the truth but, making them possible in their remainder, it marks in the poem the hiatus of a wound of which the lips never close or come together. (Derrida 2003a: 54)

What Derrida timidly called a postscript to Gadamer has, within the space of a few pages, declared its dissatisfaction with any hermeneutic project. It is time to do something else.

4. Derrida begins section four of *Béliers* by announcing the desire to be faithful both to "the hermeneutic demand" as well as to "that singular alterity" on which the search for communicable meaning falters (Derrida 2003a: 57). Derrida will attempt "timidly" (Derrida 2003a: 57) to pick out some of the elements of the poem. He finally names the *bélier* (ram) which gives his book the title. To be sure, the German word which it translates, *Widder*, had already been quoted as early as page 26, since it occurs in the poem Derrida discusses; yet its link to the title of the book was not explained, and would therefore only be available to readers familiar with German. In case we might have thought that the rams here could be Derrida and Gadamer, clashing horns over the interpretation of Celan, Derrida now goes on to examine the resonance of the word. The ram may be a sacrificial animal, a battering ram, or a sign of the zodiac (Aries). These associations open up numerous further links. The ram may evoke the biblical ram sacrificed by Abraham after he had been led to believe he should kill his son Isaac, or the ram which God tells Moses that Aaron should sacrifice to expiate the sins of Israel. Derrida explores these and other possibilities before returning, at the end of the section, to the final line of the poem, "Die Welt is fort, ich muss dich tragen" (The world is gone, I must carry you). Picking up once again the question posed in the title to Gadamer's book *Who Am I and Who Are You?*, Derrida wonders who the I and the You of this final line might be, and he suggests that they are all the figures, named and unnamed, who might be evoked in the poem: the ram, Abraham, Isaac, Aaron, their descendants, God, the poem and its reader. As Derrida probes it ever more searchingly, the poem makes itself available, entrusts itself to its reader, even as it remains enigmatically, unrepeatably singular. It speaks of, and enacts, the non-relational relation between self and other through which something like a responsible dialogue occurs without the shared ground of understanding or consensus.

Derrida's performance in this section, which is likely to delight some readers as much as it irritates others, illustrates the divide between himself and Gadamer. In *Who Am I and Who Are You?* Gadamer argues that the common source of failure in interpretation is "that one obstructs one's way to the poem by attempting to understand it on the basis of something external, something brought in from the outside, or even one's subjective impressions" (Gadamer 1997: 144). We should distinguish rigorously between what is genuinely *inside* the poem and what is external to it. Like much else in Gadamer, this seems sensible and intuitively right. Yet from Derrida's perspective it only works if we have a rock-solid sense of what is inside and what is outside. Is the reference to the sacrifice of Isaac inside Celan's poem, or merely read into it by Derrida? Is Derrida bringing out something which is latently present, or abusively imposing his own subjectivity on the poem? By what criteria would we resolve these questions? Gadamer's recommendation that we should not bring in anything external to the poem is caught in a hermeneutic circle, in that it presupposes that we already know, or at least know how to ascertain, what is in the poem and what is not. Derrida has no such assurance. So, he may alight on Gadamer's reference to interpretation as an infinite process, but he gives it an emphasis which Gadamer does not. Gadamer knows that there is a risk to interpretation, the risk that he may be wrong, yet his aim is still to achieve some degree of correctness, so that he can confidently announce "I believe I have more or less understood these poems." At this point, interpretation is, if not curtailed for ever, at least stilled for the time being.

It would be unimaginable (to me, in any case) for Derrida to announce that he had more or less understood Celan's poems, or even a single poem, or even a single line or a single word of a poem. Derrida's characteristic anxiety as a reader is that there is never enough time to address the poem as patiently as it demands: "We *cannot* do here what we *should* do . . . . Its plurivocity would demand hours and years of deciphering" (Derrida 2003a: 59–60; emphasis in original). Gadamer looks forward to the time when he as commentator can withdraw and let the poem speak; for Derrida there will always be something *other* to find in the poem, so the commentary can never come to rest in the quiescence of settled understanding.

5. Yet commentary must, of course, come to an end, even if only because the commentator runs out of breath, time or listeners. Derrida begins his fifth and final section by promising his audience "a simulacrum of a conclusion" (Derrida 2003a: 71). He simultaneously knows that he has not said nearly enough and that he has gone on too long: "I wouldn't want to abuse your patience" (Derrida 2003a: 71). In his final pages he sketches five points, all linked to the line "Die Welt ist fort, ich muss dich tragen." In these closing points, what is at stake in the poem escalates rapidly. The

first two points relate to the word *tragen*, to carry or bear. Derrida notes (a) that *tragen* evokes an address to the future, insofar as a mother bears a child and (b) that it might also entail an address to the dead or to a ghost insofar as it suggests mourning (Derrida uses the French expression *porter le deuil*, to wear or carry mourning) and melancholia. Three final points relate to this dual possibility of reading, and each is now linked to the name of a major thinker. With reference to Freud, Derrida develops the theme of melancholia, which he had introduced in the second sentence of his book in relation to Gadamer. In what is for Freud the "normal" process of mourning, the grieving subject overcomes the loss of the dead other. Derrida insists instead on the necessity of melancholia, since it entails a refusal to get beyond grief and thereby it is the only way of clinging to the lost other. Derrida next invokes Husserl. The poem's claim that "Die Welt ist fort, ich muss dich tragen" is confronted with Husserl's claim in his *Cartesian Meditations* (1931) that the other is an *alter ego*, another self accessible in an originary intuition. When the world is lost, there is no common ground which makes of self and other merely interchangeable versions of one another; I bear the other, but do not incorporate her or include her in myself in any direct act of comprehension.

Finally, Derrida looks to Heidegger's reflection on *die Welt* (the world), and particularly to his attempt in *The Fundamental Concepts of Metaphysics* (lectures delivered in 1929 and 1930) to distinguish between what is *weltlos* (worldless), *weltarm* (poor in world), and *weltbildend* (world-forming). Heidegger argues that the stone is worldless (there is no sense in which it "inhabits" the world), the animal is poor in world (it inhabits the world but has only limited access to it) and man is world-forming (he can constantly extend the range and manner in which he relates to the world). But one line of Celan's poem throws doubt on Heidegger's patient analysis. Derrida suggests that Celan's "Die Welt ist fort" exceeds and problematises Heidegger's distinctions. If the world is gone, the distinctions between worldless, poor in world and world-forming fall away. Where does this leave us? Derrida ends with a final reference to Gadamer, the dead other with whom he would have wished to discuss these problems, and a quotation from the poet Hölderlin: "Denn keiner trägt das Leben allein" (For no one bears life alone) (from "The Titans," Hölderlin 1965: 395; quoted in Derrida 2003a: 80).

This final section of *Béliers* is brilliantly, outrageously provocative. Having worried away at Celan's poem for some time, Derrida now takes a single, and one might think wholly opaque, line and makes startling claims for its philosophical reach. It resists and challenges Freud, Husserl and Heidegger in some of the key areas of their thought. What Derrida offers here is not really a reading of a poem; rather, it is a virtuoso demonstration of how, when a poem is exposed to minute scrutiny, it comes to pose more and more searching questions of its reader. Derrida wants to encounter, and to countersign, the poem's unnerving strangeness rather than to hear a thematisable message. And his concluding section is teasingly, knowingly rapid. After a slow beginning, he brings his discussion to an abrupt conclusion, or "simulacrum of a conclusion" (Derrida 2003a: 71), drawing attention to how much analysis still remains to be done. Heidegger's distinctions between worldless, poor in world and world-forming must be questioned, but Derrida defers this urgent enquiry to another time: "For reasons on which I cannot elaborate here, nothing seems to me to be more problematic than these theses" (Derrida 2003a: 79). More remains to be said; the dialogue is not finished.

This insistence on keeping the dialogue open entails both receptiveness and infidelity to the other. Whilst declaring his reading to be a postscript to Gadamer's book on Celan, Derrida's approach here is anything but Gadamerian. The postscript effectively disavows the script, even as it calls for the necessary but now impossible response of the dead interlocutor. In his reading of Celan, Gadamer remains modest in front of the work, careful to exclude errors in his reading and to find only what is there so that he can finally stand back and let the poem speak. For Derrida, the stakes of the poem are greater than they could ever be for Gadamer. His *timidity* before the poem, which at another moment he also calls his *temerity*, is neither a sense of the commentator's inferiority nor a fear of falsifying the work; rather, it is an anxiety about being inadequate in face of the poem's exorbitant call. It is not so much a question of shadowing the poem in a faithful commentary as the urgency of encountering in it something which is singular and unrepeatable, and which demands thought to the precise extent that it resists appropriative understanding.

Does *Béliers* make up for the missed encounter between Derrida and Gadamer in 1981? Derrida's reply is adamant: *the missed encounter is a suc-*

cessful encounter. It succeeds because it fails. Understanding and agreement are not the conditions of the encounter, because the common, shared world they require is not assured. Celan's poem asserts that "Die Welt ist fort": there is no shared world, only a profusion of inscrutable singularities. So the condition for successful-failed encounter is the interruption between self and other, which ensures that *something happens*, even if what happens might not readily be described as understanding. The melancholia which is named so insistently in *Béliers* is an attempt to preserve the lost other, to keep tangible the sense that the other cannot be assimilated but that proximity to its unspeakable strangeness can nevertheless be maintained. This is, Derrida insists, an *ethical* position; it does not diminish the gap between self and other, and it does not consign the other to oblivion: "So melancholia *is necessary*" (Derrida 2003a: 74; Derrida's emphasis). The poignancy of the missed encounter is that it is only *as missed* that it remains open to the future ("But I was sure that a strange and intense sharing had begun," Derrida 2003a: 10). The melancholia of Derrida's text derives from its endeavour to maintain the breach that preserves the other as other; and the other here may be Gadamer whilst he was alive or after he has died, as it may be Celan's enigmatic poem. In all cases, the endeavour is not to curtail what Derrida, following Gadamer, calls a dialogue, but to trace the dark sayings and residues which keep it going.

Rather than to understand the poem, or the other, Derrida wants to let its enigma resound, ratcheting up the stakes of non-comprehension as he goes. Perhaps Derrida's commentary tells us more about him than it does about Celan's text. But to be sure of this would mean already to have resolved those questions that Derrida strains to keep open: what is inside the poem and what is outside it, what does it mean to encounter, to interpret and to understand otherness, and how can something speak in the poem which resists the claims of critical method? Derrida welcomes Gadamer's view of interpretation as an infinite process, and he embraces it more eagerly than Gadamer himself. This shows up a crucial difference of emphasis between hermeneutics and deconstruction, at least in their Gadamerian and Derridean forms respectively. Hermeneutics would like to bring interpretation to a close, at least provisionally, though it knows it may not be able to; deconstruction would like not to stop, though it knows it will have to, certainly, in some simulacrum of a conclusion.

CHAPTER THREE

Deleuze: Against Interpretation

There is nothing to understand, nothing to interpret.

—DELEUZE AND PARNET 1977: 10

There is nothing to explain, nothing to understand, nothing to interpret.

—DELEUZE 1990: 17

Against Interpretation

Gilles Deleuze, no less than Derrida, was a reader of other people's work. In his early career he wrote on great figures from the history of philosophy, including Hume, Bergson, Kant, Spinoza and Nietzsche, and later he published books on Leibniz, Spinoza and Foucault. He was also a wide-ranging reader of literature, with books on Proust, Sacher-Masoch and (with Félix Guattari) Kafka, and essays or extended discussions of numerous literary authors, including Lewis Carroll, Zola, Artaud, Melville, Tournier, T. E. Lawrence, Carmelo Bene and many others. Moreover, the publication of his two-part study of film, *L'Image-mouvement* (1983) and *L'Image-temps* (1985), revealed that he also had a vast knowledge of world cinema from its origins until the latest work of his contemporaries. So the development of his own philosophy involved intensive and extensive engagement with the work of others, be they philosophers, writers or filmmakers.[1] But Deleuze repeatedly insisted that he was not an *interpreter* of texts and films. Rather than revealing their messages or intentions, he wanted to create something new through his encounters with them. He regarded the works he discussed as machines engaged in the world, not receptacles of a hidden content to be discovered by the diligent labour of interpretation. He was interested in what they *did*, not what they *meant*.

Deleuze echoes the Heideggerian move of recognising art as an essential ally in the work of philosophy. As Elizabeth Grosz puts it in her discussion of Deleuze, "Philosophy may find itself the twin or sibling of art and its various practices, neither judge of nor spokesperson for art, but its equally wayward sibling, working alongside art without illuminating it or speaking for it, being provoked by art and sharing the same enticements for the emergence of innovation and invention" (Grosz 2008: 2). Philosophy and the arts share what Grosz calls "their rootedness in chaos, their capacity to ride the waves of a vibratory universe without direction or purpose, in short, their capacity to enlarge the universe by enabling its potential to be otherwise, to be framed through concepts and affects" (Grosz 2008: 24). The key criterion for Deleuze is creativity, which characterises all the greatest achievements of philosophy, art and the sciences. As Deleuze and Guattari put it in *Qu'est-ce que la philosophie?*, "To tell the truth, sciences, arts and philosophies are equally creative, although it is the role of philosophy alone to create concepts in the strict sense" (Deleuze and Guattari 1991: 11). We might suspect that the second half of this sentence seriously modifies the claim that all the disciplines are "equally creative." Because philosophy alone creates concepts "in the strict sense," Deleuze and Guattari may imply that it is *primus inter pares*: somehow superior to art and science despite their alleged equality. Deleuze and Guattari are adamant that no such implication should be read into what they have said: "The exclusivity of the creation of concepts ensures that philosophy has a function, but gives it no pre-eminence, no privilege, because there are so many other ways of thinking and creating" (Deleuze and Guattari 1991: 13). No form of creation is inherently superior to any other.

For Deleuze as for Heidegger, then, philosophy and art are separate but equal; they are twin peaks which at their greatest both represent the highest human achievements. Commentators have disagreed, however, over whether in practice Deleuze actually maintains the non-hierarchical view on which *Qu'est-ce que la philosophie?* insists. Reidar Due argues that in Deleuze's later work aesthetics, that is, the philosophical comprehension of art, becomes the master discipline of philosophy (Due 2007: 164). Grosz does not believe that Deleuze's understanding of art should be regarded as an aesthetics; and, as the previous paragraph indicates, she follows Deleuze and Guattari in describing philosophy as the "twin or sibling" of art. Peter Hallward is less convinced of any alleged parity, suggesting that although "art has an exceptionally important contribution to make" (Hallward 2006: 104) in Deleuze's account of creation, it is only philosophy which carries it to its ultimate conclusion. Grosz counters that "Hallward's reading entails an hierarchical organization in Deleuze's understanding of the relations between science, art, and philosophy that has no textual basis in Deleuze's writing" (Grosz 2008: 5). If by "no textual basis" Grosz means that there is no *explicit* support for Hallward's reading, this does not mean that Deleuze's texts may not implicitly rely on a hierarchy which they overtly deny. With this in mind, my position in this chapter is closer to Hallward's than to Grosz's. Despite everything Deleuze says to the contrary, the ancient rivalry of philosophy and the arts has not been resolved.

Deleuze was a reader, but not (on his own account) an interpreter. This chapter explores the usefulness and ramifications of this distinction between reading and interpreting in Deleuze's work. The discussion revolves around two key issues. The first concerns Deleuze's repetitiveness. In *Différence et répétition* (1968) Deleuze argues for a positive understanding of repetition according to which what is repeated is not a stable content or structure but rather the creative power of difference. As Adrian Parr succinctly summarises Deleuze's view: "In this way, repetition is best understood in terms of discovery and experimentation; it allows new experiences, affects and expressions to emerge. To repeat is to begin again; to affirm the power of the new and the unforeseeable" (Parr 2005: 223). I am not convinced that Deleuze's repetitiveness actually instantiates this conception of repetition. The encounter with philosophy, literature or film is supposed to produce creative new results rather than hackneyed old meanings; but in practice Deleuze's analyses can sometimes seem monotonously predictable, leaving, for example, Proust looking more like Kafka or Kleist than a naïve reader might have hoped.

The near-identical form of the two epigraphs quoted at the beginning of this chapter illustrates the broader problem of repetitiveness in Deleuze's writing. Although Deleuze is by no means unique in re-using the same material in different situations (Chapter 5 of this book comments on Žižek's self-quotation, for example), the practice is particularly problematic in the context of a philosophy which claims to be constantly in search of the new. Reading Deleuze, one has the sense that the same premises and conclusions can serve any number of different occasions; and in the impression of *déjà lu* which they often arouse, Deleuze's texts fail to match the call to inventive singularity which they proclaim. In *Kafka: Pour une littérature mineure* (1975), for example, Deleuze and Guattari use the term *rhizome* to describe Kafka's letters because they contain multiple threads, connections and openings: "The letters are a rhizome, a network, a spider's web" (Deleuze and Guattari 1975: 53). A little later, it turns out that Kafka's journal is also a rhizome; in fact it is the very epitome of a rhizome: "The Journal traverses everything: the Journal is the rhizome itself" (Deleuze and Guattari 1975: 76). Moreover, in only the second sentence of the book, the authors had pronounced that Kafka's entire work is a rhizome: "How to enter into Kafka's work? It's a rhizome, a burrow" (Deleuze and Guattari 1975: 7). Parts of the work are rhizomes, and so is the work in its entirety. The term itself turns out to be rhizomatic, characterising both the components and the whole, serving as both point of entry and conclusion. Perhaps, though, it explains too much, the novelty of what it elucidates being diminished by its repetition.

The second key issue which emerges from this chapter concerns the difficulty of pursuing the kinds of criticism suggested in the previous paragraphs when Deleuze himself forecloses any discussion of the positions he adopts. Žižek opens his book *Organs Without Bodies: On Deleuze and Consequences* by referring to Deleuze's unwillingness to engage in dialogue: "Gilles Deleuze was well known for his aversion toward debate—he once wrote that when a true philosopher sits in a café and hears somebody say 'Let us debate this point a little bit!' he jumps up and runs away as fast as possible" (Žižek 2004: ix). The philosopher Alain Badiou also stresses that, "in conformity with his systematic and aristocratic orientation, Deleuze felt only scorn for debates" (Badiou 1997: 30). It is to say the least ironic that on the first page of a book on which he collaborated entitled *Dialogues* (1977), Deleuze insists that nothing is to be gained by debate or discussion; he thereby refuses to engage in the dialogue promised in the book's title. He bluntly states that there is no point at all in voicing objections to anything he says: "Objections are even worse. Every time someone makes an objection to me, I want to say : 'Okay, okay, let's move on to something else.' Objections have never produced anything positive" (Deleuze and Parnet 1977: 7). The dialogues risk becoming a series of monologues impervious to the other's contribution. Deleuze is not interested in argument and counter-argument, so on his own terms at least there is no point whatever in trying to debate what he says, or to apply to it the measures of correctness or error. His acts of reading do not constitute interpretations which might purport to reveal the truth in or of the text. They are therefore not susceptible to conventional forms of academic questioning or validation (this may be one reason why subsequent studies of Proust and Kafka sometimes do not even cite Deleuze's *Proust et les signes* or Deleuze and Guattari's *Kafka: Pour une littérature mineure*).[2] To ask whether Deleuze's reading of, for example, Proust is correct is to miss the point; but then, what is the point? Deleuze denies that what he is doing should be called interpretation, and he dismisses the interest of any possible objections. Perhaps, though, this double gesture (This is not an interpretation! Do not object to me!) can be read as a disabling and authoritarian dogmatism more than an enabling liberation from the despotism of meaning. Deleuze proposes powerful interpretations even if he refuses to name them as such, and he disallows any critical dissent.

This is not of course how Deleuze himself presents his activity. Referring to his early work on the history of philosophy, he gives a provocative account of his relation to the authors he discusses:

But most of all, my way of dealing with things at that time was, I think, to conceive of the history of philosophy as a sort of buggery [*enculage*] or, what comes down to the same thing, immaculate conception [*immaculée conception*]. I imagined myself arriving behind an author and giving him a child, which would be his and which would nevertheless be monstrous. That it should be his is very important, because it was necessary that the author really did say everything that I made him say. But that the child should be monstrous was also required because it was necessary to pass through all sorts of decenterings, slippages, break-ins, secret emissions which gave me real pleasure. (Deleuze 1990: 15)

The passage sets up a confusing array of implications. The link between *enculage* (buggery) and *immaculée conception* (immaculate conception) may in part be suggested by the fact that both contain the word *cul* (arse). The sexual act of buggery is identified with immaculate conception, producing a child which is the joint offspring of himself and the author. If this is immaculate conception, Deleuze is in the position of God, taking his partner (or victim) from behind in order to achieve his personal gratification.

In *Organs Without Bodies: On Deleuze and Consequences,* Žižek uses this passage as an occasion to comment on some of the differences between Deleuze and Derrida. He observes that for both of them, philosophy can only be practised "in the mode of metaphilosophy, as a reading of (other) philosophers" (Žižek 2004: 47). But Deleuze fiercely opposes Derrida's deconstructive "hermeneutics of suspicion," replacing it with what Žižek calls "an excessive benevolence toward the interpreted philosopher": "At the immediate material level, Derrida has to resort to quotation marks all the time, signalling that the employed concept is not really his, whereas Deleuze endorses everything, directly speaking through the interpreted author in an indirect free speech *without* quotation marks" (Žižek 2004: 47; emphasis in original). Žižek is nevertheless well aware that Deleuze's practice also entails violence: "And, of course, it is easy to demonstrate that Deleuze's 'benevolence' is much more violent and subversive than the Derridean reading: his buggery produces true monsters" (Žižek 2004: 47).

Žižek clearly enjoys Deleuze's reference to buggery, using forms of the word (including *unbuggerable* and *self-buggery*) seventeen times in the four paragraphs following his quotation of the passage. He is right, though, to see the violence inherent in Deleuze's superficially benevolent opposition to the hermeneutics of suspicion. Derrida's attitude to the texts he studies is like that of a nervous suitor shyly edging toward his beloved; Deleuze's scenario is more direct and more blatantly sexual. The author is surprised from behind, anally penetrated and impregnated with an unwanted child. This is more like a rape than an act of love. Moreover, there is also something oddly *solitary* about the coupling Deleuze describes. There is no relationship here. The sexual act (buggery) is said to be tantamount to an absence of contact (immaculate conception). The author is taken from behind, so the face remains unseen; there is no conversation, only a strained, coerced monologue ("it was necessary that the author really did say everything that I made him say"). And the final pleasure ("secret emissions which gave me real pleasure") is Deleuze's alone, a private ejaculation occasioned by the object of his (interpretive) desires but shared with no one.

My account of this passage might be accused of reading into it implications that are not there and attributing to it a meaning that it does not have. From a Deleuzian perspective I would have endeavoured to *interpret* his words by finding in them an underlying meaning, thus succumbing to an error which Deleuze spent much of his career striving against. The first edition of *Proust et les signes* (1964) conceded the value of interpretation: "you discover no truth, you learn nothing, except by deciphering and interpretation" (Deleuze 1979: 11); but subsequently Deleuze would be categorical in his rejection of the endeavour to decipher truth. The urge to interpret is likened to an illness, which Deleuze calls *interpretosis* (see Deleuze and Parnet 1977: 58). It is the activity of priests in the service of despotic Meaning, obsessed with uncovering dirty little secrets. So the questions arise of what Deleuze means by interpretation, why it is so vilified by him, and how his response to texts can avoid being categorised as interpretation. Deleuze suggests that there are two ways to read a book. One is to regard it as a box: it contains something which the reader endeavours to bring to light through interpretation. But there is another way:

a book is considered as a little a-signifying machine; the only problem is "does it work, and how does it work?" How does it work for you? If it doesn't work, if nothing comes through, then take another book. This other type of reading is a reading in intensity: something comes through or it doesn't come through. There is nothing to explain, nothing to understand, nothing to interpret. . . . This other way of reading is opposed to the former one because it relates a book immediately to an Outside. A book is a small cog in a much more complex external machinery. (Deleuze 1990: 17)

Passages such as this explain why it can be said that, whereas for Derrida there is nothing outside the text ("*il n'y a pas de hors-texte*," Derrida 1967a: 227; emphasis in original), for Deleuze there is nothing *inside* it. There is no hidden meaning or secret to be interpreted; rather, the text is part of a complex continuum with everything that is external to it. Its interest does not lie in what it contains, because it contains nothing; rather, we should be concerned with how it functions as it engages with the world. As one critic puts it, "Literary works do not mean so much as they function. When properly constructed, they are machines that make something happen" (Bogue 2003b: 187). Rather than asking what literature means, we should ask: what can it do, or even, what can it do for you/me/us (see Baugh 2001: 35, 54)?

How rigorous is this distinction between meaning and doing? The first is apparently connected to the mania for finding what is inside texts, the second with the endeavour to show how texts engage with what is outside them. In his rejection of interpretation Deleuze reproduces the simplification involved in Derrida's dislike for hermeneutics. The error of interpretation is traced to its insistence that one thing stands for another, and that in the end flux can be stabilised and reduced to a unitary core of meaning which it is the critic's job to discover. In Deleuze's writing, psychoanalytic interpretation appears to be a particularly potent and noxious instance of this tendency, as it traces the most diverse symptoms to an endlessly repeated Oedipal family drama. The previous chapter already suggested that this is an understanding of interpretation which Gadamer, for example, would not recognise as belonging to the hermeneutic tradition within which he worked. In fact, from the perspective of Gadamerian hermeneutics there is no problem in accepting much of what Deleuze says about literature and film as interpretation, even if—or because—it does not purport to represent a definitive unveiling of a stable, unified meaning lodged in the work for all time. Gadamer could readily agree that art is interesting and worthwhile because it actively engages the world rather than being an immutable repository of the same old secrets.

Sometimes, it is clear in Deleuze's writing that the description of literature as content-free is more prescriptive than descriptive. Deleuze disparages French literature because it too frequently plays along with the mania to interpret. Georges Bataille is "a very French author" because "he made the little secret into the essence of literature, with a mother inside, a priest below, an eye above" (Deleuze and Parnet 1977: 59); and French literature is described as "often the most shameless praise of neurosis" (Deleuze and Parnet 1977: 61). Rejecting the literature of "the dirty little secret," Deleuze goes on to characterise writing in terms of creation, lines of flight and becoming. His own account of the navel-gazing tendency in French literature shows that the generalising terms he uses here are questionable; clearly, not all writing actually matches up to its highest purposes. But this barely matters to his argument. As we shall see later in this chapter, Deleuze does not hesitate to suggest that cinema has an "essence" which nevertheless may be absent from most films. The same is true of literature. "Writing," Deleuze insists, "operates the conjunction, the transmutation of fluxes, through which life escapes from the resentment of persons, societies and reigns" (Deleuze and Parnet 1977: 62). For Deleuze, this could presumably be true in general even if no single instance could be brought forward to support it.

To say what literature *is* in its actual manifestations would be a dully critical, interpretive activity. Deleuze is concerned rather to create something in his writing that *might be*. To do this, he attributes to a few prestigious writers, such as T. E. Lawrence or Kafka, the achievements that he would like them to have. In the terms of the passage quoted earlier, he creates with them a child that is both theirs and his own; it claims to be descended from their works whilst being unmistakably marked by the Deleuzian appropriation. Deleuze's discussions of literature give the curious sense of being remarkably detailed and close to the text under discussion and strangely indifferent to them. In *Kafka: Pour une littérature mineure*, Deleuze and Guattari discuss the three characteristics of what they call minor literature: it "deterritorializes" language by unsettling it from within; in it, everything is political; and it constitutes a kind of collective utterance rather than being identifiable as the expression of an individual (Deleuze and Guattari 1975: 29–33). The work of Kafka is taken both to suggest and to exemplify this account of minor literature; yet as a concept it belongs so distinctively to Deleuze and Guattari that it seems imposed on Kafka, despite the close reference to some of his works. Sometimes, detailed quotation is completely absent precisely when it would seem crucial to support the case being made: Deleuze and Guattari happily discuss Kafka's style without quoting a single word of German. Even a sympathetic critic concedes that, at times, "it seems as if Deleuze and Guattari are merely willing Kafka into being the writer they want him to be" (Bogue 2003b: 114).

Deleuze develops a strikingly original conception of literature in his own distinctive vocabulary. Despite the counter-example of French writing, literature should not be understood as being about the memories, experiences, identities or opinions of its authors. It is a rhizome or a machinic assemblage which is political and experimental; it deterritorialises, creates lines of flight, transmutes flux; writers are diagnosticians more than patients; as practitioners of minor literature they make language stammer, writing as if in a foreign idiom even when they have no other. Characteristically, these views tend to be powerfully asserted rather than patiently explicated. As we have seen, Deleuze was not interested in debating his positions or defending them against criticisms. Nevertheless, there are a number of problems which run like fault lines through Deleuze's work. One which has already been suggested is a repetitive element in his writing which is in performative contradiction to his call for the creatively new. The freedom of creation is also, sometimes, constrained by an impulse to classify and to categorise which can be surprisingly normative in its implications. A further problem arises from Deleuze's conception of writing as an anonymous, depersonalised, collective process not directed by any individual consciousness. In practice authorship is anything but anonymous for Deleuze, as he constantly returns to a fairly fixed canon of prestigious writers. He is aware of this apparent contradiction between the anonymity of writing and the use of proper names to designate certain privileged texts. Speaking in one's own name, he suggests, has nothing to do with the reference back to an ego, person or subject: "On the contrary, an individual acquires a real proper name, at the conclusion of the most severe exercise of depersonalisation, when he opens himself up to the multiplicities which traverse him right through, to the intensities which run through him" (Deleuze 1990: 15–16). However, despite his insistence on depersonalisation, Deleuze runs the risk of appearing to subscribe to something like a cult of genius. Art may be anonymous, but some artists are so outstandingly good at being anonymous that their names deserve to be known.

Finally, in this list of quibbles with Deleuze, his texts are more ambivalent towards literature than they might appear. They seem to host an amicable resolution of the ancient quarrel between literature and philosophy. The great artists take their rightful place alongside the great philosophers. However, if in Deleuze's writing there is no longer any conflict between philosophy and literature, philosophy has nevertheless *not quite* relinquished its aspiration to know more about art than art knows about philosophy, or about itself. The rest of this chapter traces some of the effects of these issues on Deleuze's writing, first in his book on Proust and then in his work on cinema.

For Interpretation: Proust

Deleuze's *Proust et les signes* was first published in 1964. In the second edition, published in 1970, a substantial new section entitled "La Machine littéraire" (The Literary Machine) was added; and in 1976 that section was subdivided into chapters and augmented by a new conclusion, of which an earlier version had appeared as a free-standing article. The first sentence of *Proust et les signes* explicitly poses the question of the unity of Proust's work: "In what does the unity of *A la recherche du temps perdu* consist?" (Deleuze 1979: 9); and one might ask the same question of *Proust et les signes*. Is it one book, or two books, or more? The work in its final form has two parts, each with independently numbered chapters and each with its own conclusion. Ronald Bogue reassures us that the difference between the two parts is "finally one of degree and emphasis rather than substance. The emphasis in the first part is on what one might regard as a reader's activity, that of receiving and processing signs, whereas part two would seem to stress the writer's activity of generating and configuring signs" (Bogue 2003b: 57). Part 2 "helps dispel possible misunderstandings" of part 1, clarifying what Deleuze meant by some of his earlier arguments (Bogue 2003b: 58). However, this smoothing over of differences between the two parts risks falsely unifying a work which itself posits unity (the unity of Proust's novel, or of Deleuze's study of it) as an issue and a problem. In this section I want to suggest that the two parts of *Proust et les signes* do not simply say the same thing, albeit with shifts of emphasis. Even their understanding of unity is not the same; and the differences between the two parts can be linked to tensions within Deleuze's relation to literature more generally.

In the first part of *Proust et les signes* Deleuze is certainly not as resolutely opposed to interpretation as he would be in his later texts. As noted earlier, interpretation is accepted as essential to the quest for truth; indeed, the temptation to curtail interpretation is described as "the worm in the apple" (Deleuze 1979: 43), produced by the deluded belief that the meaning of a sign resides in the object which bears or emits it. Here, Deleuze does not identify interpretation, as he would later, with the fallacy of a single, fixed and obtainable truth; on the contrary, interpretation appears as a restless activity which opposes that fallacy. And since Deleuze does not reject interpretation at this stage, it is hardly contentious to say that what he is himself producing here is an interpretation of Proust, moreover a very distinctive and powerful interpretation. With remarkable panache, the book opens by telling us that those of us who might have thought *A la recherche du temps perdu* was a book about memory have got it quite wrong: "It's a matter, not of an exposition of involuntary memory, but of the narrative of an apprenticeship. . . . Proust's work is founded, not on the exposition of memory, but on the apprenticeship of signs" (Deleuze 1979: 10, 11). The rest of *Proust et les signes* sets out to justify and to elaborate this initial guiding claim.

As we shall see in his work on cinema, Deleuze's interpretive activity shows a structuralist influence in its endeavour to classify proliferating data into a restricted number of fixed categories. So, the Proustian apprentice will encounter four kinds of sign: worldly signs, which have no transcendent meaning and may always be misinterpreted; signs of love, which always deceive; material signs, which are truthful but empty if they do not incarnate an ideal essence; and the signs of art, which surpass and transform all the others, because they reveal the truths never fully apparent elsewhere. These different signs enter into a complex interplay with four structures of time: time lost (*le temps perdu*), in which the past is lost to us; wasted time (*le temps qu'on perd*), in which we are distracted by the world or by love from what matters most; time regained, in which what was lost is found once more; and the original, absolute time of art, in which the other dimensions of time find their truth. The various kinds of sign and temporal structure may interact and overlap in numerous ways, but art brings them all together and binds them into a higher unity. This is why Deleuze claims that art has an "absolute privilege" (Deleuze 1979: 64). The apprenticeship in signs is an apprenticeship in art: an initial state of ignorance is followed by a period of learning, which leads to an ultimate revelation through art.

The privileged role of art comes from its capacity to overcome the division of subject and object. Deleuze insists that what is revealed through interpretation is not objective or subjective, though neither is it entirely separate from the interpreted object or the interpreting subject: "It's that the sign is probably deeper than the object that emits it, but it is still attached to that object. And the meaning of the sign is probably deeper than the subject who interprets it, but is still attached to that subject, is incarnated in half measure in a series of subjective associations" (Deleuze 1979: 48). The sign is neither fully independent of the object which emits it nor entirely separate from it; meaning is not entirely separate from the subject who produces it nor fully explicable in subjective terms. To escape the choice between identifying the truth of interpretation as objective (a property of the interpreted object) or subjective (produced by the inter-preting subject), Deleuze requires a third term. That term is *essence*; and the medium in which it is revealed is *art*. Essence turns out to be the answer to the question posed by Deleuze, "what is there in addition to the object and the subject?" (Deleuze 1979: 49):

Beyond the designated objects, beyond the intelligible, formulated truths; but also beyond the subject chains of association and resurrections through resemblance or contiguity: there are the essences, which are a-logical and super-logical. They tran-scend the states of subjectivity no less than they do the properties of the object. It is the essence which constitutes the true unity of sign and meaning; it is what constitutes the sign as irreducible to the subject who grasps it. It is the final word of the apprenticeship or the final revelation. (Deleuze 1979: 50)

The strategic importance of this notion of essence in Deleuze's argument is clear enough. Drawing on analyses in Proust's text, it introduces a third term which escapes the dichotomy of subject and object and provides a name for what is revealed in art at the end of the apprenticeship in signs. But in my understanding at least, that is where the clarity ends. Through part I of *Proust et les signes* Deleuze makes a number of attempts to answer the question, "What is an essence?" His various responses entail a complex web of quotation from or allusion to Proust and dense interplay with a philosophical vocabulary. Deleuze wants to use an established philosophi-cal term without fully endorsing any of its received, traditional senses:

What is an essence, as it is revealed in the work of art? It is a difference, the ulti-mate and absolute Difference. It is what constitutes being, which makes us con-ceive of being. (Deleuze 1979: 53)

It is not the subject who explains the essence, it's rather the essence which is im-plied, enveloped, rolled up in the subject. Even more, as it rolls itself up in itself, it is what constitutes subjectivity. It is not individuals who constitute the world, but the enveloped worlds, the essences which constitute individuals: "Those worlds which we call individuals, and which without art we will never know." The es-sence is not only individual, it individualises. (Deleuze 1979: 56)

Other passages specify that the two powers of the essence are difference and repetition (Deleuze 1979: 83), and that it may assume the generality of a Theme or Idea, serving as the law governing a series (Deleuze 1979: 93). When, in Proust's novel, Combray appears "in its essence," it is not as it ever was in a historical past, not as it is remembered or could ever be or have been experienced, not as it was or is "in reality"; rather, it appears "in its truth," or "in its internalised difference" (Deleuze 1979: 76). Quoting these passages without their full context certainly does not help to make them more intelligible. But my point is that I am not sure how intelligible they really are, or are meant to be.

Critics who discuss Deleuze's conception of essence in Proust's novel tend to quote him, or to quote him quoting Proust, without adding much by way of further explanation.[3] Peter Hallward is more helpful when he distinguishes between the Platonic essence, which remains general or typical, and "a Proustian or Deleuzian essence [which] is always radically singular. It is always, again, a matter of *an* event, *an* essence, *a* life, *this* life" (Hallward 2006: 123; emphasis in original). Hallward also observes that the essences of *Proust et les signes* are "another vehicle for those virtual creatings that Deleuze describes in terms of events in *Difference and Repetition* and in terms of sense in *Logic of Sense*" (Hallward 2006: 123). So the apparent familiarity and philosophical heritage of the notion of *essence* may be misleading. Deleuze's use of the term is inflected by his own work. It could be argued that it *serves a purpose* in his argument rather than being a receptacle with a content which can be uncovered.

In line with his lack of interest in the cut and thrust of debate and objection, Deleuze's engagement with other readings of Proust is minimal. The first part of *Proust et les signes*, that is, the whole of its first edition, makes no single reference to any of Proust's former critics.[4] Deleuze seems unconcerned about what anyone else might have said about Proust. He offers his own reading of *A la recherche du temps perdu* and refrains from conventional critical debate. Deleuze talks about interpretation as an issue in Proust's novel, and his reading certainly seems to entail an interpretation of Proust; but it is by no means certain either that his interpretation is *persuasive*, or even that it aims to be so. And it is equally unclear whether Deleuze invites or permits us to interpret his own text, if through interpretation we were hoping to pin down quite what Deleuze means, for example, by key terms such as *essence*. In other words, to anticipate what Deleuze will say of Proust in part 2 of *Proust et les signes*, and what elsewhere he will say of Kafka and others, the Deleuzian text is more like a machine which produces effects than a vehicle for conveying arguments, intentions and meanings.

The conclusion to part 1 of *Proust et les signes* (which is the first conclusion to the book, and the original conclusion to its first edition) brings an interesting twist. So far, Deleuze has argued that the absolute privilege of art lies in its ability to reveal the essence, which is also the unity of sign and meaning: "Art gives us true unity: the unity of an immaterial sign and a quite spiritual meaning. The Essence is precisely this unity of sign and meaning, such as it is revealed in the work of art" (Deleuze 1979: 53). In terms of the ancient quarrel between philosophy and literature, this absolute privilege would appear to give the definitive victory to literature. Philosophy might *talk* of the essence, but literature makes it present to us. And yet, the conclusion to part 1 couches the significance of Proust's achievement in philosophical terms. The first paragraph states that Proust's *Recherche* is first of all a search for truth: "Thereby is manifested the 'philosophical' import of Proust's work: it rivals philosophy" (Deleuze 1979: 115). The rivalry between literature and philosophy is re-established here, despite what appeared to have been the unmatchable capacity of art to reveal the essence. Moreover, Proust's rivalry with philosophy assures the philosophical dimension of his work rather than, for example, simply unseating the philosopher's pretensions to dominance. Proust's philosophical importance comes from the fact that he attacks what Deleuze calls "what is most essential in a classical philosophy of a rationalist kind" (Deleuze 1979: 115): the presupposition that the thinker naturally wants, loves and seeks the true. Proust shows how, on the contrary, thought is provoked only when something does violence to it, when something forces us out of our quiescence. The painful contingencies of jealousy and desire constrain us to seek the truth. We are led to essences despite ourselves rather than by some natural inclination.

Proust's art, then, rivals philosophy because it proposes an alternative to its image of thought as the love for truth. Socrates serves to represent the tradition which Proust unsettles. Despite the uncertainty suggested by Socratic irony, Deleuze suggests that Socrates is too sure of himself:

his understanding precedes and survives any contingent encounter which might challenge it (Deleuze 1979: 123). Proust opposes this with the insight that understanding comes only after the encounter with an alien object or agency. It is provoked and forced to appear by something over which it has no control or authority. But Proust's opposition, as characterised by Deleuze, is to a certain kind of philosophy, not to philosophy as such. Thus, the assault on philosophy may take place within philosophy: "It is possible that the critique of philosophy, such as Proust conducts it, is eminently philosophical" (Deleuze 1979: 122). It is unremarkable to suggest that philosophy might be attacked from the inside; more interesting here is the claim that *Proust's* critique of philosophy is philosophical. If the privilege of art is absolute, it has nothing further to gain by being designated as philosophy; yet this is precisely Deleuze's (provisionally) closing gesture. Proust's crowning achievement thus appears to be not in the revelation of essences through art, but in the creation of a new image of thought. Ultimately, then, he seems to interest Deleuze because of what he offers philosophy rather than as an artist, despite everything that has been said about the privilege of art. And in this conclusion, the quarrel between literature and philosophy, which seemed to have been resolved by Deleuze in favour of literature, is implicitly re-opened. Deleuze now heralds the artist Proust as a distinctly Deleuzian philosopher; and philosophy has the final word, even if that final word is self-critical and self-contesting. The quarrel is back on, and as we shall see, it is resumed in Deleuze's work on cinema.

Part 2 of *Proust et les signes* is as much an interpretation of the first part of the book as it is a re-interpretation of Proust. The title, "La Machine littéraire" (The Literary Machine), signals that Proust will now be read through Deleuze's view of the text as a machine producing effects rather than guarding over more or less hidden meanings. References to lines of flight and bodies without organs link the study to other texts by Deleuze from the late 1960s and 1970s. The use of his later vocabulary in the second part of his work on Proust does not mean, however, that Deleuze is merely saying the same things in different words. The question of the unity of Proust's *Recherche* remains a guiding thread, but what is conveyed by the term *unity* has changed. In part 1 it entailed the unification of signs and dimensions of time that could only be effected in the work of art. Part 2 speaks much more insistently of the internal heterogeneity of Proust's work, which bears "fragments which can't be stuck back together again, pieces which are not part of the same puzzle, which do not belong to a prior totality, which do not emanate from even a lost unity" (Deleuze 1979: 137). This does not imply that it is wrong to speak of the unity of the work at all, so long as the term is re-defined:

> What makes the unity of a work? What makes us "communicate" with a work? What makes the unity of art, if there is any? We have given up the attempt to find a unity which would unify the parts, a whole which would totalise the fragments. For it is the attribute and the nature of the parts or fragments to exclude the Logos as much as a logical unity as an organic totality. But there is, there must be a unity which is the unity *of* that multiple, *of* that multiplicity, as a whole *of* those fragments: a One and a Whole which would be not the principle, but on the contrary "the effect" of the multiple and its disconnected parts. One and Whole which would function as an effect, an effect of machines, instead of acting as principles. (Deleuze 1979: 195–6; emphasis in original)

The claim for unity has been dramatically toned down here. It is no longer the unique property of the work of art; rather, it is an effect which art produces, but also a kind of perspectival error. Fragments may seem unified when experienced in a certain way without ever actually being genuinely totalised. Unity in this sense is not so much a harmonious reconciliation as a still discordant conglomeration. The re-conception of unity also entails a denial of the unmatched status of art. In part 1, art was deemed to have an absolute privilege; in part 2, Proust's originality is still acknowledged, but there is no reason to think that the work of art is inherently or necessarily more capable of producing creative effects than any other form of text, artefact, experience or event. If art is a machine, then so is everything else; and art loses at least some of its former prestige.

 Proust et les signes is an internally conflicted work which, like Proust's novel as it is described in part 2, cannot be totalised into a harmonious whole. The differences between parts 1 and 2 do not just involve clarification and a change in vocabulary. As Paul de Man observed, part 1 postulates a textual coherence in Proust's novel, as it leads through apprenticeship from ignorance to revelation (De Man 1979: 72, 77). Part 2 denies any such coherence, except as an effect which it might or might not produce. The tensions between the two parts can be related to Deleuze's attitude to art more generally. There are in Deleuze's writing strong traces of a structuralist tendency to classify and to contain.[5] This impetus to rein in the waywardness of signs is countered by a sense of their freewheeling delirium, epitomised by Proust's Charlus, whose speeches are character-ised by "involuntary signs which resist the sovereign organisation of lan-guage, which cannot be mastered in words and phrases but put the logos into flight and drag us into another domain" (Deleuze 1979: 209). This self-contradictory stance of containment and liberation mirrors Deleuze's curious combination of both utter respect and strange indifference for the specificity of the work. Deleuze exhibits a desire both to dominate Proust's novel by showing its underlying laws and categories, and to liberate it from any such domination. Through an intense focus on detail, he tends to reach always the same conclusions. The work of art is given an absolute privilege, and subordinated to the philosopher's conceptual armoury. The ancient quarrel is settled and revived. As we shall see in the next section, the same tensions appear again in Deleuze's extraordinarily influential work on film.

Philosophy and Film

There is no doubt that Deleuze's two volumes on film, *L'Image-mou-vement* (1983) and *L'Image-temps* (1985), represent a massively impressive and important achievement in the philosophical study of film. Deleuze displays an extensive knowledge of film and its history. From the very beginning he compares filmmakers to thinkers: "The great cinema au-thors seemed to us to be worth confronting [*confrontables*] not only with painters, architects, musicians, but also with thinkers. They think with movement-images or time-images instead of with concepts" (Deleuze 1983: 7–8). So filmmakers *think*. The means by which they do this are different from but not inferior to those of the philosopher. As Deleuze and Guat-tari argued in *Qu'est-ce que la philosophie?* the philosopher's role is to invent concepts.[6] The thought of cinema, on the other hand, is non-conceptual, and it provides the impetus for philosophers to exercise their conceptual inventiveness. Such inventiveness is certainly on show in Deleuze's cinema books. Claiming in his opening sentence that he is attempting to create "a taxonomy, an attempt to classify images and signs" (Deleuze 1983: 7), he goes on to offer us the key concepts of *movement-image* and *time-image*, as well as a dizzying array of others such as *opsigns, sonsigns, chronosigns, noosigns* and *lectosigns*.

So filmmakers are thinkers, and film is part of the history and process of thought. However, the passage from Deleuze's introduction quoted above perhaps suggests that he is more ambivalent than he might at first appear about the philosophical standing of cinema. He refers to "the great cinema authors," thereby indicating from the very beginning an inclination towards an *auteurist* analysis in which film is the product of an individual creator. He talks about filmmakers rather than about film. Moreover, to say that these authors may be *confronted* ("confrontables") with thinkers is not quite to give them equal status; and when he tells us that they think with movement-images and time-images rather than with concepts, he is also very markedly using *his own concepts* to describe the non-conceptual thinking of the filmmakers. Although his formulations sometimes suggest otherwise, Deleuze is not claiming that film per se thinks, rather that filmmakers think. Moreover, they think non-conceptually; as soon as they start talking about what they do, they become philosophers (Deleuze 1985: 366). So film can do something that philosophy can't, but only philosophy can actually *say* what film does.[7] Indeed, the philosopher (Deleuze) can even tell us about the *essence* of cinema: "But the essence of cinema, which isn't what is found in most films [*qui n'est pas la généralité des films*], has thought for its highest goal, nothing other than thought and its functioning" (Deleuze 1985: 219). Thought is the essence of cinema; but Deleuze insists that he is not talking about what occurs in "most films." The philosopher knows what the essence of cinema is, although most films do not realise that essence. It might even be possible in principle that no actual film had *ever* fulfilled Deleuze's demand for cinema, without this local hitch in any way necessitating a revision of the philosopher's claim to know the essence of film.

If, in Deleuze's account, film is thought, it is thought which is waiting for philosophy to raise it to the dignity of the concept. As he says in his Conclusions, film consists in "prelinguistic images" and "presignifying signs" (Deleuze 1985: 342). The use of the prefix *pre-* implies that the images and signs in question are not yet, but are destined to be, linguistic and signifying. They are not properly realised until they have been turned into language and signification; and the preconceptual thought of film can be conceptualised only by a philosopher. In the highly ambiguous closing paragraph of the two volumes, Deleuze claims that "the concepts of cinema are not given in cinema. And yet they are the concepts of cinema, not theories about cinema" (Deleuze 1985: 366). Whatever this means (and it is really not clear), the concepts of cinema belong to cinema but are not fully present in it; something else—philosophy—must intervene if they are to be formulated in conceptual language. So the suspicion arises that the equal status of cinema in the process of thought is not so equal after all. The great *auteurs* of cinema may be *confronted* with philosophers, but philosophers retain their precedence. This can be seen, for example, in Deleuze's comparison of Orson Welles to Nietzsche. Deleuze argues that "There is a Nietzscheanism in Welles, as if Welles were covering again the principal points of Nietzsche's critique of truth" (Deleuze 1985: 179). Welles has something of a Nietzschean about him. But it is only "as if" he is going over the same ground as Nietzsche; and in any case he is a latecomer because he is covering *again* ground that Nietzsche has already covered. Welles's critique of judgement is "in the manner of Nietzsche" (Deleuze 1985: 180), rather than Nietzsche's work being in the manner of Welles. The philosopher maintains the superior position; and when it comes down to it, Welles "does not have the same clarity as Nietzsche even though he deals with the same theme" (Deleuze 1985: 184). Welles may be a Nietzschean, but this certainly doesn't make him Nietzsche's equal.

Deleuze's work on film has been criticised on a number of grounds. Even a sympathetic critic such as D. N. Rodowick describes some aspects of the cinema books as "indefensible": he points for example to Deleuze's attitude towards authorship, the disjunction between subtle philosophical arguments and the thinness of their demonstration in analysis of actual films, his cultural elitism, and his lack of attention to the problem of difference in spectatorship (such as sexual, racial or class difference) (Rodowick 1997: xiii–xiv). In the present context, there are two problems with deriving an understanding of film as philosophy from Deleuze's writing. First, his exclusive interest in and reverence for what he calls "the great authors of cinema" indicate a surprisingly unproblematised *auteurism* which makes of a film (or at least the films in which Deleuze is interested) the creation of a gifted individual. As we saw in the case of literature, there is an implicit cult of the great artist, which fits uneasily with the claim that creation is anonymous. Great films are made by great filmmakers; and if thought occurs in film at all, it can be traced back to a creative genius who is ultimately responsible for it. Just as, earlier in his career, Deleuze's history of philosophy was a history of great philosophers (Plato, Leibniz, Spinoza, Hume, Kant, Nietzsche), his history of cinema is a history of great directors (Eisenstein, Hitchcock, Welles, Antonioni, Fellini, Godard). A great director might make a bad film, but a bad director could never make a film that really contributed to the history or process of thought.

The second problem in this context is the lingering suspicion that, despite what Deleuze sometimes says, he does not actually put film and philosophy on an equal footing. Film needs philosophy to establish its credentials as thought more than philosophy needs film in the invention of concepts. Not all commentators agree with this reading. Paola Marrati concludes her study of Deleuze's books on cinema by insisting that "in his work an encounter with cinema truly takes place, leading Deleuze in directions which are in many respects new" (Marrati 2003: 126).[8] Dominique Chateau, on the other hand, argues that for Deleuze, "Cinema is ultimately dismissed by philosophy which has appropriated it, by philosophy which never finds itself so much as in itself, in the solitude of its mastery and its tools" (Chateau 2003: 107); Hallward concurs that Deleuze's cinema books are "books of philosophy and of philosophy alone" rather than being about "actual cinema" (Hallward 2006: 140); and Alain Badiou argues that what Deleuze found in film was little more than the confirmation of his own philosophy: "what is finally produced returns to the reservoir of concepts which, from the beginning, he instituted and linked together: movement and time, in their Bergsonian sense. . . . [T]he whole enterprise maintains a creative resumption of concepts, and not an apprehension of the art of cinema as such" (Badiou 1997: 27–28).

The issue here is whether or not there is actually an encounter with film and whether the thought of film, in whatever state it might exist, can enter into a productive dialogue with the institution and discipline of philosophy. For Marrati, there is such an encounter in Deleuze's work; for Chateau, Hallward and Badiou this is less certain. For my part, I am doubtful about Deleuze's ability to encounter and to account for something entirely unforeseen in the works he analyses. To take a single test case, the discussion of the director Jean Renoir in *L'Image-temps* suggests Deleuze's reliance on his own, highly questionable criteria. Deleuze turns to Renoir in his chapter on what he calls "the crystals of time." The work of four directors (Max Ophuls, Renoir, Fellini and Visconti) is taken to delineate four types of crystalline state instantiated in film. Whereas Ophuls's films exemplify perfect, self-contained, flawless crystals, those of Renoir always contain a flaw or "a point of flight [*un point de fuite*]," so that the crystal is "cracked [*fêlé*]" (Deleuze 1985: 113). This means that, in the complex play of internal self-mirroring through which masters and servants, theatre and reality, actual and virtual all reflect one another in Renoir's films, there is nevertheless always something which escapes this imprisoning system of correspondences. Characters such as Boudu in *Boudu sauvé des eaux* (1932) and Harriet in *The River* (1951) are locked in confining roles, but in the end they emerge into life: "One leaves the theatre to attain life" (Deleuze 1985: 117); and, on this account Renoir turns out to be the most Sartrean of directors: "It is Renoir who had a sharp awareness of the identity of freedom with a future, collective or individual, with an impulse towards the future, an openness to the future" (Deleuze 1985: 117).

It is at best problematic to claim there is a single key (the cracked crystal) to a body of work as diverse and varied as Renoir's.[9] It looks as if Renoir's entire output is being forced into a preconceived scheme in order to exemplify one of the four "crystals of time." In detail also, Deleuze's observations are unpersuasive or possibly just wrong. In relation to *La Règle du jeu* (1939) he claims that it is the gamekeeper Schumacher who represents the flaw in the crystal. Schumacher is "the only one not to have a double or reflection. Bursting in despite being banned, pursuing the poacher-servant, killing the pilot by mistake, he is the one who breaks the circuit, who shatters the cracked crystal and makes its contents spill out, by gun shot" (Deleuze 1985: 114). It is hard to see how it can be argued that Schumacher has no doubles or reflections in the film. In fact the character fits in perfectly with the film's system of parallels and inversions: he is servant to his master; his role as gamekeeper is inverted in that of the poacher Marceau; and in the erotic dramas of the film his role as jealous husband makes him the double of the La Chesnaye, who is also trying to cling on to an errant wife. It would perhaps be more true to say that, of the major characters in the film, all are doubles and reflections of the others, or that none is a double or reflection of any because none is quite the same as any other. Deleuze's global reading of Renoir's films, though, requires some "point of flight," so Schumacher is called upon to fulfil a need. And yet Deleuze also claims that *La Règle du jeu*, despite being a fine film, is untypical of Renoir's work because of its pessimism and violence. Here, Deleuze chooses the corpus that suits his reading, and has nothing to say about other violent and bleak films amongst Renoir's output, such as *La Chienne* (1931) or *La Bête humaine* (1938).

The reading of Renoir is questionable in detail and in general, as the director's entire output is made to fit into a single category which does little justice to it. Deleuze is both admirably attentive to the films he discusses, and strangely negligent, even high-handed, towards them. He insists that the critic must not apply to films concepts that come from outside. The concepts used must be "proper to the cinema," even if they "can only be formed philosophically" (Deleuze 1990: 83). His dislike for linguistic and psychoanalytical readings ("there as elsewhere it does not add much," Deleuze 1990: 84) stems precisely from the fact that (he believes) they impose ready-formed conceptual frameworks onto their objects of study. The same criticism can be made of Deleuze. If he genuinely succeeded in not applying pre-existing concepts onto film, it would be a remarkable achievement. It is not certain, though, that he even tries in any convincing way. The philosopher retains the upper hand.

The Return of the Same

What is repeated, Deleuze tells us in *Différence et répétition*, is difference. As Adrian Parr puts it, "repetition dissolves identities as it changes them, giving rise to something unrecognizable and productive" (Parr 2005: 225). Maybe so; but what if the difference that is repeated were also monotonously the same? Deleuze places the highest value on singularity and creation, yet the great creators about whom he writes end up appearing surprisingly similar to one another. What Kafka says about minor literatures is the same as what Melville says about American literature (Deleuze 1993: 114); great novelists are all prophets with common goals (Deleuze 1993: 105); in the volumes on film, the whole of world cinema can be classified according to the two epochs of image-movement and image-time. Multiplicity is contained within fixed categories. Peter Hallward summarises why it is that Proust, for example, turns out to be comparable to artists as different as Kafka or Bacon or Artaud: "However divergent their medium and material, Deleuze tends to read his privileged artists as contributors to one and the same creative project" (Hallward 2006: 117). Out of the profusion of singularities and difference emerges, according to Hallward, a single question, "the question of absolute creation, elaborated through the distinction of actual creatures and virtual creatings" (Hallward 2006: 159). This single question gives unity to Deleuze's intellectual project, but also risks tying it down. Across Deleuze's massive output, the repetition of difference can become disappointingly familiar. He seems to learn little that is new from the creators to whom he nevertheless attends in such careful detail.

This can be related to Deleuze's revival of the ancient quarrel between philosophy and literature, and his intervention in the more recent quarrel between philosophy and film. Deleuze's explicit pronouncements do not fit easily with some implications of what he says and does. According to *Proust et les signes* art has an absolute privilege shared by no other human activity. Yet this privilege is attenuated in Deleuze's work. Great filmmakers are said to be comparable to great thinkers; and art, science and philosophy are "equally creative" (Deleuze and Guattari 1991: 11). Art appears here to be equal rather than supreme; and although Deleuze does not claim the superiority of philosophy, he nevertheless tends to measure the value of other disciplines from a philosophical perspective. The essence of film is, he says, *thought*; and although art, science and philosophy are deemed to be equally creative, Deleuze goes on to specify that only philosophy creates concepts "in the strict sense" (Deleuze and Guattari 1991: 11). So all the disciplines are equal, though at least in some respects philosophy is more equal than others. Hallward neatly summarises the reason for the privileged position of philosophy: "If being is creation and if being becomes more creative the less its creations are obstructed by creatures, then the privilege of philosophy is that it is the discipline most adequate to our expression of being as such. Philosophy is our most becoming expression of being. Philosophy simply *is* the expression of being, insofar as it articulates absolutely pure creations, i.e. creations liberated from any residual mediation through the creatural or the actual" (Hallward 2006: 127; emphasis in original).[10]

Deleuze attempts to erase the apparent incompatibilities between difference and repetition, singularity and seriality. But the repetitiveness of his own writing and the predictability of his conclusions belie the un-fettered creativeness which is embraced in principle. His work reproduces elements of the stand-off between deconstruction and hermeneutics discussed in the previous chapter, not methodologically, but in the tension between the desire to open a work up to ever new potential (difference, singularity, creativity, becoming) and a tendency to close it down by finding in it endlessly repeated effects (repetition, seriality, classification). Philosophy is dislodged from its dominant position, but quietly clambers back so that it nevertheless re-conquers a privileged perspective on all that it surveys. Deleuze's writing can itself be read as one of the literary machines he describes, more interesting for what it does than what it says. It can be exhilarating, fascinating, annoying or dull; and what makes it worthwhile are not so much the insights it offers as the blind spots which drive it energetically, relentlessly, onwards.

CHAPTER FOUR

Levinas and the Resistance
to Reading

Many of you are will be thinking, with good reason, that at this very moment, I am in the process of rubbing the text so that blood spurts out of it. I accept the challenge! Has anyone ever seen a reading that was anything other than this effort carried out on a text?

—LEVINAS 1968: 102

The Phenomenology of Reading[1]

Levinas might have been surprised, and perhaps not hugely flattered, to find his work discussed in the context of literary theory.[2] His own comments on the subject were sparse; his forays into literary criticism were rare and on the whole unimpressive; and his general assessment of art and literature was to say the least disparaging. And yet, a vital strand in his work consisted in reading and in writing about his experiences as a reader, initially in the 1930s as an exegete of Husserl and Heidegger, and later as a commentator on the Talmud from the 1960s until his death in 1995. Moreover, the act of reading brings into play the most important issue of his ethical philosophy, namely the possibility of a transforming encounter with someone or something entirely other. In part, this chapter compares Levinas's account of the reading process with other reader-response theories; then, by examining more closely one of Levinas's relatively rare discussions of secular literature—his 1947 essay on Proust—it considers the extent to which his practice as reader supports or subverts his theoretical position. This has broader repercussions for his philosophy because what is at stake is whether or not an encounter with otherness actually takes place. Can the text can be experienced as truly other or does it serve merely as a screen onto which readers project their assumptions and pre-understandings?

The guiding insight of the phenomenology of reading and related branches of study such as reception aesthetics and reader-response criticism is that texts do not "mean" in some sort of vacuum, but that meaning is produced through the interaction of a text with a reader or community of readers. A central problem then becomes: how is it possible to explain that texts mean different things to different people without simply abandoning any normative sense of correct reading and endorsing a sort of semantic free-for-all in which a work might mean anything we want it to mean? No one (with rare exceptions) argues that texts have only one meaning, but no one (with rare exceptions) argues that they have none either. What is required, if interpretive anarchy or nihilism are to be avoided, is an account of how something is supplied by the text and something by the reader, so that individual acts of reading are unique, but not for that reason arbitrary or completely unrelated to other such acts. For the purposes of understanding Levinas's position on this, the work of Wolfgang Iser is a useful point of reference. Iser builds judiciously on the phenomenology of Roman Ingarden and the hermeneutics of Hans-Georg Gadamer in order to describe the co-implication of text and reader in the production of meaning. In brief, Iser argues that some aspects of a literary text are determinate whilst others are indeterminate. As he famously puts it, comparing determinate elements to the stars in the sky, which we might connect together in different patterns, "The 'stars' in a literary text are fixed; the lines that join them are variable" (Iser 1988: 218).

In Iser's account, readers are free to fill out the indeterminate, variable parts of a text in different ways. At the same time, because the text never quite matches up to our expectations of it, it reminds us that something remains indeterminate. It surprises us and puts us in the presence of something that does not entirely reflect the world as we believe it to be. It negates the familiar, and so it challenges and revises our preconceptions and thereby allows us to gather new experiences. Thus, the act of reading becomes an exemplary encounter with the unknown: "Reading reflects the structure of experience to the extent that we must suspend the ideas and attitudes that shape our personality before we can experience the unfamiliar world of the literary text. But during this process, something happens to us" (Iser 1988: 225). This "something" that happens to us turns out also to have important consequences for our identities as human subjects: "The production of the meaning of literary texts . . . does not merely entail the discovery of the unformulated, which can then be taken over by the active imagination of the reader; it also entails the possibility that we may formulate ourselves and so discover what had previously seemed to elude our consciousness. These are the ways in which reading literature gives us the chance to formulate the unformulated" (Iser 1988: 227).

Iser's insights can fairly readily be translated into a more dramatic Levinasian idiom: reading is an encounter with otherness which shatters self-understanding and re-orientates our very subjectivity. However, Iser has been criticised on grounds which, as we shall see, also have an important bearing on Levinas's account of reading. Terry Eagleton, for example, argues that Iser already *presumes* as given the values that are supposed to result from reading: I can only be challenged as a reader if I am pre-disposed to read in a manner which allows me to be challenged. As Eagleton puts it, "we can foray into foreign territory because we are always secretly at home" (Eagleton 1983: 80). There is no real encounter with otherness because the consequences and effects of any such encounter are already taken for granted and known in advance. Stanley Fish has proposed a model of reading quite contrary to Iser's, which he explicitly engages in his polemical essay "Why No One's Afraid of Wolfgang Iser" (Fish 1989: 68–86). Fish insists that Iser relies on a rigid distinction between the determinate and the indeterminate, whereas, Fish argues, in fact that distinction is itself an interpretive assumption which *produces* the effects it claims to describe. In Fish's alternative account there is no happy collusion between text and reader, with each supplying part of the impetus for the production of meaning; indeed, there is no *encounter* with the text at all, since the text is never more than an occasion for us to externalise the interpretive norms that we bring with us when we begin to read. Moreover, these norms are defined by the communities to which we belong, so they are not in any sense individual to us as private subjects. As Fish puts it in *Is There a Text in This Class?*, "Interpreters do not decode poems; they make them" (Fish 1980: 327). And interpreters are themselves *made* by the broader forces which mould their interpretations:

Thus while it is true to say that we create poetry (and assignments and lists), we create it through interpretive strategies that are finally not our own but have their source in a publicly available system of intelligibility. Insofar as the system (in this case a literary system) constrains us, it also fashions us, furnishing us with categories of understanding, with which we in turn fashion the entities to which we can then point. In short, to the list of made or constructed objects we must add ourselves, for we no less than the poems and assignments we see are the products of social and cultural patterns of thought. (Fish 1980: 332)

What is at issue in this disagreement between Iser and Fish is, in Levinasian terms, the very possibility of an encounter with otherness in the act of reading. Does something happen when we read, or has everything significant already happened before we even pick up the text? Does the text have the capacity to transform us, or do we simply appropriate it as our reflecting mirror? Are we constituted through our encounters with the other, or can the other only be encountered insofar as it already conforms to what we want of it? The next section will examine how Levinas's account of the reading process takes distinctive positions on these issues.

Sacred and Secular Texts

Of all the thinkers considered in this book, Levinas comes closest to formulating explicitly something like a theory of overreading, even if he would not call it or conceive of it as anything of the sort. Importantly, it arises in the context of his commentaries on the Talmud, and markedly not with reference to secular literature.[3] From 1960 onwards, Levinas's talmudic commentaries became a regular feature at the annual Colloque des intellectuels juifs de langue française, which had been inaugurated in 1957. Levinas's Judaism is essentially talmudic, and talmudic commentary provides him with an opportunity to combine religious devotion with sustained intellectual enquiry.[4] It also allows him to exercise an interpretive boldness, or what he calls "imprudence" (Levinas 1968: 16), which rarely surfaces in other parts of his work.

Levinas suggests that the Talmud is no less authoritative than the Bible, though the texts are very different in nature (see Levinas 1982a: 165; 1987: 8). The Talmud constantly refers to and elucidates the Bible, thus becoming the obligatory conduit through which the Bible is to be understood. Levinas shows the greatest possible respect for the Talmud and for the intellectual powers of the Rabbis whose words it transcribes. In the Talmud, he suggests, the potential for thought has been fully and definitively realised. In a phrase which Levinas repeats, "everything has been thought [*tout a été pensé*]" (Levinas 1976b: 102; Levinas 1968: 16); everything, even the most unforeseeable aspects of the modern world (Levinas 1976b: 102), has been anticipated and theorised in advance; all wisdom and knowledge can be discovered by the student of the Talmud. However, the explanatory role of the Talmud in respect of the Bible and of modern life does not make of it a set of unquestionable rules, prescriptions and interpretations; on the contrary, the essence of the text lies in its restless questioning. Levinas constantly emphasises the plurality of meanings to be found in the Talmud. Even opinions which are rejected are nevertheless recorded, as if nothing that has been or could be thought should be obliterated (Levinas 1982a: 141). And on issues of the utmost importance for religious Jews, divergent views are offered. The first two talmudic commentaries published by Levinas deal with Judaic conceptions of the Messiah, and here the reader is confronted with numerous competing options. According to different talmudic masters, in the messianic epoch social injustice will, or will not, be abolished (Levinas 1976b: 91–97); it will be a return to Eden, or to something better than Eden (Levinas 1976b: 99–101); those who repent will be privileged over the morally pure, or vice versa (Levinas 1976b: 98); the coming of the Messiah depends upon human action, or is independent of it (Levinas 1976b: 102–14); the Messiah's name will be Silo, or Yinon, or Hanina (Levinas 1976b: 124). Each of the Rabbis who defend or reject these views can justify his opinion with biblical authority. The debate becomes what Levinas calls "a combat that trades verses like blows" (Levinas 1976b: 108). More problematically still, the Rabbis cite the same verses but interpret them differently (Levinas 1976b: 98). This is made possible both by the nature of Hebrew as a consonantal language, which allows for diverse readings of the same word,[5] and by variant readings of context. According to Levinas, in such detailed disputes over meaning lies the essential strength of the Talmud, as it strives to examine every angle of the questions under discussion. Its authority derives not from its dogmatic prescriptions, but from its spirit of enquiry: "This concern to take 'opinions' and 'options' back to the crossroads of the Problem, where they are given their dignity as *thoughts*, is the true spirit of the Talmud" (Levinas 1976b: 98; emphasis in original).

In this account of the Talmud, then, contradictions, disagreements and ambiguities do not appear as unwanted disturbances to be overcome; they are precisely what gives the Talmud its vitality, permitting it to escape the specific historical circumstances of its compilation. Levinas's method of commentary endeavours to respect and exploit the plurality of meaning rather than to reduce it. In this, he is defending the Talmud and the practice of Rabbinic commentary against the historical, philological and positivist approach which he traces back to Spinoza's *Tractatus Theologico-Politicus* (1670).[6] Denying the inspired origin of the Bible and rejecting the interpretations of what he calls the Pharisees, Spinoza outlines a number of principles for discovering the true meaning of Holy Scripture:[7] (a) The tongue in which it was written should be fully understood; (b) contents should be analysed and organised under thematic headings, so that all texts that deal with a given subject may be compared, and ambiguous, obscure or mutually contradictory passages can be isolated; (c) and finally, a history of various parts of Holy Scripture should be compiled, analysing the life of the original author, the transmission of the text, and how the various parts were united into a single work. Spinoza lays out a rational path for understanding Scripture, shorn of all superstition and based on the original context of text and author. He thereby makes himself one of the most important forerunners of the historical study of the Bible, which acquired a central position in biblical studies from the nineteenth century onwards.

Although Levinas acknowledges that historical criticism and philological criticism have a role to play (Levinas 1976b: 102), any attempt to uncover the single, original meaning of the sacred texts is in his view misguided. This does not entail rejecting Spinoza's rationalism in favour of recourse to irrationalism or intuition. On the contrary, the Talmud is a most rational text which addresses the intellect, even though the mode of address is different from what we might expect of a philosophical work (Levinas 1968: 33). What Levinas disputes, then, is not Spinoza's rationalism, but the model of textual meaning that underlies his view of Scripture. In Spinoza's account, ambiguities and obscurities should be resolved by better knowledge of the language spoken by the author, and inconsistencies may be explained by the fact that different parts of the text had different authors with contradictory intentions. Spinoza regards meaning as static and entirely located in the past; for Levinas, this approach neglects the importance of the reader, an indispensable participant in the process of meaning: "But Spinoza will not have conferred a role in the production of meaning on the reader of the text" (Levinas 1982a: 206; 1994a: 173).[8]

In a well-known talmudic story, Moses is transported into the future to hear a lesson given by Rabbi Akiba; disconcerted that he cannot understand the lesson, he is surprised to hear Akiba's wisdom attributed to the revelation made to Moses himself on Mount Sinai (Levinas 1982a: 163–64). So Moses did not recognise the message which he transmitted to his successors. The story illustrates how the author does not command, nor even necessarily understand, the full meaning of his text. The reader finds meanings which may not have been consciously placed there. Levinas frequently describes the two-way process between text and reader as *solicitation*: the reader solicits the text with his or her current interests in mind, and is in turn solicited by the text to an exploration of meaning to which those current interests make an indispensable contribution. The Talmud contains a surplus of meaning, which ensures its ability to speak to the concerns of modern commentators.

To explore this surplus and its contemporary resonance, Levinas adopts a mode of reading which concentrates on precisely the obscurities, ambiguities and contradictions which Spinoza had sought to eliminate, for it is in these that new possibilities of meaning may be developed. Several important principles guide the commentary:

a. The first of these concerns the coherence and unity of the text. However disparate their historical origins, the Bible and the Talmud are not to be regarded as random compilations. The text is treated as a coherent whole, with all its parts interrelated by links which are necessary even if they are also difficult to establish (Levinas 1977: 29, 167; Levinas 1982a: 166).[9]

b. Second, whilst respecting the religious content of the Talmud, Levinas starts from the assumption that the text contains a rational discussion of problems with philosophical significance (Levinas 1976b: 101; Levinas 1968: 10). Although the language of the Rabbis is different from that of an academic philosopher, it can readily be transposed into it; and the casuistry of the Rabbis' thought (arguing from individual cases rather than abstract ideas) goes together with an abiding concern for general principles, though these cannot be separated from the individual examples which suggest and limit them (Levinas 1968: 48; Levinas 1982a: 21).

c. Third, a quotation of a verse from the Bible does not represent a recourse to an unquestionable authority but rather invites the reader to explore the context of that quotation, to find the relationship between it and the context of the current discussion; hence it opens up new possibilities of meaning within the text (Levinas 1968: 47–48).

d. Fourth, the reader should always solicit the text in the light of his or her current concerns, despite the anachronisms that doing so may seem to entail (Levinas 1976b: 101; Levinas 1977: 9). Levinas's standard move in his commentaries is to address the theme of the conference at which he is speaking through a text which has little apparent connection to it. So a text on the damage caused by fire elucidates the theme of war (Levinas 1977: 149–80), a text on haircutting is made relevant to the theme of the youth of Israel (Levinas 1977: 54–81), the question of forgiveness prompts a reflection on Heidegger's attitude to Nazism (Levinas 1968: 56).

e. Fifth, all opinions and interpretations should be respected, none should be overlooked or dismissed out of hand (Levinas 1982a: 141). Contrary views may all have validity because their proponents each have access to an aspect of the truth, as a talmudic formula implies: "These and those alike are the words of the living God" (Levinas 1982a: 167; 1994a: 137).

f. Finally, nothing in the Talmud is arbitrary or fortuitous, so anything may be taken as a legitimate subject for interpretation. In his commentaries Levinas draws upon similarities between words, unusual spellings, the numerical values of words,[10] etymologies (even dubious ones) or ambiguities deriving from Hebrew syntax. This entails an intense attention to the letter of the text, with all its associations and peculiarities, based on the conviction that everything is, or may be, significant.

These guiding principles evidently leave a great deal of space for interpretive freedom. Levinas acknowledges that in some of its aspects Jewish interpretation resembles the hermeneutic waywardness of deconstruction (Levinas 1982a: 66). However, this is not dissemination conceived as the destruction or dispersal of meaning. Talmudic commentary rests upon the presumption that the text has something to say, but that its message cannot be restricted to its obvious or surface meaning.[11] Further levels of meaning will only be discovered by exerting pressure on the written word. In the passage used as an epigraph to this chapter, Levinas suggests the degree of violence that this may entail by his development of a talmudic reference to Raba, who was so immersed in study that he rubbed his foot until the blood spurted out:

As if by chance, to rub in such a way that blood spurts out from it is perhaps the way one must "rub" the text to reach the life which it conceals. Many of you may be thinking, with good reason, that at this very moment, I am in the process of rubbing the text so that blood spurts out of it. I accept the challenge! Has anyone ever seen a reading that was anything other than this effort carried out on a text? To the extent that a reading rests on the trust granted the author, it can consist only in this violence done to words to tear from them the secret that time and conventions cover over with their sedimentations as soon as those words are exposed to the open air of history. It is necessary, by rubbing, to remove that layer which impairs them. (Levinas 1968: 102)[12]

The graphic violence of this passage is worth noting. The reader causes himself pain in the act of reading. Moreover, the reader's self-inflicted wound also entails an act of violence against the work he is studying, since it is now from the text that the blood is said to spurt. The extreme pressure exerted on the text in the act of reading nevertheless aims to restore meanings which have been lost or obscured through the passage of time. So, Levinas implies that the meanings he uncovers are genuinely present in the texts he analyses. At the same time they are also the commentator's meanings, the specific answers to his or her questions, and potentially unique to each reader. Each commentary adds to the meaning of the text or realises something that without the unique character of the commentator would have remained undiscovered. Commentary is thus necessary to the text (Levinas 1982a: 108); indeed the Talmud is already constructed as a series of commentaries, discussions and commentaries on commentaries, to which Levinas's own commentary adds yet further layers. Commentary demands interpretation (Levinas 1982a: 126), making the process potentially endless, though it is curtailed in practice by the need to make binding decisions and judgements. The number of possible readings is equal to or perhaps even greater than the number of actual readers:

It is as if the multiplicity of persons . . . were the condition for the plenitude of "absolute truth"; as if every person, through his uniqueness, were the guarantee of the revelation of a unique aspect of truth, and some of its points would never have been revealed if some people had been absent from mankind. (Levinas 1982a: 163; 1994a: 133)

There is for Levinas no contradiction between the absolute respect for the authority of the text and the uniqueness of each interpretation. The meaning of the Talmud is inexhaustible, so each reading may be both new and entirely faithful to the letter and spirit of the text. Revelation, in this account, is not something that occurred once and for all on Mount Sinai; it is repeated, continued and modified with every act of reading: "the voice of Revelation, as inflected, precisely, by each person's ear, would be necessary to the 'Whole' of the truth. . . . [T]he multiplicity of irreducible people is necessary to the dimensions of meaning" (Levinas 1982a: 163; 1994a: 133–34). Revelation and exegesis go hand in hand, which explains the extraordinary status of the Talmud in Levinas's rabbinic Judaism. God does not speak directly to the commentator; the divine word is available in the Talmud, requiring interpretation, and offering different nuances to every reader. Exegesis is an act of devotion and adoration every bit as important as prayer, and the Sacred Texts require a practice of interpretation that entails both an "audacious hermeneutic" and "listening piously to sovereign orders" (Levinas 1987: 10).[13] This combines freedom and restraint; it is entirely respectful of the text but fully open to new possibilities of meaning.[14] Commentary thus emerges as a never-completed project, a restless activity with conclusions which can only ever be provisional. Everything has been thought in the Talmud, but its full significance will never be definitively elucidated.

The bold commentator sees in the text what no one else had, or could have, seen. Levinas's commentaries combine modesty (he usually begins with a statement of his inadequacy to the task before him), scholarship, reliance upon the work of other commentators, and a speculative daring which develops possibilities of meaning further and further removed from the obvious sense of the text. A good example of this is provided by the parable of a man with two wives, one young and one old; the young wife pulls out his grey hairs and the old wife pulls out his dark hairs, to the point that he is left bald on both sides (Levinas 1977: 176). Levinas acknowledges the faintly humorous aspect of the anecdote and then extends its significance to make of it a parable of the conflict between tradition and modernity. For the young, the past (which Levinas compares to the prescriptions of Jewish religious law) is like grey hair: pure form that has lost its colour. The young wife plucks out the grey hairs, as the young uproot traditions by interpreting texts to the point that they no longer mean what they seem to say. The old woman respects the traditional view, takes the sacred texts literally and does not regard them as requiring rejuvenation. She plucks out the dark hairs, representing the innovations to be brought from youthful vitality, impatience and interpretation. The text, then, describes the conflict within the community of Israel between the young and the old, revolutionaries and traditionalists. More generally, it condemns the bigamy of the spirit which loses its sovereignty when it becomes the site of dispute between opposing cults: "maturity as conservatism and youth as a search for novelty at any price" (Levinas 1977: 177). The commentary itself attempts to maintain a balance between innovation and tradition which eluded the hairless husband. It develops implications permitted by the text and by traditional protocols of reading, whilst attempting to find the unique resonance of the text for the commentator's current concerns. Neither tradition nor innovation, freedom nor constraint, rigid forms nor bold interpretations, are allowed to dominate as Levinas maintains an exchange between the text and his own situation, between the search for new meanings and well-established exegetic frameworks.

Levinas's reflection on talmudic commentary has important parallels in contemporary hermeneutic thought. He compares his approach to the interpretive stance implied in Ricoeur's aphorism "The symbol gives rise to thought [*Le symbole donne à penser*]" (see Levinas 1982a: 107).[15] What Ricoeur calls a symbol plays the same role as the text in Levinas's commentaries, acting as an incitement to thought which can never be exhausted, and for which no single interpretive protocol (philological, historical, formalist, structuralist, psychoanalytic and so on) is adequate on its own (see Levinas 1968: 18–20). The emphasis on the constant exchange between text and reader, and on the uniqueness of every reading, also links Levinas's practice to the hermeneutic philosophy of Gadamer. Like Levinas, Gadamer argues that every act of understanding is different from all others: "It is enough to say that one understands *differently, if one understands at all*" (Gadamer 1986: 302; emphasis in original). This does not mean that the interpreter is the sole and entire source of the interpretation. The text is not an empty vessel with no content of its own. The hermeneutic positions of Levinas and Gadamer preserve the possibility of a real encounter with the text. In Gadamer's terminology, the act of reading brings about a fusion of horizons, whereby the horizon of the text, although never fully comprehended, comes into contact with and extends the reader's horizon (see Gadamer 1986: 311–12). Interpretation is saved from arbitrariness, subjectivism, or what Gadamer calls "hermeneutic nihilism" (Gadamer 1986: 100), by the fact that it is rooted in a tradition which is to some extent shared by most interpreters at any given time or in any given country. Although each reading is new and different, it is not simply wilful and utterly unrelated to all previous readings, because it is guided by assumptions which are common to other contemporary readers. In Gadamer's hermeneutics, meaning is dynamic but not arbitrary; the same can be said of Levinas's talmudic readings, which are rule-bound, but bound by rules which leave significant space for innovation. As in Gadamer's hermeneutics, the openness of the text poses the problem of how to discriminate between different interpretations;[16] and, like Gadamer, Levinas resolves the difficulty by his insistence that all valid reading, like all genuine innovation, is firmly grounded in the continuity of tradition:

But, what is more, a distinction is allowed to be made between the personal originality brought to the reading of the Book and the pure play of the fantasies of amateurs (or even of charlatans); this is made both by a necessary reference of the subjective to the historical continuity of the reading, and by the tradition of commentaries that cannot be ignored under the pretext that inspirations come to you directly from the text. A "renewal" worthy of the name cannot avoid these references, any more than it can avoid reference to what is known as the oral Law. (Levinas 1982a: 164; 1994a: 135)

Like much contemporary literary theory, then, Levinas insists that the reader plays an active but not an exclusive role in the production of meaning. This leads to the conclusion that readers may legitimately offer interpretations which cannot possibly have been consciously intended by the original authors. Levinas's belief that in the Talmud "everything has been thought" depends upon the implication that the text inevitably and always exceeds the intentions of any given author, as well as the capacities of any individual commentator. In Levinas's talmudic commentaries, then, we have a theory and practice of reading as radical and imaginative as anything proposed by Derrida, Deleuze, Žižek or Cavell. Levinas does not apply his approach to secular literary texts or films, but this does not mean that it could not be used in the study of non-religious works. Annette Aronowicz argues that his hermeneutic "is not limited to any set of texts, be they rabbinic or biblical. It is a hermeneutic *tout court*, an approach to interpretation as such" (Aronowicz 2003: 47). In Aronowicz's view, then, Levinas's interpretive procedures can be applied to non-sacred texts, even if the philosopher himself did not make such a move.[17]

In the "Avant-propos" (Foreword) and the essay "De la lecture juive des Ecritures" (On the Jewish Reading of Scriptures) in *L'Au-delà du verset* (1982) Levinas goes some way towards extending his conception of the Talmud into a more general theory of reading and textuality. This is not to say that the sacred frame of reference is absent here. On the contrary, according to Levinas it is due to the religious nature of language that individual acts of reading are always different from one another and that the meaning of a text is never fully available. Human language, as written down in both sacred and secular texts, always means more than it explicitly says. Levinas suggests that this is because it is full of the word of God but can never fully contain that word. It is always in excess of itself, always implying, suggesting and teaching more than appears on the surface. Levinas is certainly talking *principally* about sacred texts, but he nevertheless makes the important concession here of arguing that this is true of all texts, not just Holy Scripture: "A religious essence of language, a place where prophecy will conjure up the Holy Scriptures, but which all literature awaits or commemorates, whether celebrating or profaning it" (Levinas 1982a: 8; 1994a: xi). So written texts stage an encounter with the wholly uncontainable, and as such they are an essential part of the human condition and the relation to God.

Levinas argues that the questions of textuality and reading are matters for phenomenology, because it is through them that our relation to something other comes out into the open: "My condition—or my uncondition—is my relation to books. It is the very movement-towards-god [*l'à-Dieu*]. Is this an abstract expression? Language and the book that arises and is already read in language is phenomenology, the 'staging' in which the abstract is made concrete" (Levinas 1982a: 9; 1994a: xii–xiii).

This phenomenology calls for a restless labour of commentary because no interpretation is ever final or complete. In line with the hermeneutic tradition best represented in philosophy by Gadamer and in literary theory by Iser, Levinas insists that each reader brings something unique to the text, so that each act of reading responds to the text's call in an unprecedented manner. Every interpretation (so long as it is not wilfully aberrant) finds something new, which was previously unseen but nevertheless indubitably present in potential in the text. This is because each individual may contribute to the never-totalised unity of Truth. The multiplicity of interpretations certainly does not imply, for Levinas, that meaning is ungrounded, even if one act of reading is never identical to any other:

This does not amount to identifying exegesis with the impressions and subjective reflections left by the word once it has been understood, nor to including them gratuitously in the "outside" of meaning. It does, however, amount to understanding the very plurality of people as an unavoidable moment of the signification of meaning, and as in some way justified by the destiny of the inspired word, so that can the infinite richness of what it does not say can be said or that the meaning of what it does say can be "renewed," to use the technical expression of the Rabbis. (Levinas 1982a: 136; 1994a: 110)

So reading is a means of participating in Revelation, a Revelation which is ongoing, never complete, always unique and fresh, but saved from arbitrariness by the commanding presence of the text and by respect for the rich tradition of commentary to which it has given rise. In Levinas's term, the text is *inspired*: it contains more than it contains, and it solicits the reader to participate in the realisation of its meaning. As for Iser, the reader is transformed by the experience of opening herself up to the unfamiliarity or otherness of the text, occasioning what Levinas calls a "break, in the being that I am, of my good conscience of being-there" (Levinas 1982a: 9; 1994a: xii). In other words, reading is a properly ethical encounter, because it exposes me to that which exceeds me utterly; and in my capacity to respond I discover my obligation to the other.

Like Gadamer and Iser, Levinas conflates the distinctive questions of hermeneutics (How do I establish the meaning of a text?) and phenomenology (What happens to me when I read?), so that the meaning of the text is understood precisely as the event which occurs when I read. Whereas Iser understands this exposure to the unfamiliar in a liberal humanist framework, Levinas emphasises its religious nature. Because I am unique and irreplaceable, my acts of reading are also unique and irreplaceable, and as such they constitute an experience of the sacred and play a role in the ongoing process of Revelation. To some extent, then, Levinas's account can be understood within the context of phenomenological theories of reading. He attempts to explain the experience of reading in terms of an exchange between a fixed but semantically inexhaustible text and the particularity of an individual reader, so that there is what Levinas calls "this coming and going [*ce va-et-vient*] from text to reader and from reader to text" (Levinas 1982a: 204; 1994a: 171). In the process, new possibilities of meaning are discovered in the text, and the reader is transformed through exposure to the text's otherness.

However, even in Levinas's theoretical account of the reading process, a doubt could be raised about whether there is genuinely any possibility to be *surprised* by the text that is being read. If the text has the potential to teach and to transform, it must surely offer something I could not have anticipated. Although Levinas suggests that the *meanings* produced in any individual act of reading are always different, the meaning of these meanings turns out to be always the same. Terminologically, Levinas distinguishes between *signification*, the particular meaning found in reading, and *signifiance*, the text's capacity to offer meaning. It is the latter which turns out to be most important, and the least open to dispute. The text's signification is traced back to its primordial *signifiance*, which in turn is connected to the religious, inspired nature of language, and which ultimately issues an unchanging command, that is, the imperative of ethical responsibility. Across a huge range of texts and interpretations, Levinas ultimately finds one essential message: "writing is always prescriptive and ethical, the Word of God which commands me and vows me to the other, a holy writing before being sacred text" (Levinas 1982a: 9; 1994a: xii). The "full significance" of language and texts is their "ethical truth," and Levinas is as utterly assured of this as he is non-dogmatic about any particular *signification*.

So there is at least the suspicion here that the voyage into otherness does not occur, just as it does not occur in Iser according to the criticisms of Eagleton and Fish, because the traveller has always secretly remained at home. Reading reveals only what the reader's predispositions and prior assumptions allow her to see; the shape of the text is dictated by the nature of the gaze which is directed at it. Aronowicz has noted an element of circularity in Levinas's hermeneutic: "It turns out that the responsibility he discovers as content is the very principle that leads to this discovery in the first place" (Aronowicz 2003: 39). Rather than being necessarily a failing, this is what makes his reading practice, as Aronowicz puts it, "an ethics, a vision of the interaction between specific persons, from which the principles derive or which the principles embody" (Aronowicz 1990: xxxii). Commentary proceeds from responsibility and re-discovers responsibility in the texts it addresses. This requires an act of faith, an absolute confidence that the text has something to teach, and that it will be worthy of the attention paid to it. This is why, I suggest, Levinas is wary of extending his hermeneutic to secular literature even if Aronowicz is right to argue that it could be so extended. The Talmud pays the interpreter back for his efforts by giving him a lesson in responsibility. The lesson of secular literature may not be so welcome; it may instead, sometimes, teach cruelty and isolation. It is not to be trusted in the same way as a sacred text. Its otherness, as it were, may be the wrong sort, darkly corrupting rather than beneficially transforming. It may be that Levinas cannot allow himself to read secular literature in the same way that he reads the Talmud, with the same degree of self-exposure, because what it delivers is not the message he wants to hear. I want now to turn to Levinas's essay on Proust to see how far this suspicion is justified in one of his relatively rare published encounters with a secular literary text, and to consider what broader consequences this might have for his thought.

On Proust

Why, in 1947, should Levinas publish an article on Proust? Of course, the question could be reversed: why *shouldn't* Levinas publish an article on Proust? But there are in fact a number of reasons why Levinas's article "L'Autre dans Proust" (The Other in Proust) is an odd essay for him to have written. At this time he was in his early forties, and he had so far shown no inclination towards literary criticism. Between 1940 and 1945 he had been a prisoner of war in Germany, and indeed this probably saved his life. As a Jew, had he not been in the French army when he was captured he would almost certainly have been sent to a concentration camp rather than to a POW camp, and in all likelihood, like many of his relatives, he would not have survived. Since his return from Germany he had been radically re-thinking his philosophical positions, and in 1947 and 1948 there appeared a series of publications in which his changing views on phenomenology, and the increasing centrality of the Other in his thought, could be observed: *De l'existence à l'existant* (1947), *Le Temps et l'autre* (1948), *En découvrant l'existence avec Husserl et Heidegger* (1949). These essays, books and lectures pointed backwards to his work on Husserl and Heidegger in the 1930s, and forwards to his own mature ethics, which he would elaborate in 1961 in his first philosophical masterwork, *Totalité et infini*. In 1947 Levinas also began an intense period of studying the Talmud and effectively gave up writing philosophy for a couple of years. In 1948 he published in *Les Temps modernes* an article entitled "La Réalité et son ombre" (Reality and Its Shadow), which expressed what appeared to be a "deep-seated antipathy to art" (Eaglestone 1997: 98) or "an outright dismissal" (Robbins 1999: 82) of the work of art and the illusions it fosters.[18]

This period, then, was a time of intense intellectual ferment for Levinas, and one which hardly seems propitious for a diversion into the world of literary criticism. Levinas had been introduced to Proust by his life-long friend Maurice Blanchot in the 1930s, and he read him whilst a prisoner of war in the early 1940s. But from the argument of "La Réalité et son ombre," published the year after "L'Autre dans Proust," it is hard to imagine that Levinas would waste time on literature at all. Writing in *Les Temps modernes*, a journal founded and edited by Sartre, Levinas provocatively argues against Sartre's enthusiasm for committed literature. Levinas attacks art because it is irresponsible and inhuman, it is a form of idolatry which puts the mind to sleep and shrouds it in darkness; in Seán Hand's words, it "actively promotes a pact with obscurity" (Hand 1996: 67). Literature does not escape this assault. Narrative fiction falsifies the nature of the self and the experience of time and freedom. Characters in novels are "confined beings, prisoners. Their story is never finished, it still goes on but does not advance" (Levinas 1994b: 140–41). Falsification takes place *through the very act of narration*. What is at fault is not any particular novel or any particular novelist; better writers would never be able to be more truthful. Once something is narrated, it becomes subject to an inescapable process of distortion and mystification. Even the most capable writer is condemned to sink down into the quagmire of fiction:

The most lucid writer finds himself in the bewitched world of images. He speaks as if he was moving in a world of shadows—through enigmas, allusions, suggestion, in the equivocal—as if he lacked the strength to deal with realities, as if he couldn't advance towards them without vacillating, as if, bloodless and clumsy, he always committed himself beyond what he intended, as if he spilt half the water he brings to us. (Levinas 1994b: 147–48)

Levinas is uncompromising. Literature is obscure, absurd, selfish, cut off from lucidity; and crucially it is morally pernicious because it fails to acknowledge the priority of the relation with the Other. Levinas does not pull his punches in his condemnation of artistic enjoyment: "There is something wicked and egoistical and cowardly in artistic enjoyment. There are periods when one can be ashamed of it, as if one were feasting whilst the plague raged" (Levinas 1994b: 146). There are times when taking pleasure in art is shameful, and there is little doubt that Levinas regards the late 1940s as one such period.

So I return to my earlier question: why write about Proust in 1947? In this section I will look at Levinas's essay to see what he finds in Proust. Then, I want to test Levinas's approach by turning to Proust's novel, in particular the section entitled *Un amour de Swann*, in the hope of gleaning some sense of what Levinas gets, and what he does not and cannot get, from his reading of Proust.

At the beginning of "L'Autre dans Proust" Levinas outlines two common perceptions of Proust from the 1930s. First, there is Proust the psychologist: "The master of the differential calculus of souls, the psychologist of the infinitesimal. The magician of inexpressible rhythms" (Levinas 1976a: 117). Second, there is Proust the sociologist: "The new Saint-Simon of a nobility without Versailles, the analyst of a precious and artificial world" (Levinas 1976a: 118). Both these readings can now be discredited. Proust's psychology is outdated and his sociology is unconvincing. This discredit, however, has a major advantage since, as Levinas suggests, it "takes us back to the essential" (Levinas 1976a: 118); it allows us to see Proust for what he is. The subsequent discussion depends on a distinction between the philosopher, whose theory is unequivocally directed towards its object, and the poet, whose utterances are inhabited by ambiguity because they create their object rather than expressing it. The key decision in "L'Autre dans Proust" is to designate Proust's writing as poetry. Proust is an inveterate theoriser, but theory is only ever a means and not an end in itself; rather than knowledge, wisdom or insight, it offers spells and incantations which summon reality magically in all its bewildering ambiguity. In Proust's novel everything remains in "absolute indetermination," betraying "the simultaneous possibility of contradictory things" and "a cancelling of all choices" (Levinas 1976a: 119). The contours of the known, the knowable, and the rule-bound, are eroded: "The metamorphoses and the evolutions of the characters—even the most improbable—are imposed as the most natural, in a world returned to Sodom and Gomorrah; relations are established between terms which seemed to refuse them. Everything is vertiginously possible" (Levinas 1976a: 119–20).

So what Proust offers is not psychology or sociology, which would give knowledge of the self or of the world; rather, he creates a world in which and of which all knowledge recedes the more we pursue it. The designation of Proust as poet prepares the next key move of the essay: the introduction of alterity. The subject of experience becomes strange to itself and discovers the presence of otherness: "Everything occurs as if another myself constantly shadowed the self, in an unmatchable friendship, but also in a cold strangeness which life endeavours to overcome. The mystery in Proust is the mystery of the other" (Levinas 1976a: 120). The strangeness of the self to itself is encountered both through the frustrations of introspection and in relations with others. For the narrator of Proust's novel, Albertine incarnates "that strangeness which mocks knowledge," provoking "an insatiable curiosity for the otherness of the other, which is at once empty and inexhaustible" (Levinas 1976a: 121). This in turn allows Levinas to allude to a conception of love he had sketched in *Le Temps et l'autre* and which would be developed more thoroughly in *Totalité et infini*. Rather than the fusion and communication of souls, love is a relation with the other as other, as fundamentally unknowable. And as he reaches towards his conclusion, Levinas raises the stakes even further. Designating love as a relation with otherness, Proust also sketches a decisive break with the whole Western philosophical tradition by shattering the prestige of unity as the apotheosis of being. Rather than positing unity, knowledge, and fusion as ideal achievement, he makes manifest how the mystery of otherness inhabits our selves, our relations and our world. Although on this occasion Levinas does not describe this as *ethical*, it clearly echoes the ethics of alterity that he would spend the rest of his career expounding.

Perhaps by this point Levinas feels that he has gone too far in his rehabilitation of Proust. Certainly it is strange that here he apparently ascribes an important ethical insight to a literary text whereas in "La Réalité et son ombre" he envisages no such possibility. In the final sentence of "L'Autre dans Proust" Levinas summarises his reading, but also suggests a degree of ambivalence towards it:

But the deepest lesson of Proust—if however poetry bears lessons [*des enseignements*]—consists in situating the real in a relation with what forever remains other, with the other as absence and mystery, in finding it again in the very intimacy of the "I," in inaugurating a dialectic which breaks definitively with Parmenides. (Levinas 1976a: 123)

As the rhapsodic claims made for Proust escalate, the aside "if however poetry bears lessons" nevertheless tones them down: this is what we should learn from Proust *if we can learn anything at all.* As Jill Robbins puts it, "The hesitation is important, the qualifier is enormous. For it is not at all clear that poetry—Proust's or anyone else's—*can* contain teaching" (Robbins 1999: 82; emphasis in original). Perhaps Proust has in fact taught us nothing at all, since *enseignement* (teaching), a strongly positive word in Levinas's vocabulary, is the prerogative of teachers and philosophers rather than poets. Perhaps Levinas has only found in Proust what he already knew, so that, in this essay about the discovery of otherness, Levinas has in fact discovered only his own reflection. The encounter which the essay attempts to describe would in this case be precisely what had failed to take place in Levinas's reading of Proust.

Part of the fascination of this essay comes from its uneasiness with itself, which is made most manifest in the hesitancy of its final sentence. Claims are made for Proust which the essay does not quite fully endorse. Other elements of the essay suggest that it captures Levinas's thought at a moment of flux. Key terms such as *mystery, teaching* and even *ethics* are used either in different senses or with different evaluations and associations than they would subsequently have for Levinas.[19] If there is an ethical dimension to Proust's "poetry," it occurs, according to Levinas's essay, "as soon as ethics is finished" (Levinas 1976a: 119), that is, at the moment when the text succumbs to magic; yet this link between ethics and magic is repudiated in Levinas's later thought. The references to spells and incantation, wherein seems to lie the power and teaching of Proust's writing, are precisely what, in "La Réalité et son ombre" and subsequently in *Totalité et infini*, Levinas would attack as the mystifications of poetry. Levinas's mind seems not yet to be made up. He wants to endorse Proust and the potential of literature, but only on the condition that its waywardness can be restrained.

Writing about Proust provides Levinas with an occasion to explore his own, not yet fully worked out views. "L'Autre dans Proust" is the trace of an intellectual project at a moment of indecision, and which may yet go in a number of different directions. I will return to Levinas's relation to Proust at the end of this chapter. For the moment I want to highlight two features of this reading. First, Levinas discusses Proust in terms of poetry rather than narrative. His interest is in the moment of encounter between self and other, its consequences for conceptions of selfhood, love and being, and not in the subsequent narrative development of that encounter. Second, despite all the reasons Levinas might have for rejecting the charms of literature and despite hints of reservation, the evaluation of Proust is largely positive because his work opens up an ethical perspective which parallels Levinas's own views. Later, I will suggest that these two features of Levinas's reading are interlinked. Before that, though, I want to turn to Proust's *Un amour de Swann* to see what Levinas's approach does and does not account for in that fragment of *A la recherche du temps perdu*.

Un amour de Swann

In Levinas's reading of Proust, the experience of love can be a means of encountering alterity. It is worth noting, however, that from the outset *Un amour de Swann* presents an environment which is deeply unwelcoming to otherness. The very first sentence describes the Verdurin clan as demanding of its members strict adherence to an unquestioned Credo, a set of beliefs and attitudes that all must share. Anyone who does not obey is immediately excluded. The clan occupies a fortified space in which the Same must be endlessly repeated: the same conversations, the same jokes, the same excursions, the same music. Difference is not to be tolerated. When Swann joins the group, he arouses hostility and is eventually expelled because he retains his reserve, which frightens the clan by raising the spectre of independent thought and judgement. Women in general are also, it is suggested, recalcitrant to the Verdurin cult of the Same. From the first paragraph of *Un amour de Swann* we are informed that in time all women are rejected from the Verdurin clan because of their curiosity for the new. So, Proust's text implies that women occupy the role of Other insofar as they disrupt the rule of the Same. Levinas makes the same equation between femininity and otherness implicitly in "L'Autre dans Proust" and explicitly in his other texts from the 1940s. Indeed, he was roundly and, I think, rightly criticised by Beauvoir in *Le Deuxième Sexe* for unhesitatingly adopting a perspective according to which women were placed in the position of Other to be defined by opposition to the male Same (see Beauvoir 1949: 17–18). Proust's novel on the whole shares this perspective, even if it also indicates that on occasion men, such as Swann, can occupy the role of disruptive other. In any case, through its opening description of the Verdurin clan, *Un amour de Swann* sets up an imperious norm in which otherness is treated as an intolerable transgression to be swiftly punished by expulsion.

What is at stake in *Un amour de Swann* is the possibility of escaping, intellectually and emotionally, from the strictures of repetition and sameness. In this context love is the privileged testing ground, since it is in the experience of love that the extent of our entrapment within repeated relations and patterns of behaviour will be probed. Swann appears initially as someone who seeks out the unknown. He has long since learned everything he can from women of his own class and social circle, so he engages in affairs with women of lesser standing, from whom he hopes still to discover something new. But this search for the new has itself become repetitive, as Swann has settled into what is described as "a permanent character and identical goals" (Proust 1954: 233). Love is portrayed as a stage where the same scenarios are played out with endless monotony. This is in direct contrast to the rhetoric of love through which Odette initially attempts to seduce Swann. Odette assures Swann that love may be the encounter of unique beings rather than the repetition of unbending structures:

You must have suffered because of a woman. And you believe that others are like her. She wasn't capable of understanding you; you are such an exceptional being.

That's what I first loved about you, I could really feel that you weren't like other people.—And then you as well, he had said to her, I know what women are, you must have a lot to occupy you, have little freedom. (Proust 1954: 239)

Here, then, Odette alleges that it is precisely Swann's uniqueness that she loves. She tries to persuade him that not all women are the same, and that an enriching encounter is possible between two separate beings. What we do not know, of course, and what we can only guess, is how often she has used this chat-up line in the past. The rhetoric of uniqueness is infinitely repeatable. Whether deliberately or inadvertently, Swann responds by failing to take her point. At first he looks as if he is agreeing with her ("And then you as well"), but then he bluntly puts her down by re-affirming that women are all the same ("I know what women are"). This non-exchange between the pair indicates that there is little prospect of bridging the gulf between beings, when each speaks to the other in the clichés of sameness and difference. One way of describing Swann's non-response to his future lover's overture is to say that, although Swann has *met* Odette, although in fact he knows her reasonably well, he has not yet *encountered* her as other, as a being capable of shaking his world and transforming his identity.

Before Swann can encounter Odette in this sense, he needs to learn that the experience of otherness is possible. This is brought home to him when he first hears the "little phrase" from Vinteuil's Sonata for Piano and Violin. In the passage describing Swann's response to the sonata, Proust uses of the pronoun *elle* (she) to refer to the phrase because *la phrase* is feminine in French. This has the effect of personifying the piece of music and it underpins the erotic connotations developed throughout the following passage:

This time he could clearly make out a phrase [*une phrase*] which for a few moments rose above the waves of sound. It [*Elle*] immediately offered him particular pleasures, which he had never thought of before hearing it, which he felt that nothing other than it [*elle*] could give him, and he felt for it [*elle*] something like an unknown love. . . . And it [*elle*] did indeed reappear, but without speaking more clearly to him, even causing him a less profound pleasure. But back home, he needed it [*elle*]: he was like a man in whose life a passing woman, whom he saw for only a moment, has just introduced the image of a new beauty which gives his own sensibility a greater value, without his even knowing if he will ever be able to see again the one he already loves and whose name he does not even know. (Proust 1954: 252)

The passage alludes to Charles Baudelaire's poem "A une passante" (To a Passing Woman), in which the speaker fleetingly glimpses a woman in the street with whom he believes he could have found love. So, in this passage from *Un amour de Swann* the aesthetic experience becomes entangled with, and even supplanted by, the Baudelairean motif of tantalisingly fugitive and unknown pleasures.

Swann's experience of the "little phrase" is revived when he hears it again one evening at a gathering of the Verdurin clan. It prepares and mimics his subsequent relationship with Odette in that it opens him up for the disruptive, erotic encounter with the ungraspable other. It is then, finally, at this point that Swann begins to behave something like the subject enamoured of alterity described by Levinas. Swann finds himself thinking strange thoughts and experiencing new sensations (Proust 1954: 273–74). His response to his transformed self is ambivalent:

He was forced to acknowledge . . . that he was no longer the same, that a new being was there with him, part of him, joined to him, a being of whom he would perhaps not be able to rid himself, with whom he would be forced to make accommodations as with a master or an illness. And yet since he had begun to feel that a new person had thus been added to him, his life seemed to him to be more interesting. (Proust 1954: 274)

The passage leaves open whether the "new person" who has been added to him is Odette, or the new self which has grafted itself onto his former being. In either case the encounter has transformed him, as he has accepted the challenge posed to him by the insistent other.

However, Proust's novel never entirely gives up on the suggestion that even the most disruptive, unforeseen experience of love obeys rules which can be formulated in terms of general axioms. The text wavers between tracing the shocks, surprises and inconsistencies of individual behaviour and a generalising discourse which pins actions back down to the principles which they instantiate. Even when he acts most eccentrically, Swann feels that his love "obeyed immutable and natural laws" (Proust 1954: 285), and Proust's novel enmeshes him in a discourse which strains to articulate those laws. One of the central dramas of Proust's prose is the tension and the struggle between the exception and the rule, the waywardness of the individual instance and the intelligibility of the principle, the irregularity of the particular and the repetition of the universal. So Swann's encounter with the other is a transforming experience, but the novel implies that it is still *rule-driven*, still explicable in terms of repeated patterns. Whether the novel amply proves this is the open question that it poses to its reader. Certainly, the discourse of universality retains its prestige; however, particularly as Swann's jealousy escalates, the authority of the rule is constantly strained by the excesses of the particular instantiation.

In Proust's novel it can never be taken for granted that the encounter with otherness, in Levinas's sense, can occur or be sustained. It requires a disruption of the discourse of universality which in *Un amour de Swann* and the rest of *A la recherche du temps perdu* may often be intimated, but is never fully embraced. And this leads to a point of the utmost importance for Proust's staging of the encounter between self and other. That encounter always takes place, if it takes place at all, in complex, overdetermined contexts. Moreover, and this is the issue on which Proust departs most importantly from Levinas, it is part of a narrative; it has a history with distinct stages, in the course of which the significance of the encounter constantly evolves. At first, Swann is indifferent to Odette; later he seems to be genuinely transformed by her, but he remains unconcerned by her past or what she does when he does not see her; then, as he succumbs to jealousy, he becomes gripped by an imperious desire for total possession and knowledge; by the end of *Un amour de Swann* he has grown indifferent to her again, though from other parts of *A la recherche du temps perdu* we know that this is not the end of the matter. The encounter with the other, then, is not a single event which transforms the self unequivocally and definitively; it is inseparable from a narrative in which love, desire, possession and hatred drive the relation in constantly shifting proportions. The desire for the other easily tips over into the desire for her death: "Sometimes he hoped that she would die without suffering in an accident" (Proust 1954: 418).[20] Swann's love may make him a changed man, perhaps a better one, less of a snob, more attendant to the difference of the other, but it also leads him to seek to annihilate the other in its very alterity by knowing everything that can be known about it. Odette perceives full well that the desire for the other is also a desire to kill the other: "Oh! Charles, but you can't see that you are killing me!" (Proust 1954: 430).

Conclusion

Earlier, I drew attention in particular to two aspects of Levinas's reading of Proust: his designation of *A la recherche du temps perdu* as poetry rather than narrative, and the discovery in the novel of a relation to the other which potentially opened up a positive ethical perspective. These two aspects of Levinas's reading are tied to one another. By excising the narrative element from Proust's work, Levinas can isolate the encounter with the other from the different stages it goes through. He can focus on the transformations it enables and not see the narrative connections between different phases in the relation. Proust does not entirely exclude the possibility of an ethical encounter with the other; the other is ungraspable, the encounter is improbable, and yet the beautiful equivocations of Proust's prose suggest that it *just might* occur. But Proustian love is also violent and possessive. Levinas does not see that the Proustian lover is both an ethical subject and, perhaps indistinguishably, a potential murderer. What Levinas misses, what he literally cannot read, is precisely that side of Proust's novel that would be most disruptive to the views he was developing at the time of writing his essay, as he was feeling his way towards an ethics of the encounter with alterity which would lead to responsibility and justice. In the late 1940s the Holocaust was very much in Levinas's thoughts, and it would remain so for the rest of his career. His ethics can be read as a sustained refusal to allow the events of recent history to determine once and for all the sense of the human. In this sense his mature philosophy is a denial of what he knew full well and could not afford to read in Proust: that the relation with the other is often murderous.

It is not the least irony here that Levinas's essay on Proust, which revolves around the possibility of encounter with the other, itself constitutes such a partial and flawed meeting. The missed encounter suggests an unwillingness on Levinas's part to confront equivocations and indecisions within Proust's text, a reluctance to acknowledge the space separating him from Proust, and an anxious need to avert his eyes from all-too-blatant evidence of human cruelty. Proust's novel offers an insight into the violence which haunts the relation with other; Levinas was looking for reasons to believe in generosity, so he could perhaps do nothing other than pass over what it might be better for him not to know. This raises the question of how far Levinas's failure to encounter Proust casts a shadow over the viability of his overall ethical project, in which encounter plays such a crucial role. In theory, Levinas sketches a phenomenology of reading in which text and reader renew each other. Like Iser, he wants to believe that the text transforms us as we find new meanings in it. But Levinas turns out to be, to put it bluntly, a bad reader, replicating only what he is predisposed to see. His writing clings on to a hope, the enabling and disabling hope of his mature philosophy: the unshakeable conviction that an encounter is possible, that I might learn from it, and that I will not respond to it by committing murder. It is possible to see his resilient misreadings as the trace of that hope, which conditioned his failure to acknowledge, in the texts he was reading, the evidence which contradicted it.

CHAPTER FIVE

Žižek's Idiotic Enjoyment

Slavoj Žižek came on the academic stage like a breath of fresh air; or perhaps it would be more accurate to say that he hit it like a tornado, leaving audiences enthralled, exhausted, brow-beaten, invigorated, enlightened and bewildered in equal measure.[1] He shares Deleuze's passion for film; but whereas Deleuze was unapologetically highbrow in his taste for literature and film, Žižek staunchly defends kitsch, science fiction, detective novels, film noir and Hollywood blockbusters; and whereas Deleuze had no patience with psychoanalytic criticism, Žižek aligns his work resolutely with the thought of a psychoanalytic master, Jacques Lacan. Žižek is a Lacanian just as Lacan was a Freudian: with the utmost devotion, even if their form of fidelity leaves a lot of leeway for creative appropriation. So, by his own ready admission Žižek is a Lacanian theorist, steeped in both psychoanalytical thought and popular culture, and always willing to use one to explain the other. His early work *Looking Awry* (1991) indicates his unique approach to high theory through its subtitle, *An Introduction to Jacques Lacan Through Popular Culture.* Along similar lines, *Enjoy Your Symptom!* (1992) has the subtitle *Jacques Lacan in Hollywood and Out.* Žižek's books are littered with analyses of popular literature and film, usually viewed through an openly Lacanian optic. Žižek warns us, though, that his intention is not only the pedagogic goal of explicating Lacan, since what is at stake is also his own enjoyment: "it is clear that Lacanian theory serves as an excuse for indulging in the idiotic enjoyment of popular culture. Lacan himself is used to legitimize the delirious race from Hitchcock's *Vertigo* to King's *Pet Sematary*, from McCullough's *An Indecent Obsession* to Romero's *Night of the Living Dead*" (Žižek 1991: viii).

Žižek is fully aware of the reproaches made against psychoanalytical criticism ever since Freud began to write about works of art: it turns art from a conscious, deliberate achievement of human civilisation into a dirty arena for sexual perversion; it has no conception of the aesthetic as such because it uses art merely as an example to illustrate its pre-established clinical insights; and it might be able to explain something about human motivations, but it has nothing to say about how a damaged individual becomes a great artist. Dostoevsky may have been an epileptic with an unresolved paternal authority complex, but not every epileptic with an unresolved paternal authority complex becomes the author of *Crime and Punishment* (for this example, see Žižek 1994: 176). Psychoanalysis may provide a way of understanding authors, but it tells us little about art.

According to such reproaches, psychoanalytic critics impose what they already know on art and in the process fail to learn anything new from it. Žižek's position, though, entails a provocative denial of this charge. The title of his edited volume *Everything You Always Wanted to Know About Lacan (But Were Afraid to Ask Hitchcock)* (1992) implies that it is Hitchcock who could tell us about Lacan, if only we were to ask him properly, rather than the other way around. Popular culture might know what high theory has not yet understood. This chapter considers what sense such a claim might make, and whether or not Žižek's interpretive practice escapes the routine charges made against psychoanalytic criticism. The discussion revolves around the problems of critical authority and textual resistance. Can the critic submit himself to the singular call of the work without imposing his mastery on it? Does he even want to? Who has the final word, the critic or the text, and what remains unaccounted for in the dialogue, or duel, between them?

Žižek sets out to use popular culture in general and Hollywood film in particular in pursuit of his Lacanian intellectual project. In the introduction to *Enjoy Your Symptom!* Žižek provocatively characterises the relationship between Lacan and Hollywood in Hegelian terms: "Hollywood is conceived as a 'phenomenology' of the Lacanian Spirit, its appearing for the common consciousness" (Žižek 1992a: xi). In part this merely says that Hollywood film can be used to illustrate or exemplify Lacanian theory; but the claim is also more complex, in that it suggests that Lacanian theory is as much a property of Hollywood as it is of Lacan's teaching. Spirit has a phenomenology because it requires the phenomenon in order to appear and to progress on the path towards truth. So Hollywood might benefit from being seen through a Lacanian optic, but Lacanian theory might also benefit from its collusion with Hollywood.

Žižek's mission is in some measure pedagogic, so he chooses examples of popular culture which can be used to help explain elements of Lacanian thought. But this is not quite to say that Žižek is rigidly *applying* Lacanian theory to popular culture. Žižek is not concerned with the question of what a psychoanalytic reading of literature or film would be. Rather, in this respect he is more properly Lacanian, insofar as Lacan (for example in his reading of Poe's "The Purloined Letter," which is discussed in the next section of this chapter) does not apply psychoanalysis to literary works, but rather he finds in the text a knowledge which is the same as—rigorously of equal value to—that of psychoanalysis, even if that knowledge is formulated differently. Žižek describes his practice very carefully, and with characteristic swagger, at the beginning of *Looking Awry*. He refers to the book as

a reading of the most sublime theoretical motifs of Jacques Lacan together with and through exemplary cases of contemporary mass culture. . . . We thus apply to Lacan himself his own famous formula "Kant with Sade," i.e. his reading of Kantian ethics through the eyes of Sadian perversion. What the reader will find in this book is a whole series of "Lacan with . . . ": Alfred Hitchcock, Fritz Lang, Ruth Rendell, Patricia Highsmith, Colleen McCullough, Stephen King, etc. (If now and then, the book also mentions "great" names like Shakespeare and Kafka, the reader need not be uneasy: they are read strictly as kitsch authors, on the same level as McCullough and King.) (Žižek 1991: vii)

The key phrase here is "together with and through." The different texts are read together, without one being treated as "theory" and other as "example"; moreover, Lacan is read through kitsch, rather than the other way around. In this sense it is not so much the application of Lacanian theory to popular culture, as the application of popular culture to Lacanian theory. The question is not "What does psychoanalysis tell us about film?"; rather, Žižek asks what film and psychoanalysis may tell us about one another. Žižek develops his point later with reference to the title of *Look-*

ing Awry: "What is at stake in the endeavour to 'look awry' at theoretical motifs is not just a kind of contrived attempt to 'illustrate' high theory, to make it 'easily accessible,' and thus to spare us the effort of effective thinking. The point is rather that such an exemplification, such a mise-en-scène of theoretical motifs renders visible aspects that would otherwise remain unnoticed" (Žižek 1991: 3).

Žižek is deeply immersed in Lacanian thought and vocabulary. However, it is important to stress that Lacan does not figure as the *knowledge* which popular culture *illustrates*. What Žižek's texts describe is rather a constant zigzag between psychoanalysis and film, effecting a crossover in which each elucidates the other. Popular culture may be understood with the aid of Lacan, but reciprocally Lacan makes more sense when read through popular culture. And it is in the nature of Žižek's writing that it exceeds each frame of reference, as apparently new material and forms of discourse are called upon. Thus the fall of Ceauşescu, the former communist dictator of Romania, is as much bound up with the drama of the big Other as is Lacanian analysis and popular film. Ceauşescu and his followers continued to act as if they believed in the consistency and power of the big Other (as represented by the Communist Party) even when its authority had disintegrated (Žižek 1992a: 41). Žižek implies that if they had taken a course in Lacanian analysis, or watched more film noir, things might have turned out differently.

In Žižek's account, popular culture is a form of knowledge on an equal footing with, or even sometimes superior to, analytic or philosophical discourse. At one moment he introduces Kant to explain popular culture (Žižek 1992a: 164), but at another he insists that, "What Kant did not know, . . . the vulgar sentimental literature, the kitsch of today knows very well" (Žižek 1991: 160). Where does its knowledge originate? The answer to this comes not from overstating the insights contained in popular culture, but by reassessing those which are provided by psychoanalysis. Žižek is not interested in the scientific claims sometimes made by Freud himself for psychoanalysis. Psychoanalysis is not a body of assured, disinterested knowledge subject to verification and falsification. The analyst, in Lacan's phrase, is "the subject supposed to know [*le sujet supposé savoir*]"; and what is crucial here is that the analyst's knowledge is *supposed* by the analysand. Analysis is complete only when the analysand has come to understand that the analyst, as representative of the big Other, simply does not have the knowledge with which he or she is invested.

This subversion of the analyst's authority is an aspect of Lacanian teaching which the psychoanalytical establishment finds hard to swallow; Hollywood, Žižek suggests, "has been more accommodating" (Žižek 1991: 176). This is a typical Žižekian assertion in its mixture of flippancy and seriousness. It looks like a joke to suggest that Hollywood has understood Lacan better than other branches of psychoanalysis have, but Žižek is quite serious. In the Hal Ashby film *Being There* (1979), for example, a simpleton played by Peter Sellers is mistaken for an acute political analyst because he appears in the right place at the right time. This is precisely what the analyst does. The point is that psychoanalysis is not a body of knowledge to be applied, for example to its patients or to literary texts or films. Rather, it is a practice, or a drama, of desire, subjecthood, transference and repetition. And exactly the same can be said of popular culture; even in its most unsophisticated, theoretically naïve versions, it is bound up in the same mechanisms, the same confrontations of sense and sense-lessness, order and chaos, that characterise the psychoanalytic encounter. And this is also the case with Žižek's own texts. His writing is repetitious, it takes surprising twists and turns, goes back on itself and revises what has been said previously. Žižek's style enacts a hesitant edging towards a theoretical position which is never quite finalised, in the attempt to enunciate the Real of desire when, in the Lacanian account, both the Real and desire are beyond the reach of enunciation.

Žižek's unabashed liking for popular culture and its entanglement in his theoretical project is very different from Deleuze's preference for the works of great directors. Nevertheless, Žižek invokes Deleuze in defending the study of film against critics who would tie it too rigidly to its historical context:

One often hears that to understand a work of art one needs to know its historical context. Against this historicist commonplace, a Deleuzian counterclaim would be not only that too much of a historical context can blur the proper contact with a work of art (i.e., that to enact this contact one should abstract from the work's context), but also that it is, rather, the work of art itself that provides a context enabling us to understand properly a given historical situation. If someone were to visit Serbia today, the direct contact with raw data there would leave him confused. If, however, he were to read a couple of literary works and see a couple of representative movies, they would definitely provide the context that would enable him to locate the raw data of his experience. (Žižek 2004: 15)

There is a twofold move here. First, Žižek envisages a "proper" mode of contact with a work of art which might be lost if it is swamped in context; thus, Žižek's often staggeringly brilliant readings of films characteristically endeavour to encounter the theoretical insight of cinema rather than its historical frame. Second, Žižek reverses the precedence of context and film by claiming that film explains its context rather than the other way around. This does not exclude contextual discussion; rather, it supplies it with a dose of humility, restoring to film a voice in forging understanding instead of making it the passive representation of external circumstances.

The example of Žižek's intellectual daring urges critics to be more theoretically bold and experimental in their encounters with film. A question remains, however, over whether the proper mode of contact to which he refers is in fact achievable, particularly since his own approach is so heavily inflected by his Lacanian perspective. Žižek is completely open about this. He can, however, sometimes give the impression that he is making films in a Lacanian likeness more than he encounters what might be unanticipated about them. In *The Fright of Real Tears: Krzysztof Kieślowski Between Theory and Post-theory* (2001), he is quite explicit that his aim is "not to talk *about* [Kieślowski's] work, but to refer to his work in order to accomplish the *work* of theory" (Žižek 2001: 9; emphasis in original). So the theoretical project takes precedence over the ambition of *listening* to film, even if Žižek goes on to insist that his procedure is "much more faithful to the interpreted work than any superficial respect for the work's unfathomable autonomy" (Žižek 2001: 9). He concedes here that there will not be contact with the work *as such*, that it can be encountered only by subjecting it to, in Žižek's word, a "ruthless" use (Žižek 2001: 9). This entails the paradoxical claim that the critic can only be faithful to the work by accepting to distort it. Sometimes, though, it might appear that the distortion overshadows the fidelity, and that Žižek's Lacanian presumptions direct his reading to such an extent that they stand in the way of his contact with film. In his discussion of the Judy-Madeleine figure in Hitchcock's *Vertigo* (1958), for example, the description of her changing place in each of the film's three parts is a little too neat: "In part one, she is

Phi, an imaginary presence at the site of the Real; in part two, she is S(a), the signifier of the barred Other (i.e., the signifier of a certain mystery); in part three, she is *a*, the excremental abject-remainder" (Žižek 2004: 162). Here, the Lacanian optic risks overwhelming Hitchcock's film; elsewhere, as we shall see later in this chapter, Žižek finds in the film a radical insight which echoes Lacan's teaching without merely replicating it.

Žižek's unremitting dedication to Lacanian insights is undoubtedly a strength of his approach, as it raises the theoretical stakes of film and film studies to ever higher levels; but at the same time it may also miss what he calls a "proper" contact, because the language and the optic appear to be ready-made, forming their subject (and their reader) more than they mould themselves to it. In this respect Deleuze is more persuasively inventive in his discussion of film, improvising new concepts (in accordance with his convictions about the philosopher's role) rather than applying old ones. A standard charge made against psychoanalytic criticism is that it merely uses art to illustrate what it already knows. What is at stake here is how far Žižek escapes that charge, and how far it is in any case a fair assessment of the intellectual lineage which he carries forward. The next section discusses some of the issues raised by psychoanalytic, and specifically Lacanian, encounters with art.

Why the Letter Always or Never Arrives at Its Destination

The charge that psychoanalytic critics impose rigid, pre-established notions on art may be countered by the claim that art knows something that the analyst does not (yet) know. In one of the earliest, path-breaking psychoanalytic discussions of literature, Freud's "Delusions and Dreams in Jensen's *Gradiva*," which was first published in 1907, Freud acknowledges that literary authors may be well ahead of psychoanalytic thinkers in their understanding of the human mind: "But creative writers are valuable allies and their evidence is to be prized highly, for they are apt to know a whole host of things between heaven and earth of which our philosophy has not yet let us dream. In their knowledge of the mind they are far in advance of us everyday people, for they draw upon sources which we have not yet opened up for science" (Freud 1985: 34). Moreover, Freud was acutely aware of the limitations of the psychoanalytic method, for example in explaining creative genius, even if, as Shoshana Felman observes, his followers did not always share his awareness (Felman 1987: 38). The early essay on Jensen's *Gradiva* contains a further key implication concerning the link between psychoanalysis and literature. Jensen's story tells of a delusional man who is eventually cured when a woman named Zoe draws him out of his delusion by first entering into it with him. Zoe is in love with the man; and Freud recognises in her intervention a precise reflection of how psychoanalysis works: "The procedure which the author makes his Zoe adopt for curing her childhood friend's delusion shows a far-reaching similarity—no, a complete agreement in its essence—with a therapeutic method which was introduced into medical practice in 1895 by Dr Josef Breuer and myself, and to the perfecting of which I have since then devoted myself'" (Freud 1985: 111–12).

Freud implies that the literary text may contain a pre-analytic knowledge of both the human mind and the psychoanalytic procedure. This suggestion is developed further in Lacan's best-known engagement with literature, "Le Séminaire sur 'La Lettre volée,'" in which he discusses Edgar Allan Poe's short story "The Purloined Letter." Lacan's reading of Poe has become a key text for any discussion of psychoanalytic interpretations of literature. In particular, Derrida's response to it in his essay "Le Facteur de la vérité" (The Purveyor of Truth) lays out what he suggests is a key difference between psychoanalytic and deconstructive approaches: psychoanalysis tends to pin literature down, seeking out its occluded truth, which ultimately merely exemplifies what the analyst already knows, whereas deconstruction aims to respect the text's residue, which resists critical appropriation. For Derrida as for Deleuze, classical psychoanalysis dreams of hermeneutic mastery and in the process finds nothing new. Lacan, according to Derrida, might initially look as if he breaks with established psychoanalytic practices of reading, but in fact his discussion of Poe reproduces them insofar as it uses fiction to illustrate a pre-existing body of knowledge. Derrida criticises Lacan for simplifying Poe; he has in turn been criticised for simplifying Lacan. What is at issue in the debate around Lacan's Seminar, then, is whether or not psychoanalytic reading *inevitably* constitutes an imposition of meaning onto the text.

In Lacan's Seminar, Poe's "The Purloined Letter" illustrates the constitution of the subject through the circulation of the signifier.[2] As Felman argues in her account of Lacan's reading, the psychoanalytic process is implicated in the story to the extent that the detective, Dupin, comes to occupy the position of the analyst. Poe's narrative becomes "no less than *an allegory of psychoanalysis*":

The intervention of Dupin, who restores the letter to the queen, is thus compared to the intervention of the analyst, who rids the patient of the symptom. The analyst's effectiveness, however, does not spring from his intellectual strength but—insists Lacan—from his position in the repetitive structure. By virtue of his occupying the third position—that is, the *locus* of the unconscious of the subject as a place of substitution of letter for letter (of signifier for signifier)—the analyst, through transference, allows at once for a repetition of the trauma and for a symbolic substitution, and thus effects the drama's denouement. (Felman 1987: 43; emphasis in original)

The important point about the position of the analyst-detective here is that what authority he has comes from his position in a structure rather than from any superior knowledge he may deploy. He is not a smug know-it-all; he just happens to occupy a position in which knowledge is attributed to him, like the Peter Sellers character in *Being There*. He is as much possessed by the letter as he is its possessor. As we have seen, the analyst is "the subject supposed to know"; but the fact that the analysand *supposes* him to know does not mean that he knows anything at all, and in fact the goal of analysis is to bring about the realisation that the analyst does not have a master's knowledge. The position of the analyst is a place in a transferential exchange rather than the standpoint of truth. In Jensen's *Gradiva*, Zoe cures her delusional lover by liberating his repressed love and establishing herself as its object. Zoe is in the position of the analyst, because, as Freud put it, in psychotherapy "the reawakened passion, whether it is love or hate, invariably chooses as its object the figure of the doctor" (Freud 1985: 113). This is the process of transference, even if Freud does not use the term here; and it is transference which is the key to the cure, not any specific knowledge the analyst may have. Telling a patient that he is an obsessional neurotic will not cure him; re-activating the causes of his neurosis just might.

Freud's reading of *Gradiva* ascribes to the text a pre-theoretical grasp of psychoanalytical procedures. Lacan's reading of "The Purloined Letter" specifies that the text's understanding of psychoanalysis is not so much a form of knowledge (be it conscious or unconscious, theorised or pre-theoretical) as the understanding of a process in which knowledge is not the key operator. The analyst is supposed to know, but in fact does not. His therapeutic effectiveness does not depend on what he does or does not know. Nevertheless, what is at stake in the current context is whether or not the analyst or critic strives to establish a magisterial position, even whilst insisting that he has none.

Rather than entering into a detailed account of Lacan's much-discussed seminar on "The Purloined Letter," for the purposes of the present chapter I would pick out two points:

First, although Lacan exhibits admiration and respect for the insight of Poe's brilliant story, he also suggests that his own intervention is necessary for that insight to emerge properly. He promises to reveal to us "what Poe's story demonstrates *through my efforts [par mes soins]*" (Lacan 1966b: 7; my emphasis). In other words, the story *on its own* is not sufficient to reveal the operation of the signifier; it needs Lacan's assistance to bring out what remains unspoken. Lacan suggests that the story shows how authority is only ever founded in a structure which lies outside, and defines, the subject; nevertheless, there is at least the hint here that Lacan is re-affirming his own authority over the text by stressing the effort which he has expended on it. Does Lacan aspire after all to be the delusional Master? In the 1955 seminar in which he first discussed "The Purloined Letter," Lacan began by asking his audience to raise their fingers if they had read Poe's story, thereby putting his listeners in the position of schoolchildren being quizzed on their homework. Ruefully, the Master concluded that all too few of his pupils deserved his praise: "not even half of you!" (Lacan 1978: 228).

Second, Lacan's seminar discloses, but then all too rapidly passes over, what remains unanalysed in the story. As its title suggests, "The Purloined Letter" revolves around a letter which is stolen by the Minister and then recovered by Dupin. The Minister steals the letter from the Queen with her full knowledge. Because of the presence of the King, she cannot intervene to stop him, as she does not want to draw the King's attention to the letter; so the Minister casually replaces it with another, which he happens to have with him and which is described as "somewhat similar" and "of no importance" (Poe 1945: 442). All effort is concentrated on recovering the stolen letter, whereas nothing further is said about the one which is substituted for it. But is it correct to pay no attention to the letter left behind by the Minister? Lacan observes that, in a psychoanalytic perspective, whatever appears to be a meaningless detail may in fact be what is most revealing:

A *remainder* [*reste*] which no analyst will overlook, trained as he is to retain every-thing that comes from the signifier even without always knowing what to do with it: the letter, left behind by the minister, and which the Queen's hand can now roll into a ball. (Lacan 1966b: 22; emphasis in original)

The letter which is left behind could turn out to be as important as the one which is stolen. Is it really as insignificant as it is made to seem, or might it be the key that unlocks everything else? To whom is it addressed? Could it be, for example, a love letter from the Minister to the Queen, so that his true purpose was not to steal the purloined letter but to deliver the one left behind? Lacan insists that, although the Queen might roll it up and discard it (a detail not given in Poe's story), no analyst would simply dis-miss it so unthinkingly. And yet, this is precisely what he goes on to do: he does not mention the discarded letter again. He warns his audience that it would be a mistake to neglect it, but then he neglects it himself. His Semi-nar acknowledges a remainder left behind in his reading, and it fails to ful-fil its promise not to let it slip by unnoticed. Interestingly, as we shall see in a moment, Derrida replicates Lacan's neglect whilst also criticising him for overlooking the text's residues.

Derrida's discussion of Lacan's Seminar in his essay "Le Facteur de la vérité" can be seen in the context of a simmering rivalry, even hostility, between the two thinkers. In a long footnote to his *Positions* (1972), Der-rida accuses Lacan of repeated direct and indirect aggressions against him (Derrida 1972c: 113), and he promises to undertake a patient reading of his Seminar on "The Purloined Letter" at a later date (Derrida 1972c: 118). In the Presentation to the "Points" edition of his *Ecrits,* Lacan implicitly asserts the priority of his approach over Derrida's (Lacan 1966a: 11).[3] In "Le Facteur de la vérité" Derrida finally delivered his response to Lacan's Seminar. The essay is a long, detailed engagement with both Poe's story and Lacan's reading of it, as well as a more general reflection on literature, psychoanalysis and literary theory. Early in "Le Facteur de la vérité" Derrida acknowledges that Lacan's Seminar marks an advance in relation to all post-Freudian psychoanalytic criticism, because it gives the signifier its due without rushing headlong to unveil the text's semantic content (Derrida 1980: 452). But that is more or less where the compliments stop. Derrida's critique becomes relentless: in his account, the Seminar treats "The Purloined Letter" in the classic mould of applied psychoanalysis as an example destined to illustrate a law or a truth; the status of the text is not questioned and there is no consideration of how fiction *resists* knowledge, so literature is treated as an example with a message to be deciphered by the analyst; the Seminar merely looks at the content of the story, not at its narration; the displacement of the signifier is treated as a signified; Lacan neglects the role of the narrator, which leads him to read the story in terms of repeated triangles rather than open-sided quadrangles; and the Seminar falsifies "The Purloined Letter" by taking it in isolation rather than considering it in the context of the cycle of stories to which it belongs. In short, Lacan is wrong in detail and misguided in principle. He puts things into the text which aren't there and leaves things out which are. Moreover, despite its concern for the role of the signifier, the Seminar is in the end a "hermeneutic deciphering" (Derrida 1980: 470), which as we saw in Chapter 2 in Derrida's eyes entails the fallacy of a stable, reproducible meaning lodged for all time in the literary text.

The terms in which Derrida's criticises Lacan are themselves strikingly and surprisingly *conventional*. The most conservative literary hermeneut might readily agree that an interpretation could be discredited if it could be shown (a) to be wrong in detail, (b) to fail to account for important features of the text, and (c) to neglect the proper context.[4] Moreover, Derrida's critique may backfire on him if he is not entirely free of the failings he criticises in others. In "The Frame of Reference: Poe, Lacan, Derrida" Barbara Johnson brilliantly analyses how, for all his critical acuity, Derrida replicates some of the moves to which he objects in Lacan's reading of Poe (Johnson 1980: 116–17). For the purposes of this chapter, as with Lacan's Seminar I would like to pick out two points where Derrida's performance is entangled with Lacan's:

First, Derrida, as Johnson puts it, "dismisses Lacan's 'style' as a mere ornament, veiling, for a time, an unequivocal message" (Johnson 1980: 116). Referring to Lacan's Seminar, Derrida says that "in it the logic of the signifier interrupts naive semanticism. And Lacan's 'style' was made to frustrate for a long time [*longtemps*] any access to a content that could be isolated, an unequivocal meaning which could be determined beyond the writing" (Derrida 1980: 449). The most interesting word here is *longtemps* (for a long time). Without it, Derrida would be asserting the impossibility of finding a set of determinate propositions in Lacan's often bewildering writing; but it turns out that Lacan's style blocks access to meaning only temporarily, albeit *for a long time*. In the end the content can be isolated, the unambiguous meaning can be uncovered. Rather than an intriguing instance of the dissemination or deferment of meaning, Derrida finds in the difficulty of Lacan's style little more than annoying impediment which can be overcome with patience. Derrida's *longtemps* is the key moment which enables his entire reading of Lacan's Seminar. Because Lacan's text delays access to meaning *only temporarily*, it is then possible to determine what it is his text is saying, and then to disagree with it point for point. But this admits a dizzying reflexivity into Derrida's critique, since Lacan's key mistake is precisely to bypass Poe's textuality in order to unmask the text's message. Derrida reduces Lacan's text to an inner core of meaning in order to attack Lacan for reducing Poe's text to an inner core of meaning. Here, the question of hermeneutic mastery is at issue once again. Lacan tries to master Poe; unleashing Poe from Lacan's authority, Derrida in turn tries to master Lacan by disclosing his failure to master Poe.

Second, Derrida's discussion takes us back to the problem of the residue or remainder which is left behind in the hermeneutic and psycho-analytic reduction of the text to its semantic core. Derrida picks up on Lacan's reference to the letter left behind by the Minister in place of the one he steals. Derrida suggests on the basis of this that there are two kinds of remainder in Lacan's reading:

1. A remainder which can be destroyed precisely because it is superfluous. The minister left behind a letter to replace the one he stole: "A *remainder* which no analyst will overlook, trained as he is to retain everything that comes from the signifier even without always knowing what to do with it: the letter, left behind by the minister, and which the Queen's hand can now roll into a ball" [quoting Lacan 1966b: 22; emphasis in original]. 2. An indestructible remainder, precisely because it slips away, the "unforgettable" insistence of the purloined letter which determines repetition and the "persistence of behaviour." (Derrida 1980: 451)

I am not sure that Derrida is right to distinguish between two different types of remainder in Lacan, one of which can be discarded and the other which cannot. Lacan implies on the contrary that the Queen would be wrong to discard the substituted letter (although I would point out again that Poe's text does not say that she discards it). The Queen may not realise the significance of the letter left behind by the Minister, but the trained analyst should not dismiss it as casually as the Queen does, even if he does not know what to make of it. Or indeed *precisely because* he does not know what to make of it. So the Queen should perhaps attend more closely to the Minister's letter, even if, having observed its potential importance, Lacan in the end pays it no more attention than she does. The letter is the remainder left behind by the Minister, neglected by the Queen and passed over by Lacan, who nevertheless warns his audience not to pass it over. Derrida extends this neglect of the letter even as he criticises Lacan wrongly for emulating the Queen in trying to destroy it. Derrida does not return to this remainder any more than Lacan does.

Part of the apparent disagreement between Derrida and Lacan hinges on whether or not a letter arrives at its destination, and on what might be meant by such a question. Lacan concludes his reading of Poe's story by telling us that the meaning of the purloined letter is that the sender gets back his own message in inverted form, or in other words "a letter always arrives at its destination" (Lacan 1966b: 53). Taking this as evidence of Lacan's logocentrism, Derrida counters that the letter or the signifier is divisible, fallible, and liable to go astray without assurance that it will eventually return to its proper place: "a letter does *not always* arrive at its destination, and as soon as that belongs to its structure, it can be said that it never truly arrives there, what when it arrives its could-not-arrive torments it with an internal drift" (Derrida 1980: 517; emphasis in original). Lacan insists that a letter always arrives at its destination; Derrida argues that because a letter might not arrive at its destination, then in a sense it *never* arrives at its destination. Poe's "The Purloined Letter" demonstrates this illusory arrival which is in fact a non-arrival insofar as Lacan takes himself to be its proper recipient, unveiling its real message, whereas in fact the story escapes him at the very moment when he reads it.

This disagreement may not, though, be as stark as it seems. Johnson points out that, in Lacan's reading of Poe's story, all those who hold or behold the letter find themselves addressed by it, so that "the letter's destination is thus *wherever it is read*" (Johnson 1980: 144; emphasis in original). The claim that "a letter always arrives at its destination" turns out to be rich in meaning. Johnson suggests that it may suggest, amongst innumerable other things, "the only message I can read is the one I send," "wherever the letter is, is its destination," "when a letter is read, it reads the reader," "the repressed always returns," "I exist only as a reader of the other," "the letter has no destination," and, because the one unmissable message is our own death, "we all die" (Johnson 1980: 145). In their own terms, Lacan and Derrida might both be right when they claim variously that a letter always arrives or that it never arrives at its destination. Indeed, they might be saying something quite similar to one another, all appearances to the contrary.

When Žižek takes up Johnson's discussion of whether or not a letter arrives at its destination, he is characteristically bullish. Derrida's insistence that a letter may fail to arrive at its destination is described as "a primordial response of common sense" (Žižek 1992a: 9) and "simply beside the point" (Žižek 1992a: 12): of course a letter might go astray; everyone knows that, including Lacan. Lacan's dictum has nothing to do with the belief that a letter must always arrive at a preordained goal. On the contrary, it "*lays bare the very mechanism of teleological illusion*" (Žižek 1992a: 10; emphasis in original). The recipient of the message becomes its addressee when and only when she (mis)recognises herself as such. The impression of an infallible trajectory from sender to recipient is a retrospective construction which makes a coherent narrative out of senseless contingent data. Žižek then proceeds, in Johnson's wake, to give a series of paraphrases of "the letter always arrives at its destination" which explain its meaning in a Lacanian optic: "A letter always arrives at its destination *since its destination is wherever it arrives*" (Žižek 1992a: 10; emphasis in original); "there is no metalanguage" (Žižek 1992a: 12); "the symbolic debt has to be repaid" (Žižek 1992a: 16); and (following Johnson, quoted above) "the only letter that nobody can evade, that sooner or later reaches us, i.e., the letter which has each of us as its infallible addressee, is death" (Žižek 1992a: 21).

Žižek's defence of Lacan does not mean that he merely rebuts Derrida's criticisms in order to show that Lacan was right. He stresses the need to go beyond Lacan's Seminar, because it "stays within the confines of the 'structuralist' problematic of a senseless, 'mechanical' symbolic order regulating the subject's innermost experience" (Žižek 1992a: 22). Žižek, then, reinterprets both the Seminar and "The Purloined Letter" from the perspective of Lacan's later teaching. Seen in this way, the letter which circulates in the story is, he says, "no longer the materialized agency of the *signifier* but rather an *object* in the strict sense of materialized enjoyment—the stain, the uncanny excess that the subjects snatch away from each other, forgetful of how its possession will mark them with a passive, 'feminine' stance that bears witness to the confrontation with the object-cause of desire" (Žižek 1992a: 22–23; emphasis in original). Showing the same mixture of fidelity and revisionism with which Lacan treats Freud, Žižek insists that Lacan was right to suggest that "the letter always arrives at its destination," even if it was for reasons other than the ones its writer might have had in mind when he actually wrote it. Moreover, Žižek makes explicit a crucial aspect of his ambition as a Lacanian critic: it is the "stain" or "uncanny excess" of the text which is the true object of his reading. Rather than eliminating this excess, he aims to encounter it as the trace of what he calls "the traumatic presence of the Real" (Žižek 1992a: 23).

From the earliest years of the history of psychoanalysis Freud recognised that art may know something that the analyst has not yet understood. Even so, the analyst arrogates the right to give the artist's insight its precise theoretical formulation. In his *Oedipus Rex* Sophocles might have given dramatic expression to patricide and incest, but he represents their realisation as an unwitting mistake; only Freud, it seems, could draw out the play's unspoken insight into the desire to kill the father and possess the mother. In Freud's wake, both Lacan and Žižek attribute to art a knowledge comparable to that of the analyst, yet in their work there is certainly no unambiguous abdication of authority in favour of the text or film. If Poe's "The Purloined Letter" shows the power of the signifier in the constitution of the subject, it is only, as Lacan does not refrain from reminding us, "through my efforts." At the same time he concedes that something gets left behind—here, the Minister's letter—which might have changed everything if only we knew how to read it. The letter arrives at its destination, but which letter, and which destination? So the letter also fails to arrive at its destination. The text both addresses us and withholds itself from us. In the hands of a Lacan or a Derrida it is both read (brilliantly) and unreadable; or, in Johnson's concluding words, "the true otherness of the purloined letter of literature has perhaps still in no way been accounted for" (Johnson 1980: 146). As Derrida and Lacan contend for the best reading of Poe, we can see a tension between the arrogation of hermeneutic authority and a sense that art continues to resonate from a position of uncomprehended strangeness. It is my suggestion here that this tension is not an aberration which could be eliminated with greater intellectual vigilance; rather, it is at the very core of psychoanalytic criticism at its best, and more generally of critical overreading at its best. Subsequent sections will show that it is inherent to Žižek's practice as interpreter and that it gives savour to what, following Lacan, he might call the idiotic enjoyment (*jouissance*) of interpretation.

Interpretation as Enjoyment

In the introduction to *Everything You Always Wanted to Know About Lacan (But Were Afraid to Ask Hitchcock)* Žižek distinguishes between modernist and postmodern interpretation. In both cases interpretation is inherent to its object, and without it there is no access to the work of art. Modernist art is incomprehensible and traumatic, undermining the complacency of daily routines; commentary serves to integrate the trauma into our everyday lives, showing how the apparently obscure work in fact relates to "normal" reality. The postmodern approach is completely different:

What postmodernism does, however, is the very opposite: its objects *par excellence* are products with a distinctive mass appeal (films like *Blade Runner, Terminator* or *Blue Velvet*)—it is for the interpreter to detect in them an exemplification of the most esoteric theoretical finesses of Lacan, Derrida or Foucault. If, then, the pleasure of the modernist interpretation consists in the effect of recognition which "gentrifies" the disquieting uncanniness of its object ("Aha, now I see the point of this apparent mess!"), the aim of the postmodernist treatment is to estrange its very initial homeliness: "You think what you see is a simple melodrama even your senile granny would have no difficulty in following? Yet without taking into account . . . /the difference between symptom and *sinthom*; the structure of the Borromean knot; the fact that Woman is one of the Names-of-the-Father; etc., etc./ you've totally missed the point!" (Žižek 1992b: 1–2).

The passage is as prescriptive as it is descriptive. Žižek proposes an open series of maximally improbable collisions between high theory and popular culture. In the foreword to the "Short Circuits" series which he edits, he compares critical reading to the shock of short-circuiting, when a faulty connection interrupts the network's smooth functioning (Žižek 2003: vii). In Žižek's version, the short circuit should be deliberately sought out because it reveals disavowed truths, perceptible only when wires get crossed. The familiar should be looked at in unfamiliar ways. Elsewhere Žižek describes this as anamorphosis, the technique in art whereby a seemingly distorted image can be seen in its proper proportions when viewed from an unexpected angle (Žižek 1991: 90–91; 1992a: 139–40). Texts with no apparent connection should be read in the light of one another. In this way, Lacan elucidates Hitchcock who elucidates Lacan. What psychoanalysis brings most powerfully to interpretive practice is the sense that anything, no matter how insignificant it might appear, is potentially interpretable, and that the most innocuous detail may turn out to explain everything else. Žižek comments that Hitchcock aficionados believe that everything has meaning in his films and, referring to *Everything You Always Wanted to Know About Lacan,* he concedes that "this book partakes unrestrainedly in such madness" (Žižek 1992b: 2). Effectively, what he is doing here is making an earnest plea for overinterpretation. Žižek appeals to us to take what might seem simple and to defamiliarise it, to show its exorbitant theoretical sophistication, and to transform its meaning by pronouncing its key to be the hitherto neglected detail. Žižek takes very seriously indeed Lacan's insistence that no alert analyst will overlook a hastily discarded letter.

Žižek's aim in interpretation is to coerce an unseen truth into visibility, and in the process to produce something strange, startling, yet also persuasive. The Lacanian insights of popular culture are not, though, a hidden or latent content to be made manifest by the interpreter. They are precisely what is *already* manifest in the work, albeit misrecognised. The model here is again Poe's "The Purloined Letter," in which the stolen letter is missed by everyone because it is left in plain view. Because it is there for all to see, no one sees it. Two of Žižek's favourite jokes illustrate how we may miss the truth because it is presented to us too directly. The first is discussed by Freud in his *Jokes and Their Relation to the Unconscious* (1905). Žižek frequently cites the joke about two men who meet on a train, for example in *Looking Awry*: "One of these men asks the other in an offended tone: 'Why are you telling me that you are going to Cracow, so that I'll think you're going to Lemberg, when you are really going to Cracow?' (Žižek 1991: 73). The other is Groucho Marx's line from *Duck Soup* (1933): "This man looks like an idiot and acts like an idiot—but this should in no way deceive you: he IS an idiot!" (Žižek 1991: 73). The truth risks being missed because it is *not* hidden. So with his short-circuiting, anamorphotic "looking awry" or his interpretive detours via Lacan, Žižek can suggest that he is not for a moment forcing the work of art to say what is not there, but on the contrary he merely allows it to express a meaning which was always manifest.

Žižek repeats a number of characteristic moves in the elaboration of his interpretations. One is to define a consensus or a common sense view, and then to invert it. Whatever we may think, Žižek likes to let us know that exactly the opposite is the case. Thus, in relation to Kieślowski's *Decalogue*, most interpreters agree that there is no direct correlation between each instalment and one of the Ten Commandments, whereas Žižek argues that each part refers to only one commandment (Žižek 2001: 111). Another approach is to take two opposed readings and to dismiss them both, perhaps according a little greater respect to one at the expense of the other. David Lynch's films, for example, have been read as self-reflexive exercises in making films about films, or they have been subjected to a New Age reading focused on the flow of subconscious Life Energy. Both interpretations are deemed to be wrong, but the New Age reading is at least accorded the merit of taking Lynch's films seriously (Žižek 2000: 3).

Žižek thrives on a rhetoric of uncompromising refutation which robustly dismisses foregoing views. He also revels in the intellectual daring fuelled by his Lacanian training. At their best, his interpretations can be overwhelmingly powerful, making it difficult for subsequent readers or viewers to see anything other than what he has found in the films or books he is discussing. Earlier, I suggested that some of what he says about Hitchcock's *Vertigo* may look too much as if he is imposing Lacanian terminology on the film, but his discussion of the same work in *Looking Awry* is more persuasive whilst being no less Lacanian. At first it may appear that Žižek is using Hitchcock to illustrate the Lacanian saying according to which "the Woman does not exist." However, Žižek incorporates this into a reading which also recognises the radical insight of the film. Judy and Madeleine turn out to be the same woman, but—transformed in Scottie's fantasy world—Madeleine is viewed as sublime and desirable whereas Judy remains plain and undesirable. Žižek compares the situation to an octopus, which is magnificent in the water, but appears only as a disgusting lump of slime on land. The sublime quality of the object is not intrinsic; it depends on its position in a fantasy space. If the film ended with the death of Madeleine, it would be a passionate story of love and loss illustrating that the fantasy figure cannot be possessed in reality: "The Woman doesn't exist." Madeleine's death would in fact justify her sublime, unattainable quality and ensure the hold of the fantasy over Scottie's mind.

Žižek, though, does not stop here, and neither does Hitchcock's film. Hitchcock is, Žižek insists, "incomparably more radical" (Žižek 1991: 85). In the film's second part, as Scottie tries to turn Judy into Madeleine he discovers that Madeleine was Judy all along. Rather than making the banal woman into a sublime object, the sublime object becomes banal and loses her power of fascination. It is as if the film *knows* what Lacanian analysis knows, that is, that the fantasy space is an illusion. The film stages two losses. The first loss of Madeleine confirms her fascinating power: "it is precisely through this loss that she gains her place in the fantasy space that regulates the subject's desire" (Žižek 1991: 86). The second loss is "a loss of loss" (Žižek 1991: 86): not just the loss of Judy, but the disintegration of the fantasy space itself. This is much more devastating than the first loss, because in the first one the fantasy space is reinforced, whereas in the second it is destroyed, leaving the subject with nothing. The film ends ambiguously. As he looks down into the void Scottie is cured of his vertigo, but also he is broken because he has lost the consistency that gave support to his being. Žižek likens this situation to a Lacanian version of the psychoanalytic cure. Rather than hoping for a happy resolution, it entails the acceptance of contingency: "The abyss Scottie is finally able to look into is the very abyss of the hole in the Other (the symbolic order) concealed by the fascinating presence of the fantasy object" (Žižek 1991: 86). In the direct lineage of Freud on *Gradiva* and Lacan on "The Purloined Letter," Žižek finds in *Vertigo* a knowledge of the psychoanalytic method. Hitchcock's film understands Lacanian motifs and also enacts a sort of psychoanalytic cure, leading the central character, Scottie, through a process by which he can finally traverse his fantasy and look into the abyss which it masks.

Although Žižek relentlessly assaults any commonsensical consensus he may come across, he is not always so scrupulous to defend his own views against attack. His approach wavers between patient, scholarly coherence-building and outrageous leaps of the interpreting imagination. So, at one moment he separates out Hitchcock's work into five different periods (see Žižek 1992b: 3–5) whereas at another he insists that the "postmodernist pleasure in interpreting Hitchcock" (Žižek 1992b: 127) lies elsewhere: "one invents the 'craziest' possible shift from the film's 'official' content (the actual core of the *Strangers on a Train* [1951] is the circulation of a cigarette lighter, etc.), whereupon one is expected to stand the test by proposing perspicacious arguments on its behalf" (Žižek 1992b: 127). Referring to two scenes involving shooting in the first version of *The Man Who Knew Too Much* (1934) (in one the mother misses a clay pigeon, in the other she shoots the murderer who is threatening her daughter), Žižek then goes on to say that "one is tempted to say that the film is 'actually' the story of the two shots" (Žižek 1992b: 127). Žižek's scare quotes partially distance him from his assertions: he knows his interpretive leaps are "crazy" and that *The Man Who Knew Too Much* is not "actually" about two shots. Yet this distancing also allows him to embrace the interpretation all the more fully, as if to say "I know it's crazy, but here it is, take it or leave it." The phrase "one is tempted to say" occurs repeatedly in Žižek's writing, as if the path of interpretation were littered with enticing allurements to stray from the straight route of propriety. As for the "perspicacious arguments" that one is "expected" to propose, Žižek can hardly be bothered. He relies more on assertion than argument; and between what one is "expected" to do and what one is "tempted" to do, temptation will win out every time. Like Oscar Wilde, Žižek can resist anything except temptation.

The wavering between coherence-building and "crazy" interpretation is also a tension between the pursuit of sense and enjoyment. Referring to Donald Davidson's semantic "principle of charity," Žižek suggests that there is also a Freudian charity principle which forms the basis of psychoanalytic treatment: "everything that the patient will say, even the most confused free associations, *has a meaning*, is to be interpreted"

(Žižek 2001: 98; emphasis in original). The charity principle justifies the interpreter's hounding after hidden meanings, occluded patterns and underlying truths. Yet coherence-building, however ingenious, is a way of avoiding the Real of desire, the dark inner kernel on which all meaning falters. So the interpreter is impelled onwards, searching for the secret behind the sign, but caught also between the twin dangers of saying too little and saying too much. How, for example, do we explain the glass of unnaturally white milk brought by Cary Grant in *Suspicion* (1941), handed to Gregory Peck in *Spellbound* (1945) and held again by Cary Grant in *Notorious* (1946)? To find a common core of meaning in the glass of milk would be to say too much; but if we make of the milk an empty signifier which means something different in each film, then we miss the force which makes it persist from one film to another, with the consequence that we do not say enough.

To negotiate this tension, Žižek introduces the distinction between the *symptom* and the *sinthom*, a term introduced by Lacan in the late phase of his teaching. The symptom bears a coded message for the interpreter to decipher; the sinthom, on the other hand, is a way of organising enjoyment which means nothing in itself. They are, as Žižek puts it, "formations with no meaning guaranteed by the big Other, 'tics' and repetitive features that merely cipher a certain mode of *jouissance* and insist from one to another totality of meaning" (Žižek 2001: 98). The Hitchcockian glass of milk, like other motifs analysed by Žižek, is such a sinthom. It is the excess or surplus which upsets the interpreter's construction of coherence. Such sinthoms promote the madness of interpretation whilst remaining uninterpretable: "So, paradoxically, these repeated motifs, which serve as a support of the Hitchcockian interpretive delirium, designate the *limit of interpretation*: they are what resists interpretation, the inscription into the texture of a specific visual enjoyment" (Žižek 1992b: 126; emphasis in original). The sinthom fixes a core of enjoyment in the films discussed by Žižek, and also provokes the work and pleasure of interpretation, which as we have seen Žižek characterises as "madness" or "delirium," "crazy" or just plain "idiotic." What is perhaps most crucially at stake in the sinthom is the interpreter's own enjoyment. It incites him to find and to lose himself in the production and the disarray of meaning, the sense and excess, the promise of coherence and the brute, dumb senselessness in which the interpreter wallows like a pig in mud. The interpreter's *cogito* might be: I interpret, therefore I enjoy, and therefore I am not.

Rather than entirely embracing the anti-hermeneutics of the sinthom, Žižek follows the imperatives of both the symptom (Interpret! Find the hidden truth!) and the sinthom (The Real is unfathomable, so enjoy!). In his acts of interpretation he seeks out meaning in accordance with the Freudian principle of charity, which is the psychoanalyst's *vade mecum*. But he also finds meaning to be blocked or inaccessible. What interpretation recovers, repeatedly, is the deadlock at the core of its own enterprise. Everything means something, but the thing that everything means turns out to be the Lacanian Thing, the no-thing which means nothing. This is both the condition and the limit of interpretation.

"As Every Reasonable and Cultured Person Knows . . . "

When Žižek begins a sentence with the phrase "As every reasonable and cultured person knows" (Žižek 2006: 313), it is a sure bet that he is about to say something wilfully heterodox. In this case he is about to tell us that the true greatness of Italian cinema is not neo-Realism "or some other quirk which appeals only to degenerate intellectuals," but spaghetti westerns, erotic comedies from the 1970s and—"greatest of them all, without a doubt"—historical costume spectacles. Žižek's characteristic overstatement compels our assent (Who, after all, would want to be a degenerate intellectual, apart from perhaps Žižek himself?), whilst also leaving us with the nagging sense that we may be being hoodwinked (Surely he can't be serious?). Does the rhetoric force us to agree or invite us to dissent? Is Žižek placing himself in the position of the master of interpretation here, or is he mocking any such position, or is he doing both? In any case, there is the risk that he is a little too persuasive. If we take him at what appears to be his word, we may end up assenting to something which was never more than, at best, a provocative joke. How would we react if students on a European film course started insisting in their examination answers that Italian erotic comedy is "a world-historical contribution to the European and global culture of the twentieth century" (Žižek 2006: 313) whereas neo-Realism is to be ranked alongside other quirks which appeal only to the degenerate?

A good example of Žižek being too persuasive is provided in the introduction to *The Fright of Real Tears*, when he describes his improvised response to an unexpected question:

Some months before writing this, at an art round table, I was asked to comment on a painting I had seen there for the first time. I did not have *any* idea about it, so I engaged in a total bluff, which went something like this: the frame of the painting in front of us is not its true frame; there is another, invisible, frame, implied by the structure of the painting, which frames our perception of the painting, and these two frames do not overlap—there is an invisible gap separating the two. The pivotal content of the painting is not rendered in its visible part, but is located in this dislocation of the two frames, in the gap that separates them. Are we, today, in our post-modern madness, still able to discern the traces of this gap? Perhaps more than the reading of a painting hinges on it; perhaps the decisive dimension of humanity will be lost when we lose the capacity to discern this gap . . . To my surprise, this brief intervention was a huge success, and many following participants referred to the dimension in-between-the-two-frames, elevating it into a term. This very success made me sad, really sad. What I encountered here was not only the efficiency of a bluff, but a much more radical apathy at the very heart of today's cultural studies. (Žižek 2001: 5–6; emphasis in original)

Žižek's stance here is fundamentally ambiguous. He mocks both his own pretentiousness and his audience's credulity, yet there is perhaps also a tinge of boastfulness here. On the one hand he insists that he feels sad that his audience could be taken in by such a preposterous bluff. At the same time he seems proud of his response and of the brilliance with which he pulled it off. What was for him mere verbiage improvised on the spur of the moment is greeted with huge success, and establishes a term that others will subsequently cite. Žižek is saddened that we are taken in, but also gratified by this dramatic demonstration of his superior persuasive powers. The key stakes of mastery and imposture are at play here. The master is an impostor who declares himself to be an impostor and thereby finds his mastery confirmed, strengthened by the knowledge that it is founded in imposture. Godlike, Žižek stands above the fray, deceiving us and feeling the deepest sadness that we are so fallible as to be deceived by him.

Things, though, are about to get even more complex. In the introduction to *The Fright of Real Tears* Žižek cites his improvisation on the two frames of the work of art as a bluff which brings to light both his audience's credulity and a deep apathy within cultural studies. It is certainly not offered as something we should take too seriously as an insight into modern art. We are likely, then, to be surprised when we come across the following passage in chapter 7 of *The Fright of Real Tears*:

One of the minimal definitions of a modernist painting concerns the function of its frame; there is another, invisible, frame, the frame implied by the structure of the painting, which frames our perception of the painting, and these two frames by definition never overlap—there is an invisible gap separating them. The pivotal concern of the painting is not rendered in its visible part, but is located in this dislocation of the two frames, in the gap that separates them. (Žižek 2001: 130)

Žižek then claims that this "dimension in-between-the-two-frames" (*Fright* 130) is obvious in works by Malevich, Hopper and Munch. What was initially cited as a bluff which we would be fools to take seriously is here repeated in apparent earnestness. Žižek now even uses the term "dimension in-between-the-two-frames" which earlier he had claimed was invented by gullible listeners in response to his intervention. The near word-for-word repetition of the earlier passage has an uncanny feel to it. It is as if Žižek has now become the credulous dupe of his own persuasive brilliance, taken in by his own bluff. The effect of this is extremely disorientating. Should we pore over Žižek's words in a scholarly attempt to understand them properly, has the text set us a deliberate trap to see whether we will be misled again by its preposterous claims even when we have been warned against such naivety, or is Žižek inadvertently revealing his own imposture? Who is the butt of the joke here, the reader or the author? We may be further surprised to find the same passage quoted again, almost identically, in Žižek's later work *The Parallax View* (Žižek 2006: 29). But here the context is transformed; the passage is used to support a quite different point from the one made in *The Fright of Real Tears*. Its "frame," as it were, has been replaced, leaving its earlier frame as the invisible second frame characterised by the gap that separates it from its new one. And yet, the pages which precede and follow the passage *do* reappear in *The Parallax View*, here serving a different purpose even though practically identical in formulation apart from the fact that the enframed passage on framing has now been taken out of its frame and placed elsewhere (compare Žižek 2001: 129–34 and Žižek 2006: 70–73).

Žižek's writing displays an ingrained distrust of power and received opinions whilst at the same time claiming for itself a position of high authority. If his practice as interpreter often suggests the most wayward, freewheeling, wilful embracing of the work's semantic openness, his rhetoric on the contrary constantly ties it down to single, correct readings. The "ultimate message" of Lynch's films is the identity of Evil and the good family father (Žižek 2000: 23); Žižek spells out the "ultimate secret" and the "odious lesson" of Hitchcock's *Psycho* (Žižek 2006: 257), as well as its "ultimate social-ideological lesson" (Žižek 2006: 262); and repeatedly he tells us how we *should* read: "One should refer her to the Freudian-Lacanian notion of the 'fundamental fantasy'. . . . Against this background, one should conceive of the Mystery Man [in Lynch's *Lost Highway*] as the ultimate horror of the Other who has a direct access to our (the subject's) fundamental fantasy" (Žižek 2000: 20). We could take such expressions as mere verbal tics revealing a characteristic tendency to overstatement rather than a serious claim to reveal the sole and single truth. A more Žižekian approach, though, would be to take Žižek entirely at his word. These are not loose phrases which conceal or obscure his meaning; they are very precise expressions of exactly what he wants to say: he *has* got it all right, everyone else *is* wrong, he *is* the Master. Like the purloined letter which is misperceived because it is too visible, Žižek's meaning may mislead because it is openly displayed. To paraphrase Freud's joke: why does Žižek tell us that he knows the ultimate truth, so that we may think he is a modest relativist like the rest of us, when in fact he knows the ultimate truth? Or to paraphrase Groucho Marx: this man talks as if he knows everything and acts as if he knows everything; but don't be misled, he does know everything. Or at least he thinks he does.

This arrogation of critical authority is contained, perhaps obstructed, by a textual practice which suspends the assertive force of any given claim, since there hovers over it the prospect that it should always be read within quotation marks. Žižek has taken the lesson of recycling very much to heart: everything is to be used twice over, at least. The unnerving repetitiveness of his writing has become part of its distinctive texture. As he cuts and pastes and leaps from topic to topic with breathtaking urgency, we might begin to suspect that repetition is a marker of excess, displaying an irreducible surplus of meaning in pursuit of its own idiotic enjoyment. Žižek impels us to take seriously the stories and films he discusses, to believe that they really do encapsulate an advanced theoretical understanding of Lacanian psychoanalysis; but he may leave us unsure whether to suspend disbelief or to resist allowing ourselves to become the text's dupe. The Master, Žižek tells us, *adds no new content*; he invents a signifier through which others change their world: "Therein lies the magic of a Master: although there is nothing new at the level of positive content, 'nothing is quite the same' after he pronounces his Word . . . " (Žižek 2006: 37). The Master is a self-confessed, perhaps also self-duping, impostor whose performative Word *does* more than it *means*. Žižek's writing sometimes warns us of the dangerous power of the delusional Master and sometimes surrenders itself to its own heady exuberance.

Žižek's texts are a bracing, unsettling experience. He warns us of the Master's imposture and celebrates the impostor's mastery. His prolific, repetitive, omnivorous, breathtakingly bold writing embodies perfectly its subject: the obscene, idiotic, crazy enjoyment of (over)reading.

CHAPTER SIX

Cavell and the Claim of Reading

I assert this as obvious and do not argue it.

—AUSTIN 1962: 6

I must now put the uncontroversial aside and put forward a bunch of assertions.

—CAVELL 1984: 162

The phrase "the claim of reading" echoes the title of Stanley Cavell's book *The Claim of Reason* (1979) and deliberately draws on some of its resonance. Cavell is a reader who attempts to remain attentive to the claims made by the work he is reading, and specifically by its claim on him, its pretension to teach him, to know something of importance to him which he did not previously know. The issue for him is not to ask what we might know of a text, but rather to ask what it is that a text we care about might know, and how it might call on us to receive its instruction.[1] At the same time, Cavell is a reader who makes claims about the works he is reading. To claim is not to prove or to argue, but to assert as one's own, even when the message identified as one's own is articulated in another's voice. So the claim of reading is the text's claim on its readers, its claim to possess and therefore to dispossess us in the act of reading; and it is also the reader's repossession of a voice in the claim to speak for a text which speaks to and of its reader.

Reading is essential to Cavell's understanding of what it means to be a philosopher.[2] Whereas his intellectual inspiration, J. L. Austin, reportedly read few works of philosophy, Cavell conceives of philosophy "not as a set of problems but as a set of texts" (Cavell 1979a: 3). Philosophy is not so much about solving problems as about reading texts which might help us to live with our still unsolved quandaries. Cavell's language does not have the dramatic hyperbole of Derrida, Deleuze or Žižek. Rather than deconstructing the metaphysics of presence, overturning Platonism or hunting out the traumatic kernel of the Real, he sets out, as the title of one of his books puts it, "in quest of the ordinary," to discover that the ordinary is strange and unfamiliar to the precise extent that it is our everyday habitat.[3] Though the philosophical timbre may be very different from the high-stakes urgency of Derrida, Deleuze and Žižek, the ambition is no lower; like them he works to release something which has gone unperceived, perhaps because—to evoke again Poe's "The Purloined Letter" (discussed in Chapter 5)—it was hidden in full view, too obvious to notice. If for Lacan "The Purloined Letter" is an allegory of psychoanalysis, for Cavell it is an allegory of ordinary language philosophy: what we seek (to possess, to understand) is right in front of us, invisible to us or stolen from us because we do not know how to hold on to what is our own (see Cavell 1988: 160–69). What is to be encountered, then, is the uncanny in the Freudian sense of that which is both utterly close to us and utterly mysterious; and reading is the means of encountering it.

So for Cavell doing philosophy means reading texts, with the greatest predilection for those of Wittgenstein and Austin, but also the works of major figures from Plato through to Kant and up to Lacan and Derrida; and it also entails asserting the claim of certain less canonical authors to be allowed into the mainstream of philosophy, most notably Emerson and Thoreau.[4] This is not yet enough, though. Cavell also seeks his philosophical instruction from literature and from film. His interest in literary texts is indicated by numerous references and detailed discussions, and in particular by his essays on Shakespeare which are collected in *Disowning Knowledge in Seven Plays of Shakespeare* (2003).[5] He has also been increasingly recognised as one of the founders of philosophical film criticism, thanks to a series of books in which he makes strong claims for the philosophical seriousness of film. Gerald Bruns suggests that "film-watching and philosophizing are not different things for Cavell," because both involve "careful attention to particular human situations and to what people say and do in them vis-à-vis each other" (Bruns 1999: 200). This is not to say that Cavell corrodes or dissolves the conventional distinction between work in philosophy and art. He bemoans philosophers' lack of interest in literature, and also what he calls "philosophy's indifference to the literary conditions of its own existence" (Cavell 1984: 31); but this is not to advocate the subversion of disciplines. Cavell turns Plato's "ancient quarrel" between philosophy and literature into his own "lifelong quarrel with the profession of philosophy" (Cavell 1984: 31). Rather than a quarrel between philosophy and its outside, it is now a quarrel within philosophy concerning its reluctance to learn from what does not, at least at a disciplinary level, belong to it. He is dismayed at philosophy's failure to engage with literature. This is not, though, to say that literature and film are or should be counted as philosophy; rather, they partake of a mode of existence which is philosophical, and from which the philosopher might find instruction. Like Martha Nussbaum, Cavell suggests that the relation between literature and philosophy might be one of alliance and companionship rather than rivalry (see Cavell 2003a: 2).

Along with other thinkers discussed in this book, Cavell resists the suggestion that he is *applying* his ideas to literature or merely using literature to *illustrate* them. He argues that any model or practice of reading which involves applying a pre-existing position seriously misses the point or, worse still, becomes dull. Psychoanalytic interpretations of texts, he says, "have seemed typically to tell us something we more or less already knew, to leave us pretty much where we were before we read" (Cavell 1984: 52); in reference to Shakespeare's *Coriolanus* he comments that political reading is similarly "apt to become fairly predictable once you know whose side the reader is taking" (see Cavell 2003a: 145). Cavell wishes to unsettle philosophy's implicit assertion of priority borne by the concepts of illustration and application: in re-activating the ancient quarrel, they restore first place to thought and allow literature only an ancillary role (see Cavell 2003a: 1). The companionship he seeks between different modes of discourse and responsiveness entails a sensitivity to what he calls their "interplay," for example in his essays on Shakespeare:

the burden of my story in spinning the interplay of philosophy with literature is not that of applying philosophy to literature, where so-called literary works would become kinds of illustration of matters already independently known. It would better express my refrain to say that I take the works I am drawn to read out in public (beginning with those I have listed of Shakespeare) as studies of matters your philosophy has (has unassessably, left to itself) intellectualized as skepticism, whether in Descartes's or Hume's or Kant's pictures of that inescapably, essentially, human possibility. (Cavell 2003a: 179)

Tentativeness belongs to the intimate texture of Cavell's prose. "Interplay" is an imprecise word to name a relation which Cavell cannot yet or cannot here characterise with greater precision; the non-committal guardedness of "*so-called* literary works" and "*kinds* of illustration" holds him back from attempting to resolve issues which are not here the crux of the matter. He offers a "story," albeit what he might hope to be a plausible one, rather than purporting to tell us an incontrovertible truth; and he is aware that he is indulging in a perhaps tiresomely repetitive "refrain" rather than something refreshingly new. And yet, there is compulsion and responsibility here which lurk behind the tentative phrasing. He is "drawn" to speak of Shakespeare, and his story bears a "burden." When he distances himself from "*your* philosophy," he discreetly alludes to Shakespeare; after encountering the ghost of his father Hamlet insists that "There are more things in heaven and earth, Horatio,/ Than are dreamt of in your philosophy" (*Hamlet*, Act 1, scene v). Philosophy left to itself may miss what is most important. This is not, though, to advocate withdrawing from philosophy and from the summons to thought altogether; it is rather to displace the locus of thinking from its most privileged homes, in the work for example of Descartes, Hume or Kant. No less than theirs, Shakespeare's texts are "studies." Their genre may be different, but their intellectual seriousness should not be mistaken.

Cavell writes against, but also to some extent from within, the Anglo-American tendency in philosophy to accord little intellectual weight to literary works. Contrary to this predisposition, he insists that Shakespeare could not be the great writer he is "unless his writing is engaging the depth of the philosophical preoccupations of his culture" (Cavell 2003a: 2). Shakespeare's plays are treated as essays in skepticism, restlessly exploring what can be known of the world, of oneself and other selves in an unfathomable world of illimitable desires. It is not simply, though, that skeptical issues can be discerned in Shakespeare's plays. Cavell's key claim is that Shakespeare registers a shift in the skeptical problematic from its earlier formulations, a shift to which Descartes's *Meditations* (1641) would give decisive expression for the future development of Western philosophy. Moreover, Shakespeare writes about, and thinks through, these issues decades before Descartes would set them down in a form usually recognised as philosophy: "My intuition is that the advent of skepticism as manifested in Descartes's *Meditations* is already in full existence in Shakespeare, from the time of the great tragedies, in the generation preceding that of Descartes" (Cavell 2003a: 3). For modern thinkers, the skeptical problem is no longer, or not only, "how to conduct oneself best in an uncertain world"; it is now "how to live at all in a groundless world" (Cavell 2003a: 3). Cavell does not use Shakespeare to illustrate, to exemplify or to explain pre-existing ideas, because those ideas did not exist, or they had not been lucidly articulated, before Shakespeare gave them dramatic form. In this case at least, philosophy comes *after* literature's great achievement.

In his resistance to philosophy's neglect of literature, Cavell sometimes knowingly exacerbates the power of surprise potentially aroused by his claims in the institutional and disciplinary contexts in which he makes them. In fact, he deliberately cultivates and underlines the polite excessiveness of his readings. He warns the readers of his essays on Shakespeare that "[he] may well from time to time, in [his] experimentation, speak incredibly or outrageously" (Cavell 2003a: 5). Given the studied care and precision with which Cavell writes, I take the "or" here ("incredibly or outrageously") to offer a genuine alternative: what he says will sometimes be incredible even if it is faintly reassuring; or, it may be entirely credible, but nevertheless outrageous. The alternative is not between comfort (credibility and reassurance) or subversion (incredibility and outrageousness); rather, the familiar and the disturbing will be held together in different ways and unpredictable ratios. Here again, Cavell hints that his theme is the uncanniness of the ordinary. Later sections of this chapter will look in more detail at Cavell's practice as an interpreter; for the moment I want to underline Cavell's description of his readings as "experimentation" and his readiness to entertain what might seem outrageous or wilfully odd. His aim is to follow through what he calls an "intuition" (a term to which I shall return later) as far as possible, and then to assess, or to leave it to his readers to assess, whether that leaves us with something that is worth retaining.

Cavell's project entails a staunch and explicit defence of overreading.

We cannot know in advance what power of discovery may be unleashed by our preposterous-seeming interpretations, so we might as well try them out to see where it leaves us. The introduction to *Pursuits of Happiness* gives the best defence I know of overinterpretation. Cavell is not overly concerned, at least as a starting point, about the danger of "reading in," that is, finding in a text something that is not actually there, or more than is verifiably there:

Naturally I do not deny that some readings are irresponsible in fairly straightforward ways. But "reading in," as a term of criticism, suggests something quite particular, like going too far even if on a real track. Then the question would be, as the question often is about philosophy, how to bring reading to an end. And this should be seen as a problem internal to criticism, not a criticism of it from outside. In my experience people worried about reading in, or overinterpretation, or going too far, are, or were, typically afraid of getting started, or reading as such, as if afraid that texts—like people, like times and places—mean things and moreover mean more than you know. This is accordingly a fear of something real, and it may be a healthy fear, that is, a fear of something fearful. It strikes me as a more discerning reaction to texts than the cheerier opinion that the chase of meaning is just as much fun as man's favorite sport (also presumably a thing with no fear attached). Still, my experience is that most texts, like most lives, are underread, not overread. And the moral I urge is that this assessment be made the subject of arguments about particular texts. (Cavell 1981: 35)

The fear of overreading is a desire for containment, a longing for the familiar, the stable and the knowable unspoiled by the taint of uncanniness. This would be a world from which the possibility of skepticism had been forever banished. For Cavell, though, the standing threat of skepticism resides in the prospect that, at any moment, our most cherished certainties (about life, ourselves, or those we love) might collapse, leaving us knowing far less than we thought. Uncanniness may erupt from the heart of the everyday. Cavell's quest for the ordinary requires him to entertain the outrageous, in order to know the ordinary better than an unthinking familiarity can achieve. Literature is one companion in this endeavour. The next section considers how film is another insofar as, in Cavell's words, "film exists in a state of philosophy" (Cavell 1981: 13).

Philosophy and Film

Stanley Cavell has explored his experience of and care for film in a series of books and papers, most notably *The World Viewed: Reflections on the Ontology of Film* (1971), *Pursuits of Happiness: The Hollywood Comedy of Remarriage* (1981), *Contesting Tears: The Hollywood Melodrama of the Unknown Woman* (1996), and *Cities of Words: Pedagogical Letters on a Register of the Moral Life* (2004).[6] Cavell like Žižek is a lover of Hollywood, as is suggested by the subtitles of *Pursuits of Happiness* and *Contesting Tears*; but whereas Žižek confesses to his "idiotic enjoyment" of popular culture (Žižek, 1991b: viii), Cavell wants his enjoyment to go together with a full engagement of his intellect. He insists that the best Hollywood films are comparable in theme and intelligence to Shakespeare's plays, and that there is amongst them a body of first rate and near first rate work larger than the whole canon of Jacobean drama. Žižek's Hollywood may appear to be a guilty pleasure boldly confessed; Cavell's, on the other hand, fully belongs to the discussion in which philosophy also participates.

What Žižek calls the "proper contact" with the work of art (Žižek 2004: 15)[7] is matched by Cavell's notion of "the good encounter" (Cavell 1981: 13). Such encounters do not engender definitive readings, and successive encounters are not cumulative because, as Cavell puts it, "a later one may overturn earlier ones or may be empty" (Cavell 1981: 13). Rather, the encounter is the sign of an ongoing *connection* or *relation*, of which the significance may remain unstable. If the encounter is to take place, we must let the work teach us how to consider it (Cavell 1981: 10). As in the discussions of Deleuze and Žižek, what is at stake here is whether or not the thinker actually learns from film, or whether on the contrary he ends by reaffirming the precedence of his own discipline and established insight. In this respect Cavell's first book on film, *The World Viewed*, is less interesting than some of his later work. The subtitle of the book, *Reflections on the Ontology of Film*, makes its ontological ambitions explicit, as it sets out to answer the question "What is film?" from a philosophical perspective.[8] Here, Cavell writes as a philosopher enquiring after the essence of film. He occupies the position of the external gaze, teaching about his subject more than he learns from it. There is little extended discussion of individual films until the very end of the enlarged edition of the book, when he analyses the closing sequence of Renoir's *La Règle du jeu*. In his later works *Pursuits of Happiness, Contesting Tears* and *Cities of Words* Cavell turns from ontology and develops instead a distinctive philosophical hermeneutics of film. This involves more focussed attention on individual films and a greater sense that they are (at least) equal partners in an ongoing dialogue.

Cavell's philosophical hermeneutics of film also, crucially, entails a conception of film as having a part to play in the process of philosophy. In his paper "The Thought of Movies" Cavell describes how films give him "food for thought," and this explains why, as a professional philosopher, he has recourse to philosophy when he writes about them: "I go for help in thinking about what I understand them to be thinking about where I go for help in thinking about anything, to the thinkers I know best and trust most" (Cavell 1984: 7). The key point here is not the (in itself unremarkable) justification for using philosophy to help in the understanding of film; rather, it is the assertion that films are themselves *thinking*. They are already thinking before the thinker thinks about them; his thought is subsequent to and consequent on their prior achievement. Cavell's central claim is that "film exists in a state of philosophy" (Cavell 1981: 13). Quite what Cavell means by this, though, is difficult to pin down. In *Pursuits of Happiness* he explains that film's state of philosophy comes about because "it is inherently self-reflexive, takes itself as an inevitable part of its craving for speculation; one of its seminal genres—the one in question in the present book—demands the portrayal of philosophical conversation, hence undertakes to portray one of the causes of philosophical dispute" (Cavell 1981: 13–14). In "The Thought of Movies" he offers a rather different explanation of the claim, relating a film's self-undermining to the fact that "it has always been the condition of philosophy to attempt to escape itself" (Cavell 1984: 20). Self-reflexive films question the conditions of their existence, just as philosophers repudiate philosophy in a philosophical manner.

Cavell's linking of the same claim to different explanations is not an inconsistency in his thought so much as a recognition that the philosophical standing of film has yet to be fully understood. We find in Cavell's writing a shifting array of partial characterisations for the ways in which he relates film to philosophy. He discusses film "in the light" (Cavell 1981:

8) of major works of thought, yet he insists that "we must let the films themselves teach us how to look at them and how to think about them' (Cavell 1981: 25); philosophy and film are "juxtapos[ed]" (Cavell 1981: 13); philosophical issues are said to be "raised" by films and by film "as such" (Cavell 1981: 73); Cavell discusses and problematises the use of film as "an *illustration* of some prior set of [philosophical] preoccupations" (Cavell 1981: 272; emphasis in original); films and thinkers have a "bearing" on one another (Cavell 1996: 24); film "invites" philosophical discussion (Cavell 1996: 62), "participates" in the ambition of self-thought or may "satisfy the craving for thought' (Cavell 1996: 72); and there are "intersections" between film and philosophical concerns (Cavell 1996: 199). It is "*as though* the condition of philosophy were [film's] natural condition" (Cavell 1984: 152; my emphasis) and the creation of film was "*as if* meant for philosophy" (Cavell 1996: xii; my emphasis). Words such as "bearing" or "intersections," as well as the non-committal "as though" and "as if," might appear to be tantalisingly imprecise, so that Cavell's key claim about film existing "in the condition of philosophy" might turn out to mean less than it seems to be saying. However, the unstable, partial, tentative nature of these characterisations is essential to their point. Cavell reproduces for his reader his own hesitant edging towards an acceptance of film as philosophy, and his own knowingly incomplete understanding of what the claim means. He readily admits that his own conviction on the matter is unsteady, and that he seeks to persuade himself as much as his audience. The tentativeness in his prose reflects the unsettled nature of his conception and a readiness constantly to rethink it.

Deleuze's assertion that great filmmakers are "confrontable" with philosophers does not make of them equal partners in the project of thought; Žižek's description of Hollywood as the "phenomenology" of Lacanian Spirit does not quite accord it the same status as the psychoanalytical master. Cavell's position, on the other hand, gives precedence to neither philosophy nor film. If anything, Cavell tends to let film rather than philosophy have the final word. The difference between Žižek and Cavell on this point can be illustrated by the similar but different structures of Žižek's *Enjoy Your Symptom!* and Cavell's *Cities of Words*. Each chapter of Žižek's book takes a problem in Lacanian psychoanalysis and deals with it first through examples from Hollywood film and then in a more purely theoretical manner. Cavell's book pairs a series of essays on major world thinkers with discussion of a film. Whereas in Žižek's book film comes first but theory has the final word, in Cavell's it is precisely the other way around.

We saw in Chapter 3 that when Deleuze compares Orson Welles to Nietzsche, the great director is presented as approaching elements of Nietzschean thought without matching Nietzsche's originality, clarity or insight. This contrasts with Cavell's comments on the link between Nietzsche and the director Leo McCarey. Most would agree, I think, that McCarey is not as significant a figure in the history of film as Welles; nor is he as well-known as Hollywood contemporaries such as Frank Capra and Howard Hawks. Yet he had a very distinguished career in film, winning three Oscars and directing classics such as the Marx brothers' *Duck Soup* (1933) and one of Cavell's favourite films, *The Awful Truth* (1937). Renoir is widely quoted as having said that "Leo McCarey understood people better than any other Hollywood director" (quoted, for example, in Cavell 1981: 231). In his discussion of *The Awful Truth* Cavell compares the end of the film to Nietzsche's vision of becoming a child, overcoming revenge and accepting Eternal Recurrence. He defends this link between McCarey and Nietzsche:

All you need to accept in order to accept the connection are two propositions: that Nietzsche and McCarey are each originals, or anyway that each works on native ground, within which each knows and can mean what he does; and that there are certain truths to these matters which discover where the concepts come together of time and of childhood and of forgiveness and of overcoming revenge and of an acceptance of the repetitive needs of the body and the soul—of one's motions and one's motives, one's ecstasies and routines, one's sexuality and one's loves—as the truths of oneself. (Cavell 1981: 262)

In Deleuze's comparison between Welles and Nietzsche, Welles appears as a paler version of his philosophical precursor. There is no such implicit privileging of the philosopher over the filmmaker in Cavell's link between McCarey and Nietzsche. Each is an "original," and each discovers the same truths by separate, distinctive paths. The works of both are of strictly equal status. Cavell's respect for film does not reveal itself only in his wish to *speak* of it philosophically; his practice consists in a willingness to attend to it in such a way that he can *learn* from it philosophically also.

Cavell explains the particular philosophical significance of American film by reference to America's lack of the established "edifice of philosophy" stretching from Plato onwards which informs European intellectual self-awareness. America, though, craves thought no less than Europe; so, Cavell insists, "American film at its best participates in this Western cultural ambition of self-thought and self-invention that presents itself in the absence of the Western edifice of philosophy" (Cavell 1996: 72). Film is doing philosophical work; its key themes of knowledge, perception, relation, and the existence of other minds are also the stuff of philosophy. On Cavell's account, however, an unprepared public is as certain to misperceive the philosophical call of film as film is bound to instantiate the yearning for thought: "[film] has the space, and the cultural pressure, to satisfy the craving for thought, the ambition of a talented culture to examine itself publicly; but its public lacks the means to grasp this thought as such for the very reason that it naturally or historically lacks that edifice of philosophy within which to grasp it" (Cavell 1996: 72). Cavell here is talking specifically about American film and American audiences. He describes an unavoidable mismatch between films and their spectators, so that film becomes a site where the craving for thought is both realised and overlooked. However, despite what Cavell suggests about the more settled philosophical tradition in Europe, there is little reason to assume that European audiences are any more ideally attuned to their films than their American counterparts. So Cavell can be taken as providing an explanation both for the philosophical significance of film (not just American film) and for the inevitability that it will be misunderstood.

On occasion Cavell's vocabulary can be every bit as specialised and technical as that of Deleuze and Žižek in their discussions of film; but of the three Cavell gives the most persuasive sense that he allows himself to be taught by the films he considers, using his writing as the place of an encounter between his own philosophical outlook and the film's wisdom. His views seem less settled than theirs, more capable of being shaken and refined by the experience of film. And because it is the *experience* of film which concerns him—its ability to inform a life—he even stands by his mistakes: a failure of memory may be as interesting and as central to an experience as accurate recollection (see Cavell 1979b: xxiv). Moreover, Cavell's philosophical conversation with film reflects what he takes film to be about: the discovery of other minds, learning to converse, the invention of viable modes of being with others, the readiness to teach and to be taught and to forgive.

The Knowledge of Film

Cavell's endeavour to be taught by film requires a form of attention to the work which allows it to speak of matters which may not have struck viewers as its most immediate concerns. The rest of this chapter looks in more detail at how Cavell elicits meaning from a film, referring in particular to his discussions of Capra's *It Happened One Night* (1934) and, in the next section, Hitchcock's *North by Northwest* (1959). *It Happened One Night* starred Claudette Colbert and Clark Gable, two of the biggest stars of the time, and it won Oscars for best actor, best actress, best director, best film and best adaptation. Cavell discusses the film in the context of the first of what he calls two "genres" of film, the comedy of remarriage and the melodrama of the unknown woman, which he elaborates respectively in *Pursuits of Happiness* and *Contesting Tears*. Since these genres inform much of what Cavell says about the films he admires, it will be useful briefly to outline his understanding of them.

The comedy of remarriage contains films such as *His Girl Friday* (1940), *Adam's Rib* (1949) or *The Awful Truth*, in which a couple facing separation manage to repair or to re-create their relationship before it is irretrievably lost. The lovers are reunited by their willingness to participate in a conversation with one another, exploring both their differences and their desire to be together. The remarriage comedy typically ends with the couple back together; it is nevertheless haunted by the prospect that they will fail because the problems between them, the simmering violence that emerges at moments even in comedy, may turn out to be insurmountable. In *Contesting Tears*, which is a kind of sequel to *Pursuits of Happiness*, Cavell explores a companion genre, the melodrama of the unknown woman (named after Max Ophuls's film *Letter from an Unknown Woman* (1948)), in which couples fail or are unwilling to overcome the gulf between them. In the remarriage comedies, the woman wants to learn, to be known, and to participate in a conversation; in the melodrama of the unknown woman, which includes films such as *Gaslight* (1944) and

Now, Voyager (1942), the woman chooses instead to be isolated and to remain unknown, refusing the false solution of marriage or remarriage. The comedy of remarriage is a struggle for acknowledgement, whereas in the melodrama of the unknown woman that struggle is abandoned or renounced. This is not because woman is figured as inherently or ontologically unknowable; rather, as Cavell puts it, the choice of solitude is "the recognition that the terms of one's intelligibility are not welcome to others" (Cavell 1996: 12). Woman's desire is unacceptable to men. She does not desire what men would want her to desire, so she chooses to remain separate, unknown and unpossessed.

One of Cavell's key claims is that psychoanalysis and film are connected by the facts that both emerge at roughly the same time (the last years of the nineteenth century), and that a crucial aspect of both of them is that from their earliest years they were more interested in the study of individual women than individual men (see Cavell 1996: 98). Both are driven to some extent by the question of what we (that is, men) can know about women. Woman's unknownness, in this context, is what drives man's desire to know woman and to know what a woman knows. At the same time this male desire is deeply ambivalent, since it both insists on and dreads knowing what a woman knows. What we (again, men) discover may be the last thing we wanted to know. Self-consciously working within the Freudian question "What does a woman want?" (to which Cavell alludes in Cavell 1996: 19), Cavell gives it an epistemological twist. In both the comedy of remarriage and the melodrama of the unknown woman, the issue is not just "What does a woman want?," but also "What does the woman want to know and to be known?" (Cavell 1996: 23). In this extension of the Freudian question, Cavell recognises that the libidinal drama is also an epistemological one; moreover, he suggests that woman is not just the *object* of the question, because she is also the *subject* of desire and knowledge, and she is the source of decisions about her willingness to be known by men. In the remarriage comedies, the woman wants to know men (amongst other things) and to be known by them; in the melodrama, she chooses to remain unknown rather than settling, for example, for what Cavell calls "a marriage of irritation, silent condescension, and questionlessness" (Cavell 1996: 11).

Cavell counts *It Happened One Night* as a member of the genre of remarriage comedies.⁹ This designation is not self-evident, because the couple in the film do not actually get remarried, though the female lead does marry twice. Even so, Cavell argues that the key features of the film are the same as those of other remarriage comedies. One such feature is the fact that the film concerns the education of a woman, a woman who is willing to learn, and who through the acknowledgement of her desire can emerge as an autonomous human being. This claim in itself may be relatively uncontroversial; what marks out Cavell's reading, though, is his treatment of the film and its themes in the context of the thought of Immanuel Kant. The chapter on the film in *Pursuits of Happiness* begins with an exposition (actually a very clear, succinct exposition) of Kant's theory of knowledge. In the introduction to the book Cavell shows that he is fully aware of the provocative nature of this juxtaposition:

I am not insensible, whatever defenses I may deploy, of an avenue of outrageousness in considering Hollywood films in the light, from time to time, of major works of thought. . . . This essay [on *It Happened One Night*] begins with the longest consecutive piece of philosophical exposition in the book, concerning the thought of Immanuel Kant, whose teaching has claim to be regarded as the most serious philosophical achievement of the modern age. And what follows this beginning is the discussion of a Frank Capra film, not even something cinematically high-minded, something sad and boring, something foreign or foreign-looking, or something silent. Evidently I meant my contribution to a discussion of limits and their transgressions to be an essay that itself embodies a little transgression in its indecorous juxtaposition of subjects. (Cavell 1981: 8)

Cavell is aware that he is rubbing against convention by juxtaposing Kant and Capra, and we can see here an instance of Cavell's thematic concerns spilling over into his own practice. His essay deals with barriers and the possibility of their transgression, and it tests those barriers through its readiness to bring together material normally kept apart. So, a complex web of themes and aims links Kant, the film, and Cavell's exploration of the boundaries of film and philosophy. For Cavell reading entails cultivating, or as he says here *courting*, the outrageous: "I gave reasons in the Introduction for my refusing to disguise, even for my wishing somewhat to court, an outrageousness in the subjects of film and of philosophy, especially at what I think of as their mutual frontiers" (Cavell 1981: 73). Once again, Cavell's self-characterisation overlaps with the themes of his essay.

It Happened One Night is about courtship as it is about barriers and their transgression. Moreover, courtship now joins companionship as terms to define the bond between art and philosophy. In Capra's film two very different characters from very different backgrounds learn that, despite everything that separates them, they can nevertheless want the same things, in respect for rather than annihilation of their strangeness to one another. The process of learning and reciprocal acknowledgement which they undergo is also the hesitant edging towards one another that Cavell promotes between art and philosophy.[10] In Cavell's settlement of the ancient quarrel, the outrageousness which he pursues entails encouraging the courtship of two incompatibles, not brought together in a relationship of full and open knowing, but facing each other in affection or love for each other's unfamiliarity.

The key interpretive move here consists in establishing a link between the concerns of philosophy and the themes of comedy or melodrama. Early in the essay on *It Happened One Night* Cavell achieves this by relating the problem of knowledge to that of marriage: "Two of the fundamental human properties that human societies have been most anxious to limit are the capacity to relate oneself to the world by knowledge and the capacity to relate oneself to others by marriage" (Cavell 1981: 74). In one sentence Cavell collides epistemology with Hollywood romance by linking together their key questions: what can we know, and whom should we marry? This also brings together the two aspects of skepticism which have been Cavell's career-long concern, namely the knowledge we can have of the external world and the knowledge we can have of other selves. These issues are in turn related to divisions between the public and the private, that which is intimate and untouchable and that which is open and available to all. This then leads into a discussion of Kant, the philosopher most associated with the limitation of human knowledge. In Kant's *Critique of Pure Reason* (first edition, 1781) the restriction of knowledge is envisaged as both a loss and a gain. The world of things in themselves is forever closed to us; we can know things only as they appear, not as they are truly and immutably. In the terms used by Kant, the phenomenal is knowable to us whilst the noumenal remains forever outside our grasp. But in understanding the impenetrability of the noumenal we have also learned something of the greatest importance: we have acquired a knowledge of the very conditions of knowledge insofar as it is available to us. Cavell calls this "a traumatic increase of human knowledge" (Cavell 1981: 76). There is an unmoveable limit to what we can know, a barrier for ever separating the knowable from the unknowable. We can survey that barrier from the standpoint of our human finitude, but we can never step beyond it.

Cavell's first bold interpretive move is to link the problem of knowledge to the comedy of remarriage. A few pages later he makes a second bold move, one which he himself does not expand upon but which effectively underpins the rest of the essay. He considers how a teacher of philosophy might picture our inaccessibility to the realm of things in themselves. The teacher might, for example, draw a circle or a line on a blackboard to indicate that our faculties cannot penetrate outside the circle or below the line. Such means might be effective, but Cavell does not entirely endorse them: "But if now I ask myself how I picture the barrier to the realm of ends, I find I draw a blank" (Cavell 1981: 79). This almost throwaway sentence introduces a play on the word *draw* which will return later in the essay. One might draw a picture; and a picture might also be a moving picture or a motion picture, that is, a film (as in the expression *to go to the pictures*). Drawing is also something that happens in a lottery, but Cavell says here that he draws only a blank, that is, a losing ticket. So in the attempt to draw a picture, he draws a blank. What is drawn, then, is nothing; the picture is a blank space. But one might also draw a curtain, which might mean to close it, to set up a barrier, or to pull it back, to open up the division between two spaces. And what might serve as a curtain is not a blank but a *blanket*; and a blanket does indeed serve as a curtain, or a barrier separating two private spaces, in *It Happened One Night*. The blanket and its role in the film now become the central issues in Cavell's reading. Whereas Cavell, attempting to draw a picture of human knowledge, draws a blank, in the moving picture *It Happened One Night* the male protagonist draws a blanket to establish the clear yet transgressable barriers between selves.

In the key scene from *It Happened One Night*, the runaway heiress played by Claudette Colbert and the reporter played by Clark Gable prepare to spend a night together in a motel room. The Gable character attaches a cord between the twin beds in the room and hangs a blanket over it, thereby dividing the room into two separate spaces. Gable explains that he does not want to be overseen: "Well I like privacy when I retire. Yes, I'm very delicate in that respect. Prying eyes annoy me." He describes the blanket as "the walls of Jericho" and proceeds to undress, at which point Colbert withdraws to her own side of the room. On his own side of the blanket, Gable can see signs of her undressing as the blanket moves when she touches against it. She hangs some of her clothes over the blanket, but moves them when asked to do so by Gable. With them both lying in their separate beds, Colbert realises that she does not even know the name of the man with whom she is spending the night. She asks "Who are you?," as if setting up the barrier between them is the condition by which they might begin to learn each other's identity. The scene ends with a shot of Gable and Colbert in their beds, kept apart by the blanket which divides the room. The drama of the rest of the film is whether and how the walls of Jericho, that is, the barrier separating private selves, can be breached.

We know full well, of course, that a blanket is only a blanket, and Cavell knows it too. It is "a comic barrier, hardly more than a prop in a traveling salesman joke" (Cavell 1981: 80). Yet Cavell wants it to be more, as according to him it invokes issues of metaphysical isolation and the possibility of community; indeed, he insists that it "*must* invoke them if this film's comedy is to be understood" (Cavell 1981: 80; emphasis in original), even if he immediately tempers the authority of such a claim by confessing to his own doubt and stating that "it is still in part myself whose conviction I seek" (Cavell 1981: 81). This oscillation between categorical assertion and the disclosure of doubt is the very condition of the experimental nature of Cavell's procedure. He advances as if his claims were assured, absolutely indispensable for proper understanding, whilst also undercutting such certainty in self-questioning asides. These asides buy him the right to go forward, dispensing him from further caution. They have to be there to save his writing from crazed dogmatism, but they have to be set aside if his self-exposure to the film, his courting of hermeneutic outrageousness, is to get anywhere new. He has set himself up as a divided subject of his own text, both the author of wild interpretations and the skeptical addressee who awaits to be convinced of them. With the latter lodged in place, the former can now proceed to press the film for its meanings as rashly as he dares. The confession of doubt serves also as a self-incitement to boldness.

In the ensuing exploration of the senses borne by the blanket, three strands in particular emerge, and are intertwined. The blanket is a limit to knowledge, separating us from what we cannot know; it is the transgress-able boundary between selves; and it serves to represent the movie screen onto which are projected our uncertainties and desires. I will say a little more about each of these in turn:

1. The blanket is a limit to knowledge. It prevents Gable and Colbert from seeing each other, from seeing each other undress and seeing each other naked. So it stands in the way of their (carnal) knowledge of each other. It is the barrier separating subjects from what they cannot or should not see; but as such it is also, picking up the Kantian theme, the very condition of the knowledge a subject can have. By barring knowledge of the unseen world, it also creates and delimits a space that *can* be known. Neither Colbert nor Gable can see beyond the barrier, but each of their separate worlds is fully visible and knowable to them.

2. The blanket is a boundary between selves. Gable insists on his privacy, being delicate and annoyed by prying eyes. He does not wish to be seen as he undresses, though the camera dwells on him as long as it dares; and he accords the same right to Colbert, though again, the camera dwells as long as it dares (and interestingly, although Gable makes no attempt to see her undress, in the sequence he shows a surprisingly comprehensive knowledge of *men's* habits of taking their clothes off). This insistence on privacy is a refusal of intimacy, an unwillingness to see or to be exposed to the too-present other. Even when asked, not unreasonably, what his name is, Gable initially talks around the question before giving it a straight answer, as if to speak his name is already to reveal too much of himself:

—By the way, what's your name?

—What's that?

—Who are you?

—Who, me? I'm the whippoorwill [an American nocturnal bird named after its call] that cries in the night. I'm the soft morning breeze that caresses your lovely face.

—You've got a name haven't you?

—Yeah, I got a name. Peter Warne.

—Peter Warne. I don't like it.

Even the arousal of desire may be an unwelcome intrusion into one's privacy. Gable puts up the blanket not just out of politeness or respect for Colbert's modesty, but perhaps because he does not *want* to see her undress. He asks her to remove her clothes from his sight because they are too distracting; they make him too aware of the disquieting proximity of the other.

However, insofar as the blanket stands for the walls of Jericho, its fate is to be brought down once Joshua has sounded his horn. The film depicts this transgression of limits as possible even if it is no easy matter. In a later scene from the film, set in another motel room, Colbert listens to Gable's dreams of an ideal woman and, wanting to be that woman, steps around the blanket to enter his side of the room. Here, though, real and imaginary lives are too brutally confused, and Gable rejects Colbert as she walks into his dreams. Later, after she has returned to her separate bed, he reflects and changes his mind. He wants to accept her as both a dream figure and a reality, to let her into his dreams and to make of his dreams a reality. Yet he continues to withdraw from her even as he longs to accept her. Strangely, rather than telling her that he has changed his mind, he leaves her asleep and goes off to secure some money which will enable them to be together, hoping to return before she awakes. In other words he leaves her temporarily so that they can be together permanently.

Cavell notes that Gable's actions at this point are not adequately explained; and although the film ends happily for the couple, with the walls of Jericho breached, his mysterious abandonment of Colbert is a failure which "remains an eye of pain, a source of suspicion and compromise haunting the happy end of this drama" (Cavell 1981: 101). In Cavell's account, the "happy ending" of the comedy of remarriage cannot definitively eliminate the reasons why a couple might split up; the possibility of a future failure always haunts the couple's success in the present.

3. The blanket acts as a screen, standing for the movie screen, onto which fantasy is projected. It does not give access to a full vision of the thing itself, but it allows reality to be guessed at even whilst it withholds it. Gable does not see Colbert undressing, but the hint of her body as the blanket moves when she brushes against it may be all the more erotic for being largely in the imagination. As the blanket both shows the presence

of Colbert and the poignancy of her absence, Gable is in the position of the film's viewers:

That the barrier works like a movie screen means that our position as audience is to be read in terms of the man and woman's positions with each other, and especially in terms of the man's, for it is with him that we first watch the screen take on the characteristics of a movie screen, and his problem of putting together a real woman with a projected image of her seems a way of describing our business as viewers. (Cavell 1981: 105)

What Gable sees, and what we see, is both real and not real enough, the mark of something that it would be nonsensical to deny, but which is presented to us as out of our reach. This can be related to Cavell's complex understanding of film's realism elaborated in *The World Viewed* and "More of *The World Viewed*," an essay added to the second edition of the work. Cavell is often depicted as a realist, because his theory of film relies on the photographic link between cinema and reality; but if he is a realist, he is also, in the words of one commentator, "probably the subtlest realist ontologist of film to date" (Carroll 2006: 53). For Cavell, reality may be in some sense captured on film, but it is also inaccessible and problematic. He insists that film has a particular bearing on skeptical doubt concerning the existence or intelligibility of the world: "Film is a moving image of skepticism: not only is there a reasonable possibility, it is a fact that there our normal senses are satisfied of reality while reality does not exist—even, alarmingly, *because* it does not exist, because viewing it is all it takes" (Cavell 1979b: 188–89; emphasis in original). Looking at the screen, we have an experience of the senses which meets our expectations and requirements of the external world, yet the world is not fully present to us. This presence-absence of the world, and our absence from the world that seems present unto itself, encapsulates the skeptical dilemma insofar as it realises the fear that the world we hope to know is unavailable to us as we are unavailable to it. It places reality in front of us, but keeps us separate from it.

This is not to say that for Cavell there is no representation of reality in film; such a view is in his opinion a "fake skepticism" (Cavell 1979b: 188), since it is blatant to him that photography, painting or film may represent reality. To deny it is to deny the obvious. But this does not mean either that film refutes skepticism by offering to us a world which is available for us to know and to possess; that would be, as it were, a fake realism as flawed as fake skepticism. Film is a moving image of skepticism precisely because it does not resolve the stand-off between the desire to know the world and a sense of its retreat from us. Cavell's text is particularly dense here, in part because the complexity of his thinking is conveyed by a rich exploration of and play upon the multiple meanings of words. This is apparent in the description of film as "a *moving* image of skepticism" (my emphasis), which simultaneously suggests that film presents an image that moves and an image that moves *us*, in that it presents us *movingly* with the skeptical dilemma. The final sentence of the same paragraph summarises the argument that film neither gives us the world as knowable nor removes it from us (or it does both). The "sense of reality," Cavell insists, "is neither enforced nor escaped through film: one might say that it is there entertained" (Cavell 1979b: 189). The word "entertained" captures precisely the ambiguity of Cavell's point: the sense of reality is both kept open as a possibility, toyed with as something we might genuinely experience, and also *distracted*, kept occupied by a fiction rather than attending to its proper business.

The point of such ambiguities is that Cavell declines to defuse the tension between skepticism and realism. It is what he calls "a farce of skepticism" to deny "that it is ever reality which film projects and screens" (Cavell 1979b: 189).[11] Both *projects* and *screens* here are (at least) double-edged. Film projects reality by putting it up before us, but *as a projection*: something constructed rather than merely reflected. And reality is *screened*: both presented to us on a screen, and screened from us, made inaccessible even as it is offered to us. This play on *screening* is picked up in the following paragraph in a key sentence which perfectly encapsulates the complexity of Cavell's position. "In screening reality," he says, "film screens its givenness from us; it holds reality from us, it holds reality before us, i.e., withholds reality before us" (Cavell 1979b: 189). The screen puts reality before us and bars our way towards it; film "withholds reality before us" because reality is at the same time held up for our attention and withheld from us. Film gives us a world, but it is a world which we do not possess, and to which we do not belong.

The blanket in *It Happened One Night* becomes, then, a means for Cavell to engage with the dilemmas of skepticism, understood not as a philosophical position to be proven or refuted once and for all but as a standing threat which can never be fully expelled from our relation to the world and others. The final paragraph of the essay on Capra's film in *Pursuits of Happiness* brilliantly brings together the three aspects of the blanket as a restriction of knowledge, a barrier between selves, and a screen on which the world is projected:

I would read the instruction of the barrier along these lines. What it censors is the man's knowledge of the existence of the human being "on the other side." The picture is that the existence of others is something of which we are unconscious, a piece of knowledge we repress, about which we draw a blank. This does violence to others, it separates their bodies from their souls, makes monsters of them; and presumably we do it because we feel that others are doing this violence to us. The release from this circle of vengeance is something I call acknowledgement. (Cavell 1981: 109)

The passage again plays carefully on words, and in particular on the earlier sentence where Cavell referred to drawing a blank when attempting to draw a picture of the barrier which separates us from the realm of ends. The "picture" of the final paragraph is surely the motion picture Cavell has been discussing. It draws a blank, or draws a blanket, in order for the characters to shield themselves from what they do not wish to know about the existence of the other. Importantly, this is "a piece of knowledge we repress." It is not something that cannot be known, but something that we choose not to know. Cavell's implicit departure from Kant here is that for Kant the barrier cannot be overcome since the truth of things in themselves can never be known. For Cavell the barrier can be transgressed, not to acquire knowledge of the noumenal or of unfathomable other minds, but to create a situation where we might *acknowledge* the presence of others, to relate to them in their otherness. The outrageousness of Cavell's essay is not really that he discusses Kant alongside a Hollywood comedy; it is rather that he gives the final word in the debate to the Hollywood comedy, contriving to find in it a critical response to Kant, an insight as profound as Kant's and one which is perhaps more humanly useable.

A Bunch of Assertions

It is essential to Cavell's stance that, with the right kind of receptive attention, one might learn something from a film like *It Happened One*

Night which is every bit as incisive, persuasive and relevant as what one might learn from Kant about the limitations of knowledge, about skepticism, and the possibilities of improving the self and creating a human society worth living in. Has Cavell gone too far? Can so much really be at stake in the blanket? Cavell would wish to argue that we grossly misunderstand the achievement of Hollywood film in the 1930s and 1940s if we do not acknowledge its intellectual seriousness, even and perhaps especially the intellectual seriousness of its comedies. At the same time, Cavell accepts that he is being perhaps wilfully outrageous, conceding that he is trying to convince himself as much as anyone else. His wager is that the gains to be made in courting outrageousness outweigh what is risked in departing from common sense. How, though, are the gains to be assessed? By what criteria or authority are they to be measured and evaluated? Cavell calls for his audience's assent, and he endeavours also to persuade himself as his own self-reader. Often, though, he does not argue his position so much as present or assert it, appealing for but not compelling agreement. For this to succeed he needs to create a context in which what he says may appear plausible or worth entertaining. This section examines his essay on Hitchcock's *North by Northwest* to show how he goes about building up an argument, and how he expects that argument to be assessed.[12]

If Žižek's Hitchcock somehow seems to know all about Lacan, rather like Žižek himself, Cavell's Hitchcock also turns out to share many of his own concerns: relatedness, the formation of human couples and communities, the perfectibility of the self, and the nature of the film medium. Cavell's essay, though, entails a much more patient wooing of his audience's consent than Žižek is inclined to undertake. He begins with the complex gesture we have already observed, whereby he makes a bold claim for film's philosophical seriousness, partially withdraws from it, but nevertheless leaves the assertion firmly on the table. Film, he says, is "free of the imperative to philosophy," yet it seems "inevitably to reflect on itself—as though the condition of philosophy were its natural condition" (Cavell 1984: 152). He immediately follows this, which is after all the enabling, indispensable claim underlying his philosophical approach to film, with the disarming confession that it may appear ridiculous, even to himself: "Over and over I have had to find again my conviction in these matters, to take my experience over the same path, finding the idea of film's philosophical seriousness first to be comic, then frightening, then inescapable" (Cavell 1984: 152–53). The gambit here is both to make the claim in the most forceful way possible (it is after all "inescapable') whilst also allowing dissent from it or wariness towards it (it may also be found to be "comic" or "frightening'). The aim of the essay is to lead both the reader and its author, insofar as the author is a skeptical observer of his own performance, to be convinced (again) of film's philosophical seriousness.

Cavell does not rush his reader into assent. He refers to a possible connection between *North by Northwest* and Howard Hawks's *Bringing Up Baby* (1938) which he had suggested in *Pursuits of Happiness*, but he does not ask us "out of the blue to believe this connection," and he asks us "still less" to accept his contention that Hitchcock's film contains an allusion to George Cukor's *The Philadelphia Story* (1940) (Cavell 1984: 153). Cavell's tactic in this essay is to work slowly towards conviction. So he begins by being so uncontroversial that he states the blindingly obvious: "But let us begin as uncontroversially as we can. *North by Northwest* contains as one of its stars Cary Grant" (Cavell 1984: 154). Who could argue with that? Cavell suggests that Grant's presence is stressed in the film by remarks about how he is good-looking and vaguely familiar, and by specific allusions to other films that Grant made with Hitchcock; and Cavell then sketches a reflection on film acting and acting in general. But after only a couple of pages, he reins himself in, as if he were at risk of becoming too speculative too quickly: "But I was trying to begin uncontroversially" (Cavell 1984: 156). The essay now sets out to recover the uncontroversial stance which it had promised, and from which it may have strayed. It starts again, with a statement as bland as the observation that one of the film's stars is Cary Grant: "The film is called *North by Northwest*" (Cavell 1984: 156).

At this point Cavell embarks on a discussion of possible allusions to Shakespeare's *Hamlet* in Hitchcock's film. In the play Hamlet describes himself as "but mad north-northwest" (Act 2, scene ii). However, Cavell does not yet demand of us that we accept the film's title as an allusion to the play. Instead, he begins to amass what he calls "facts" (Cavell 1984: 157) to support the possibility of a link: Grant's character is described as "an ageless male identifying himself first of all as a son"; he is abducted by a man who has usurped another man's house and name; the name of Laertes from *Hamlet* is echoed in that of Leonard from *North by Northwest*, an echo strengthened (a footnote suggests) by the fact that the Laertes character was called Leonhardus in an alternative version of the story (Cavell 1984: 157–58). Cavell introduces more and more "facts" of this sort in the expectation that no single one of them will settle the matter, but that together they will add up to a strong case. Different readers might be persuaded at different points, or not at all. Cavell tells us that what clinched it for him was the observation that the name of Grant's character has the initials ROT, about which he quips that "rot" is his trademark; to Cavell this "irresistibly suggests" (Cavell 1984: 158) Hamlet's sense that "something is rotten in the state of Denmark" (Act 1, scene iv).[13]

Starting from the uncontroversial, indeed the undeniable ("The film is called *North by Northwest*"), Cavell has proceeded to supply evidence for something which may be a little more contentious, namely, the possibility that *Hamlet* may be "present in the film in some fashion" (Cavell 1984: 158). He does not even require of us that we take this point to be definitively established, merely that we allow it "for the sake of argument" (Cavell 1984: 158). The next step is to ask, "So what?," or, as Cavell puts it, "Of what interest is this, I mean of what interest to Hitchcock?" (Cavell 1984: 158–59). The essay now departs from the uncontroversial and shades further and further into the frankly speculative. It is as if, by expressing his own doubts and beginning by offering something like conventional evidence, Cavell has acquired for himself the right to open the interpretive throttle. This is especially significant in this context because, as he speculates on Hitchcock's relation to his sources, his desire to compete with Shakespeare as the supreme artist of his chosen medium, and his particular reasons for invoking *Hamlet*, Cavell perceives an address to interpreters. He observes that *Hamlet* is the subject of perhaps the most famous Freudian interpretation of a work of art, Ernest Jones's *Hamlet and Oedipus* (1949), and suggests that this may help to explain Hitchcock's invocation of the play:

Given the blatant presence of Freudian preoccupation and analysis in Hitchcock's work I see in his allusion to *Hamlet* a kind of warning to Freudians, even a dare, as if to say: of course my work, like any art, is subject to your interpretations, but why are these interpretations so often so obvious, unable to grasp the autonomy,

the uniqueness, of the object? (Hitchcock would not be the first artist of this century to feel he has to pit his knowledge of human nature against the thought of the
man who is said to have invented its science. (Cavell 1984: 160)

So Hitchcock sets out to rival Freud as much as he rivals Shakespeare, as-
piring to be the greatest artist in his medium as well as the greatest analyst
of human nature. What is not clear is how far Cavell wants or expects the
assent of his listener at this point. His statement that "I see in his allusion
to *Hamlet* a kind of warning" leaves a great deal unsaid. Has he in fact established that there is an allusion to *Hamlet*, or are we still only entertaining the possibility "for the sake of argument'? Does that fact that *he* sees
a warning mean that he wants or requires or hopes that we will share his
view, or for current purposes is it sufficient that he sees it, without need for
his audience's corroboration?

    This is a pivotal moment in Cavell's essay. After beginning, as he
claims, uncontroversially, that is, in a manner which might command the
ready assent of his audience, Cavell has now reached a point where Hitchcock's film demands and resists interpretation, as it both issues a warning
and accepts a dare. The challenge to interpretation which Cavell sees is
evidently not restricted to Freudian critics. Hitchcock's work attacks the
interpreter for stating the obvious whilst being unable to grasp the autonomy of film. It follows from this that interpretation can only match up
to the challenge of its object if it eschews the obvious, and therefore if it
abandons the consensual terrain of the uncontroversial. Cavell's essay begins cautiously but reaches a point where the film itself seems to insist that
the interpreter should cast caution to the wind. As quoted in one of the
epigraphs to this chapter, Cavell now renounces his earlier determination
to court, as far as he could, the audience's agreement: "I must now put the
uncontroversial aside and put forward a bunch of assertions" (Cavell 1984:
162). In the following paragraph Cavell begins this bolder phase of his
reading by, as he says, "reinterpreting, or interpreting further" the famous
scene from *North by Northwest* in which Thornhill, Grant's character, is
attacked by a crop-dusting plane the day after he and the female lead, Eve,
played by Eva Marie Saint, have spent the night together on a train:

Something cataclysmic happened to Thornhill and Eve the night before, and *I understand* the attack the next day to be simultaneously a punishment for the night
and a gaudy visual equivalent of it. Then *I understand* the crop-dusting plane, in-

strument of victimization, as a figure for a movie camera: it shoots at its victims and it coats them with a film of something that both kills and preserves, say that it causes metamorphosis. *I claim* evidence for the association of the prairie with the, let us say, inner landscape of the train compartment, in the way a close-up of Eve's face at the Chicago train station dissolves into the establishing aerial shot of the road and fields of the plane attack. The conjunction of color and mood *I claim* asks for an allegorical identification of the woman and this stretch of land, but this is just something further *each viewer must try out on his or her own.* (Cavell 1984: 162; my emphasis throughout)

The more speculative interpretive stance here does not entail giving up on evidence and argument; but the presentation of the evidence incorporates the awareness that some will not find it compelling. The repetition of "I understand" and "I claim" effectively signs the interpretation as Cavell's and simultaneously acknowledges that others may not be persuaded. The film's call to the interpreter to be less obvious, to seek out what is unique in it, results in Cavell inscribing himself more fully in his readings, taking responsibility for them even whilst insisting that they are a response to the call of the work. The film provokes the interpretation but cannot come good as its final, unequivocal guarantor. The ultimate judge of its truth or plausibility must be the interpreter or his audience. Cavell claims what his says is adequate to its object without insisting that his audience should agree; instead, he asks that each viewer should try it out on his or her own.

This notion of "trying it out" is of the utmost importance to Cavell's interpretive approach and his philosophical stance. His abiding concern is with the everyday and the ordinary, which is at once fully familiar to us and also strangely unknown. From J. L. Austin, whom he encountered as a graduate student, he learned and inherited the task of prospecting what is all around us, so obvious that it usually goes unseen or unprobed. Cavell's attitude to the texts and films he examines is the same as Austin's in his treatment of examples. They are not illustrations of something already known; rather, they are the raw material from which he seeks instruction. What validates that instruction are not impeccable syllogisms so much as an appeal for our recognition and assent. I know the difference between killing a donkey by mistake or killing it by accident, even if I do not know that I know it, or quite know what it is I know.[14] Austin calls our attention to what is already obvious, though we may not have observed it. Similarly, Cavell's interest "depends upon circling the obvious" (Cavell 1995: 83). "Circling" does not mean merely presenting; it entails testing, estranging, questioning, trusting and distrusting. In these matters there is no arbiter of validity outside oneself. Cavell states that, to accept what he says, "you can only consult yourself, not expect an independent confirmation" (Cavell 1995: 82). Of his essay on *Hamlet*, which some might consider to be too brief, he considers that it would be "the soul of witlessness" to strengthen or lengthen it by adducing further evidence: "Either it has an initial plausibility or it is, and must remain, nothing; and my commitment to it is such that I leave as naked as I can the difficulty of accepting it" (Cavell 2003a: 13). In other words, take it or leave it; or more precisely, run it past an inner court rather than hoping to be given clinching proof. Cavell proceeds from what, following Emerson, he calls "intuition." Whereas a hypothesis demands proof according to explicit criteria for what will be allowed as evidence, an intuition is not verifiable in the same way; it "does not require, or tolerate, evidence but rather, let us say, understanding of a particular sort" (Cavell 2003a: 4). It calls to be followed through, to be completed in what, again following Emerson, Cavell calls a "tuition." It needs to be tried out, taken as far as it can go, and then assessed for whether or not it will hold. And since Cavell is his own first reader, the doubter whose conviction he seeks, it will be put to the test of his own judgement before being submitted to an audience. No certain criterion allows him or us to know in advance whether it will achieve assent or merely arouse indifference.

Cavell's characteristic speaking position is that of someone who makes claims which appeal for but do not demand assent. This is not to say that he abandons any attempt to persuade his reader of the truth of his claims; but it will be an interpretation's aptitude to stick, not its demonstrable validity, which will decide its usefulness. To read, in this sense, is to yield to partiality: "This has nothing to do with—it is a kind of negation of—an idea of reading as a judicious balancing of all reasonable interpretations. My reading is nothing if not partial (another lovely Emersonian word)" (Cavell 2003a: 5).[15] However knowingly outrageous the resulting interpretations may be, they are not—or at least they aim to avoid being—wilful or arbitrary. This is because the key claim of reading is not the claim a reader might make about the work, but the claim that the text or film makes on the reader, so that what Cavell might feel he needs to say comes as a compulsion *from outside*. His interest is not in what a text means, but in what it *knows* or seems to know. If a claim about a text hits home, it is because it strikes us as attuned to what the text itself already knows. And its knowledge is finally a knowledge *about us*. It speaks uncannily, if it speaks at all, to that which is both most familiar and most strange, closest and most distant: that is, ourselves. Cavell's modesty is that he tells us only of what we already know. His immodesty is that he tells us only of what we do not know that we know. Like the books and films for which he cares, his writing speaks to us insofar as it knows something about us, about our ordinary lives of what Thoreau calls "quiet desperation,"[16] which we are entirely free not to recognise.

CHAPTER SEVEN

Conclusion: In Praise of Overreading

Reading works of literature forces on us an exercise of fidelity and respect, albeit within a certain freedom of interpretation. There is a dangerous critical heresy, typical of our time, according to which we can do anything we like with a work of literature, reading into it whatever our most uncontrolled impulses dictate to us. This is not true.

—ECO 2006: 4

The Avoidance of Error

This book began by quoting Johann Martin Chladenius, according to whom hermeneutics teaches us "to avoid misunderstandings and misrepresentations" (Chladenius 1985: 64). Contrary to how it is sometimes depicted, hermeneutics certainly does not claim that texts have only one, unambiguous meaning, but it insists that some interpretations are better and more valid than others. It is necessary to avoid the sense that we can say anything we like. As Eco says in the epigraph to this chapter, it is "a dangerous critical heresy, typical of our time" to assume that we can read whatever we want into a literary work. There is nothing new in the discovery that texts have multiple meanings; the issue is to avoid interpretive anarchy. Early Christian commentators, for example, distinguished between four senses of Holy Scripture (literal, allegorical, moral and anagogical) and thereby provided a code for its proper understanding which could be overseen and sanctioned by the authority of the Church (see Eco 1984: 147–53). From its origins, the role of hermeneutics was to combat the

"Babel of Interpretations"[1] by striving to establish ways to assess what is sound and what is aberrant by way of interpretation.

Peter Szondi observes that the focus of hermeneutics has changed in recent times; once it was, he says, "exclusively a system of rules, while today it is exclusively a theory of understanding" (Szondi 1995: 2). The difference, though, is not as stark as it might seem. If modern theorists tend not to draw up rules for assessing the plausibility of interpretations, this does not mean that they give up on the regulative function of hermeneutics. The most prominent twentieth-century exponents of hermeneutic thought in Germany and France, Hans-Georg Gadamer and Paul Ricoeur respectively, both oppose arbitrariness in interpretation or what Gadamer calls "hermeneutic nihilism" (Gadamer 1986: 100). Their theories of understanding are also theories of what it means to understand *correctly*, without error. Interpretation may be, as Paul de Man glumly put it, "nothing but the possibility of error" (De Man 1983: 141). If that is the case, however, hermeneutics is its necessary corrective: the promise that with due caution we might avoid error and perhaps even attain the truth.

Is truth, though, to be discovered by exercising due caution, or by abandoning it? Perhaps, as Alain Badiou has suggested, real thinking has to be *reckless* if it is to exist at all (Badiou 2009: 84). Perhaps the possibility of error is so inherent to human existence that we should learn to live with it rather than trying to eliminate it. Perhaps it is only when we take risks and court outrageousness that we discover anything worth saying. These are in part the lessons of the overreaders presented in this book.

From a hermeneutic point of view, one of the questions underlying the book has been whether any regulative constraints can be applied to the readers discussed here, starting with Heidegger. Is "overreading" governed by principles and susceptible to validation, or is it merely the idiosyncratic and inimitable practice of prestigious, charismatic readers? Derrida rejects "the hermeneutic project postulating the true sense of a text" (Derrida 1978: 86); Deleuze denies that what he does should be called interpretation, and disdains any debate aiming at correction and consensus; Žižek recommends a "ruthless" use of artistic pretexts (Žižek 2001: 9); Levinas endorses an "audacious hermeneutics" (Levinas 1987: 10), at least when dealing with Jewish sacred texts; and Heidegger and Cavell both argue that the potential gains of overinterpretation outweigh the risks. The positions and practices of these thinkers are all different from one another. Levinas typically begins his talmudic commentaries with a statement of modesty in respect of the text; Derrida and Cavell are patiently respectful toward the objects of their study; Heidegger, Deleuze and Žižek present themselves more as heroic adventurers setting out on unmarked paths, blustering through the dry protocols of scholarship. Each of them, though, positions himself outside the disciplinary boundaries of literary or film criticism in order to increase the philosophical yield of reading.

This final chapter returns to some of the debates concerning interpretation in order to spell out how the overreaders discussed here change the terms of the discussion. The chapter contrasts the hermeneutic aim of avoiding error with the apparent assault on truth and interpretation implied in some treatments of art. It then considers whether there are shared and shareable traits in the very disparate practices of the overreaders; and it analyses what I call the hermeneutics of overreading, which follows from the overreaders' unshakeable faith that the text *knows something* that it will reveal to us if only we ask it in the right way. The title of this final chapter, "In Praise of Overreading," alludes to Jonathan Culler's response to Eco published as "In Defence of Overinterpretation." Here, though, my aim is to express admiration for the work of the overreaders rather than to defend them. They do not stand in need of my defence. The other source of my title is of course Erasmus's *In Praise of Folly*, and perhaps what I am asking for is indeed a little more folly in our academic undertakings.

If hermeneutics is the avoidance of error, it requires a *theoretical* justification which will permit the *practical* discrimination amongst competing possibilities of reading. From its origins in the exegesis of Christian and Jewish sacred texts and Christianising allegorical interpretations of Homer, through its re-orientation as a general science of understanding during the eighteenth and nineteenth centuries in the work of German thinkers such as Friedrich Schleiermacher and Wilhelm Dilthey and up until the twentieth-century contributions of Gadamer and Ricoeur, the history of hermeneutics has been a quest to safeguard interpretation against bewilderment in the face of proliferating meanings.[2] Opinions may differ over how or whether this is achieved, but the ambition remains the same. To take an issue which for a period was hotly debated in literary critical circles, authorial intention has been sometimes embraced, sometimes rejected as a suitable regulative principle for interpretation.

For Enlightenment hermeneutic theorists such as Christian Wolff and Chladenius, an author's intention is a necessary reference point in interpretation (see Mueller-Vollmer 1985: 4–9). In their classic essay "The Intentional Fallacy" (1946) Wimsatt and Beardsley reject authorial intention not because it constrains interpretation too much, but because it is not sufficiently reliable or accessible to act as an effective constraint; only analysis and exegesis of the literary work itself can provide "the true and objective way of criticism" (Wimsatt and Beardsley 1972: 344). In *Validity in Interpretation* (1967) E. D. Hirsch retorted that the author is "the only compelling normative principle that could lend validity to an interpretation" (Hirsch 1967: 5). The disagreement is not about whether or not there should be normative principles; it concerns the question of whether authorial intention can serve as such a principle, or whether the regulative function is best served by the text in isolation from the uncertainties and obscurities of its author's intentions. In his infamous essay "La Mort de l'auteur" (The Death of the Author) (1968) Roland Barthes may have more radically entertained the possibility of discarding any notion of interpretive correctness underpinned by authorial intention, but in the process— as is indicated in some of his later work on literature such as *Le Plaisir du texte* (1973)—he risked excluding his practice from anything recognisable in conventional terms as literary criticism. In the critical and hermeneutic mainstream, something must serve to control the proliferation of meaning, be it the text (Wimsatt and Beardsley), the author (Hirsch), tradition (Gadamer), or the pressure of interpretive communities (Fish).[3] The answers may differ, but the purpose remains the same.

The Italian theorist and author Umberto Eco, whose views were touched upon in the Preface, comes out clearly in favour of reining in the freedom of interpretation. From his early writings, Eco is still associated with the notion of the "open work," according to which the reader collaborates with the text to ensure that its meaning is never settled once and for all. Eco insists, though, that this does not imply that in matters of interpretation anything goes. It may be hard to say what makes for a good interpretation, but we can more easily recognise some as bad or just plain wrong. Rather than the author's or the reader's intention, Eco proposes as a regulating principle what he calls the *intentio operis*, the intention of the work. This notion aims to avoid interpretive free play without recourse to the intentions of an empirical author. It acts as a constraint on the reader and attempts to construct him or her as the text's model addressee, who makes conjectures about meaning and tests them against the work without exceeding the bounds of what might reasonably be said. Eco argues that sometimes, when the author's intention is unattainable and the reader's intention is arguable, we may nevertheless discover "the transparent intention of the text, which disproves an untenable interpretation" (Eco 1992: 78).

Giving the *intentio operis* a Latin name might endow it with an element of intellectual glamour, but its usefulness is limited. It is not clear, for example, that it represents an advance on Wimsatt and Beardsley's account of how meaning is to be established by close reading of the literary work rather than by appealing to authorial intention. The strategic point of Eco's notion is to support his claim that the rights of interpreters have been overstressed by providing what he calls a "parameter" (Eco 1992: 141) for acceptable interpretations. This does not in itself solve the problem of how to tell a good interpretation from a bad one. Eco argues that the way to identify a bad interpretation or overinterpretation is not to begin by defining criteria for a good reading: "I think, on the contrary, that we can accept a sort of Popperian principle according to which if there are no rules that help to ascertain which interpretations are the 'best' ones, there is a least a rule for ascertaining which ones are 'bad'" (Eco 1992: 52). At this point Eco is not far from the conservative hermeneutics of E. D. Hirsch. Like Eco, Hirsch refers to Karl Popper to support his view that "there cannot be any method or model of correct interpretation," but that there can be "a ruthlessly critical process of validation" (Hirsch 1967: 206). If hermeneutics cannot tell us how to construct a good interpretation, it can at least give us the tools to help spot readings which are improbable. We may never know with absolute certainty that a given reading is correct, but we can be pretty sure that some are wrong. Eco suggests, for example, that if Jack the Ripper claimed that he did what he did on the grounds of his interpretation of the Gospel according to Saint Luke, we would be inclined to think that his reading was preposterous; and for Eco this "proves that there is at least one case in which it is possible to say that a given interpretation is a bad one" (Eco 1992: 24–25).

All this seems reasonable enough. Perhaps it is even a little too reasonable, and in any case it is not clear how far it actually helps us in assessing the plausibility of competing readings. Whereas Hirsch offers some criteria by which we might assess the validity of an interpretation, Eco goes little further than suggesting that we will recognise a bad reading when we see one. His position becomes more awkward, and more theoretically interesting, in the third and last of his lectures in *Interpretation and Overinterpretation* when he turns to discussing interpretations of his own novels *The Name of the Rose* and *Foucault's Pendulum* (originally published in Italian in 1980 and 1988, respectively). Eco signals that he is moving into theoretically difficult territory by his slightly embarrassed, jocular introduction to this section of his lecture. He calls his procedure "risky" and describes it as "a laboratory experiment," urging his listeners to keep what they hear to themselves: "Please do not tell anyone about what happens today: we are irresponsibly playing, like atomic scientists trying dangerous scenarios and unmentionable war games" (Eco 1992: 73). Faithful to his argument that the work's intention matters more than the author's, Eco does not try to refute what he regards as wrong interpretations by reference to his aims whilst writing his novels; rather, he puts himself in the position of a reader, assessing the claims of other readers by considering how persuasively they elucidate his novels. As his own reader, he may be persuaded of the validity of an interpretation which does not correspond to any intention he may have had as an author. So he insists that when he gave the name Casaubon to one of the characters in *Foucault's Pendulum*, he did not intend it as a reference to the character of the same name in George Eliot's *Middlemarch*, and indeed he included a passage in his novel which aimed to discourage readers from making any such connection. Subsequently, however, a critic pointed out that Eliot's Casaubon was writing *A Key to All Mythologies*, a fact which makes a strong link to Eco's novel. Eco is obliged to accept the validity of this observation: "Text plus standard encyclopedia knowledge entitle any cultivated reader to make that connection. It makes sense. Too bad for the empirical author who was not as smart as his reader" (Eco 1992: 82). Here, the reader wins out over the author, and the interpretation stands.

On other occasions there is no such internal conflict between Eco's position as both author and reader of his own work. He refers to an essay written in Russian by Helena Costiucovich which points to four similarities between his *The Name of the Rose* and a novel by the French writer Emile Henriot entitled *La Rose de Bratislava*: the hunting of a mysterious manuscript, a final fire in a library, reference to Prague, and the fact that Henriot's book contains a librarian called Berngard and Eco's contains a librarian called Berengar (Eco 1992: 75). From the standpoint of the author, Eco insists that he had never read Henriot's novel and did not know of its existence. As a reader also, he does not find anything compelling in the connection: the search for a mysterious manuscript and fires in libraries are common literary *topoi*; the reference to Prague does not play an important role in *The Name of the Rose*; and the similarity of Berengar and Berngard could be a coincidence. Fundamentally, Eco does not dismiss the connection because it is inherently implausible. He concedes that a reader might find the presence of four coincidences to be "interesting" (Eco 1992: 76), but for his own part he remains unmoved by it: "As an uncommitted reader of *The Name of the Rose*, I think that the argument of Helena Costiucovich does not prove anything interesting" (Eco 1992: 75). Eco is equally unpersuaded by a further suggestion made by Costiucovich that there is a link between Casanova, the author of the coveted manuscript in Henriot's novel, and Eco's character Hugh of Newcastle, who in the original Italian is called Ugo de Novocastro. Eco insists that reference to Casanova leads nowhere: "Obviously I am ready to change my mind if some other interpreter demonstrates that the Casanova connection can lead to some interesting interpretive path, but for the moment—as a model Reader of my own novel—I feel entitled to say that such a hypothesis is scarcely rewarding" (Eco 1992: 77).

Eco's reluctance to endorse these connections requires no further justification. Whilst the links made by Costiucovich are, to my mind, certainly not outlandish, neither are they compelling. The criteria Eco invokes are, however, more surprising, and they potentially unsettle the views he expresses in other parts of *Interpretation and Overinterpretation*. Elsewhere, as we have seen, Eco says that the text is the "parameter" for an acceptable interpretation (Eco 1992: 141), and he argues that "the transparent intention of the text . . . disproves an untenable interpretation" (Eco 1992: 78). Here, in reference to the interpretation of *The Name of the Rose* he suggests a rather different position, as he implies that the key terms for assessing validity are *interesting* and *rewarding*. These criteria cannot be established on grounds which are purely internal to the text. Eco does not dismiss Costiucovich's suggestions because they falsify his work; he explicitly keeps an open mind on that issue, undertaking to revise his rejection if the same observations can be made to serve a more interesting interpretation. Here at least, Eco allows his own assessment of what is interesting to decide the validity of a reading rather than its degree of concordance to the *intentio operis*. At the same time, he allows for the possibility that other readers might disagree by finding the comments interesting, and even that those comments might be made interesting to him if presented in a different interpretive context. It becomes hard to maintain the distinction between interpretation and overinterpretation, which is nevertheless the cornerstone of Eco's argument, if so vague and fluid a notion as *interestingness* is granted authority in matters of adjudication. Moreover, it is possible that all along this has been the hidden criterion guiding what is judged to be acceptable or unacceptable. Eco judges it interesting, and therefore valid, to observe that Eliot's Casaubon was writing *A Key to All Mythologies*; he does not find interest, and therefore validity, in the similarity of the names Berengar and Berngard. But we might disagree, and the notion of *intentio operis* will do nothing to help us out of this dilemma. Interestingness is only a secure means of settling the conflict of interpretations if we *also* have some secure means of deciding what is and isn't interesting. So long as we do not, we are no further advanced than we were if our aim is to distinguish between valid and false interpretations.

A further surprising consequence of invoking interestingness as a criterion of validation is that Eco begins to look more like his respondents Richard Rorty and Jonathan Culler than he seems willing to accept. In his reply to Eco, as we saw in the Preface, Jonathan Culler defends overinterpretation on the grounds that it provokes new questions. Moderate interpretation, which articulates a consensus, "is of little interest" (Culler 1992: 110); and Culler insists that Eco agrees with him, even if he doesn't know it (Culler 1992: 110–11). Rorty rejects the distinction between interpretation and overinterpretation, arguing that there are no solid grounds for keeping them separate. For Rorty, the value of descriptions or interpretations can never be gauged by their fidelity to the object to which they refer, because there is no stable object that can be independently known; rather, descriptions are evaluated "according to their efficacy as instruments for purposes" (Rorty 1992: 92). The key criteria, then, are efficacy or usefulness, not truth or adequacy. Reading Eco or Derrida, Rorty argues, might give you "something interesting to say about a text which you could not otherwise have said" (Rorty 1992: 105). *Interesting* replaces *true* because there is simply no non-tautological, grounded method for measuring a text against an interpretation and therefore of assessing the truth of the latter. For Rorty, the role of intellectuals is to say interesting things; and like Culler, Rorty suggests that Eco agrees with him even if he does not know (or admit) that he does so. Provocatively assimilating Eco's position to his own, Rorty is now able to describe the Italian author as a congenial fellow-pragmatist (Rorty 1992: 93).[4]

Eco opens the door which makes it possible for Culler and Rorty to enlist him to their own, rather different, arguments when he begins to assess interpretations by their interest rather than solely by their appropriateness to their object texts. His rejection of overinterpretation can be (over)interpreted as in fact endorsing precisely the critical excess it seems to exclude. His account allies itself with the hermeneutic tradition which seeks to eliminate error and misunderstanding; but it sits uneasily with that tradition once it allows the fluid category of the interesting to play a role in the evaluation of critical acts. He may still insist on the regulating principle of the *intentio operis*, but he risks undermining its normative power. His elaboration of his ideas, then, is shadowed by an opposing movement in which the possibility of error is positively embraced, or—more radically—truth is discarded altogether. The next section looks at more skeptical approaches to interpretation which form part of the background to the hermeneutics of overreading.

The Assault on Interpretation

In her essay "Against Interpretation" (1964) Susan Sontag described interpretation as "largely reactionary, stifling," and "the revenge of the intellect upon art" (Sontag 1972: 655). It tames the unnerving power of art by making it manageable and comfortable. Rather than the obsessive quest for meaning, Sontag calls for a more passionate, sensual form of commentary which would enable us to experience again "the luminousness of the thing in itself, of things being what they are" (Sontag 1972: 659). As a theory of understanding, hermeneutics disputes the premises underlying Sontag's position: from a hermeneutic perspective, interpretation is not something which we choose to do, and therefore could equally choose not to do; nor is there any "thing in itself" which could be experienced without the mediation of interpretation.[5] In a general sense, all experience involves interpretation, so to be "against interpretation" is an untenable position; in a more restricted sense, though, Sontag attacked what she perceived as the dominant assumption that the role of art criticism is to uncover the meaning of individual works. For different reasons, others concurred with some of her conclusions. As I suggested in Chapter 2, despite the important and well-respected work of Paul Ricoeur, in France hermeneutics has often been understood reductively as the mystified quest for the single correct interpretation of a literary work. Characterising their endeavour as an alternative to hermeneutics, the structuralists renounced interpretation in favour of a poetics which understood each particular work as one possible realisation of abstract, general structures.[6] Chapter 3 showed how Deleuze rejected the term *interpretation* altogether, on the grounds quite simply that "there is nothing to interpret" (Deleuze and Parnet 1977: 10; Deleuze 1990: 17). To some extent endorsing the structuralist project and some of its poststructuralist developments, Culler gave the opening chapter of his *Pursuit of Signs* (1981) the title "Beyond Interpretation." He argued that "one thing we do not need is more interpretations of literary works" (Culler 1981: 6), and he supported instead projects such as the systematic study of how literature signifies, or the uncanny logics of textuality explored by Derrida. Sontag was against interpretation; Culler wanted to go beyond it; and Deleuze denied that there was anything to interpret in any case. Despite the huge differences between their views, they converge at least in their conclusion: we should give up on interpretation.

Associated with this assault on interpretation is the sense that the interpreter's desire for truth is deluded. Harold Bloom conveys something of this when he bluntly insists that "There are no interpretations but only misinterpretations, and so all criticism is prose poetry" (Bloom 1973: 95). Any act of interpretation misses its object. In the context of Bloom's theory of poetry, this does not mean that all misreadings are equally valueless; on the contrary, some are better than others, just as some poems are better than others. Bloom replaces the normative distinction between right and wrong interpretations by a no less normative distinction between strong and weak acts of reading. Strong poets establish themselves as great artists by creatively misreading their precursors; and strong critics impose themselves by their powerful critical appropriations of the literary tradition. In principle the regulative criterion of correctness seems to have vanished, and Bloom opens up the prospect of infinite regress: one poet misreads another, Bloom misreads that misreading, we misread Bloom's misreading, and so on for ever. In practice, though, there is no such regress. As the title of one of his books indicates, Bloom offers us a "map of misreading," that is, a way of charting the errors of others according to fixed, repeated and describable patterns. When he speculates that "perhaps there are only more or less creative or interesting mis-readings" (Bloom 1973: 43), he adopts the criterion of interestingness which we also saw in Eco, Rorty and Culler, and he apparently evacuates any possibility of correct interpretation. However, he establishes his own speaking position as authoritative. In order to recognise a strong poet's misreading of a precursor's work, Bloom needs to be able to gauge its divergence from its source, and therefore to be able to read it accurately. To tell us what one poet changed in the work of another, Bloom must know what was there in the first place. In other words, the claim that reading is misreading does not, despite appearances, undercut the possibility that something like correct reading can be achieved.

The case of Bloom suggests that a theory of misreading does not inevitably entail either the abandonment of any hermeneutic project or the consequence that all aspiration to interpretive correctness should be relinquished. At its best, the assault on interpretation is an intelligent questioning rather than an out-and-out repudiation. The reconstruction of the viability of reading needs to pass through its radical critique. The final section of this chapter outlines some of the principles of overreading as suggested by the authors studied in this book. Before getting to that point, I want to look at reasons for problematising two of the foundation stones of successful interpretation. Overreading, I suggest, is driven by skepticism towards the key notions of context and coherence. Context roots the work in the external world; a presumption of coherence ensures that its vision is unified and self-consistent. A reading which ignores or falsifies the context of a work, or which violates its internal coherence, can usually be taken as erroneous. Overreaders, however, are not so sure what constitutes a context, or how to recognise a work's self-consistency.

Context. Context stabilises a work. If we did not know whether the Iliad was composed in the eighth century before the common era in Greece or in twenty-first century Seattle, we would be at a loss how to make sense of it. Knowing that Proust was a male homosexual of independent means writing in early twentieth-century France helps us to situate his work, giving at least some clues for understanding what and how he wrote. It does not of course tell us everything. As Sartre observed, Paul Valéry was a petit-bourgeois intellectual, but not every petit-bourgeois intellectual was Paul Valéry (Sartre 1960: 44).[7] Nevertheless, some knowledge of the historical, social and biographical context in which art works emerge surely helps us to understand them better. It allows us to reduce the polysemy of a text to manageable proportions (see Ricoeur 1986: 77).

But what is a context, and how many contexts does a given work have? In relation to the individual words of a text, Hirsch comments that "the context is not a fixed given" (Hirsch 1967: 201). It is a construction based on always questionable interpretive decisions. To construe the context of a literary text, for example, might involve examining some or all of the following: the sentence in which a word appears, or the paragraph, chapter or book in which the sentence appears, or the entire corpus of the author, and other works in the same genre by different authors in the same language or in others; the author's idiolect as well as the entire language in which the text is written, including its grammar and history, and its relations with other languages; the author's social and family background, education, sexuality and politics; the great historical events and movements of the period, including those which the work mentions and reflects upon, and those of which it may be unaware but by which it is silently structured; and doubtless much more besides. Moreover, one would also need a persuasive account of the reciprocal influence of work and context: how does the context produce the work, and how does the work transform the context and our perception of it (see Žižek 2004: 15)?

Derrida's reading of Nietzsche's "I have forgotten my umbrella," discussed in Chapter 2, is a brilliant and infuriating demonstration of how interpretive speculation is unleashed once the proper context for an utterance is missing. If we do not know whether a sentence constitutes a factual statement, an overheard quotation, a poem or a coded message, then—depending on your point of view—we are either floundering or liberated. The question that Derrida entertains is whether, to some extent, the context is *always* missing. In his discussion of J. L. Austin in "Signature événement contexte," Derrida insists that the context of an utterance can never be fully saturated or exhausted (Derrida 1972a: 389). The reassuring side of this is that context can be known *to some extent*. We can know some things about it. We might even know quite a lot about it, which for many purposes will make interpretation and understanding reasonably secure. Our knowledge of a context, and the knowledge of an utterance or work of art which that context permits, is not necessarily wrong merely because it is not complete. The other side of Derrida's point, however, is that our knowledge of the context is always partial, which means that new contexts may be introduced to transform any provisional understanding we have arrived at. Something more remains to be said, and our means of policing what can and cannot plausibly be maintained are neither practically nor theoretically up to the task.

Coherence. A second criterion for regulating interpretation is the assumption of the work's coherence. Invoking this criterion in *Interpretation and Overinterpretation*, Eco traces it back to St. Augustine:

How to prove a conjecture about the *intentio operis*? The only way is to check it upon the text as a coherent whole. This idea, too, is an old one and comes from Augustine (*De doctrina christiana*): any interpretation given of a certain portion of a text can be accepted if it is confirmed by, and must be rejected if it is challenged by, another portion of the same text. In this sense the internal textual coherence controls the otherwise uncontrollable drives of the reader. (Eco 1992: 65; see also Eco 1990: 59)

In similar vein, Gadamer suggests that all understanding is led by what he calls a "Vorgriff der Vollkommenheit" (anticipation of perfection), that is, the assumption "that only that is intelligible which truly represents a perfect unity of sense" (Gadamer 1986: 299).[8] If this assumption is frustrated by the apparent incoherence of a work, we doubt the accuracy of the text as it has been passed on to us and seek to know "how it is to be healed" (Gadamer 1986: 299). The belief that the work is a perfect unity of sense is presented as unshakeable; if the evidence does not support it, rather than revising this fundamental belief, Gadamer would prefer to question the re-liability of the version of the text that has been handed down to us.

Hirsch concurs that coherence is the key criterion in the valida-tion of interpretation. In his account three preliminary criteria must be fulfilled: legitimacy, correspondence and generic appropriateness; that is, the interpretation must be permissible within the norms of the lan-guage in which the text was composed, it must account for all linguistic components of the text, and it must respect the conventions of the genre to which the text belongs. Several competing readings might meet these demands, so a fourth, overriding principle is invoked: "When these three preliminary criteria have been satisfied, there remains a fourth criterion which gives significance to all the rest, the criterion of plausibility or *co-herence*. . . . Faced with alternatives, the interpreter chooses the reading which best meets the criterion of coherence" (Hirsch 1967: 236; emphasis in original).

The criterion of coherence requires both that the text is inherently, essentially self-consistent, and that interpreters should be able to recognise and to describe it as such. Coherent texts permit and produce coherent interpretations. Of course, this criterion does not provide a simple solu-tion to all interpretive problems. Hirsch concedes that coherence-building gets entangled in a version of the hermeneutic circle: "The procedure is thoroughly circular; the context is derived from the submeanings and the submeanings are specified and rendered coherent with reference to the context" (Hirsch 1967: 237). Competing interpretations may be equally coherent, in which case we should choose the one which is most probably right by the best possible assessment of the context of the work. In this instance, by *context* Hirsch means primarily the author's typical outlook, and the typical associations and expectations which inform his texts. Con-text and coherence reinforce one another. As we test the coherence of a reading against our best understanding of its context, we avoid, according to Hirsch, "pure circularity in making sense of the text" (Hirsch 1967: 238).

Other theorists are less sanguine about the prospects of circumvent-ing the hermeneutic circle. The discovery of a coherent unity of meaning in a work is preceded and programmed by the supposition that it exists. Perhaps we find it only because we are looking for it with such determina-tion, to the point that, as Gadamer implies, if our search is frustrated, we should correct or "heal" the text until it gives us what we wanted from it. Eco argues that the text's internal coherence puts a brake on the reader's uncontrollable drives; Rorty counters that there is no internal coherence prior to our description of it, and no anchoring of our interpretations in a secure context outside the hermeneutic circle:

> We [pragmatists] like Eco's redescription of what he calls "the old and still valid hermeneutic circle." But, given this picture of texts being made as they are interpreted, I do not see any way to preserve the metaphor of a text's *internal* coherence. I should think that a text just has whatever coherence it happened to acquire during the last roll of the hermeneutic wheel, just as a lump of clay only has whatever coherence it happened to pick up at the last turn of the potter's wheel.
>
> So I should prefer to say that the coherence of the text is not something it has before it is described, any more than the dots had coherence before we connected them. Its coherence is no more than the fact that somebody has found something interesting to say about a group of marks or noises—some way of describing those marks and noises which relates them to some of the other things we are interested in talking about. (Rorty 1992: 97; emphasis in original)

In this view, the coherence of a work is the product of interpretation rather than its source. Stanley Fish makes a similar point with characteristic provocation when he states that "interpreters do not decode poems; they make them" (Fish 1980: 327). The claim that works have inherent, internal qualities independent of their interpretation cannot be proven, since it is only by interpretation that we can point them out. It may be equally unprovable to claim that works *do not* have inherent, internal qualities; but to start from that possibility might at least keep open the prospect of encountering something raw, unanticipated and incongruous in a text or film, without the need to coerce it into a pre-existing, coherent unity of meaning.

The Hermeneutics of Overreading

Rorty's view that a work's coherence is conferred by its reader is not shared by all the overreaders discussed in this book. Some maintain that the work does have ultimate coherence, even if it is mysterious and unspeakable. As Chapter 1 indicated, Heidegger argues that the multiple meanings of a poet's work could be traced back to a single source; and from a religious perspective Levinas insists that the sacred texts of the Jewish tradition are held together by a powerful unity, albeit a unity which incorporates what might appear to us to be inconsistencies and contradictions. The various thinkers I have discussed nevertheless set out from the position that neither context nor coherence are sufficiently fixed or available to us to function as decisive limitations on interpretation. They attempt to find new possibilities of meaning in works without worrying overly about how and why they came to be there, and how they should be made to fit with some established, coherent kernel of sense which we might assume that it contains.

Problematising context and coherence as regulative constraints on interpretation is not tantamount to endorsing an unfettered relativism which evacuates all truth from the work of art and its interpretation. Quite the contrary is the case. Chapter 1 argued that the rehabilitation of the poets achieved by Heidegger in the wake of his Romantic forebears depended precisely upon the re-alignment of art with truth. Derrida, sometimes portrayed as the prince of relativists, had no compunction in invoking the value of truth when he thought his work had been misrepresented. Repudiating Habermas's attack on him, for example, he insisted that he simply did not hold the views ascribed to him: "That is false. I do indeed say *false* as opposed to *true*" (Derrida 1990: 245; emphasis in original). Derrida is sometimes depicted as dismissing out of hand any notion that texts have determinate meanings or that authors have intentions which their readers should respect. M. H. Abrams, for example, states that "Derrida puts out of play, before the game even begins, every source of norms, controls, or indicators which, in the ordinary use and experience of language, set a limit to what we can mean and what we can be understood to mean" (Abrams 1988: 268). Yet Derrida's outrage at finding his views misrepresented is by no means an inconsistency in his work. His patient attention to the detail of literary and philosophical works derives from the belief that reading entails a responsibility towards the text; and he expects others to act with the same responsibility towards him when they read or purport to read his writings. Only by exposing oneself as fully as one can to what is utterly singular about the work under consideration, only by striving conscientiously to appreciate its difference from oneself, does one earn the right to criticise it. Underpinning Derrida's commitment to the text is a sense shared by the thinkers discussed in this book, namely, that the work may contain something surprising, shocking, challenging, something un- fathomably *other* and alien, which may not be immediately apparent, but which will reward the most patient, most devoted attention.[9]

This does not mean that overreaders always succeed in remaining faithful to the works they are interpreting. The risk of error is ever-present; and no reader is secure against the oldest interpretive trap of them all: that is, the inclination to find in a text only what we are predisposed to see in it. As I have suggested on a number of occasions, the thinkers discussed in this book are certainly not immune to this danger. The en- deavour to listen to a voice from elsewhere might easily end up drowning it out. The problem, which cannot be resolved in advance by any all- purpose principle, is to distinguish between legitimate appropriation and downright falsification. Ricoeur observes that appropriation is one of the goals of all interpretation. It is the struggle to overcome distance, which may be historical or cultural, or to surmount the otherness of any person or system of values which is not immediately intelligible to us: "in this sense," Ricoeur argues, "interpretation 'brings closer,' 'equalizes,' makes 'contemporary and similar,' which is truly to make *one's own* what first of all was *alien*" (Ricoeur 1986: 153; emphasis in original). Appropriation, as the overcoming of distance, may be a universal hermeneutic aim, but its pitfalls are substantial. The otherness of the work may go unheard because we assimilate it too brutally to what we can readily conceive. At its best overreading is motivated by a fierce commitment to the singularity of the work of art and to its potential to transform our ways of thinking; but it is as prone to the risks of hasty appropriation as any form of reading.

Ricoeur distinguishes between two modes of interpretation: inter- pretation as the recollection of meaning, and as the exercise of suspicion. The former entails what he calls "a reasonable faith [*une foi raisonnable*]" (Ricoeur 1965: 37), which aims to restore what sacred texts and signs might have to say to us. The hermeneutics of suspicion, of which the modern masters are Marx, Nietzsche and Freud, suggests on the contrary that the role of interpretation is to demystify its objects because they have some- thing to hide, something that can only be brought to the surface by read- ing them against the grain. The hermeneutics of overreading does not quite correspond to either the recollection of meaning or the exercise of suspicion. Its faith in the work is exorbitant rather than reasonable—not exactly irrational, but certainly willing to depart from the familiar, well-trodden ways of thought—and it has no definitive confidence that what it finds is really there or not. At the same time it has no sense that the work is mystified in respect of its true significance. On the contrary, there is an excessive trust in the work and something approaching desperation to tease out its complex insights. This is not, then, the hermeneutics of suspicion, but a hermeneutics of conviction, guided by firm and demanding tenets of faith.

Overreading is imaginative and flexible. It may appear to disdain the standards of evidence and argument which most critics respect; and in the process it may fail to find anything new to say about the works under scrutiny. Sometimes, though, it may renew our understanding of a text or film in challenging, thrilling ways . To conclude this book, I want to sketch some of the maxims which guide overreading in its search to release the unanticipated voice of the textual or filmic Other. At the risk of falsely unifying the thinkers discussed in the book, it is nevertheless possible to see some tendencies, which might even be called principles, underlying their practice. Some of these are relatively uncontroversial, or at least they do not self-evidently run up against common sense; others might be thought bluntly to contradict the norms of ordinary scholarly enquiry.

1. *No form of evidence should be ruled out on principle.* There is no methodical or methodological purity about overreading. No form of evidence is consistently used or consistently excluded, and any information that might add to a work's yield of sense is legitimate. Heidegger sometimes uses textual variants or (sometimes questionable) etymologies, but certainly not in any systematic way. Theoretically informed criticism has often been anti-biographical, but this cannot be a tenet of overreading. Derrida can be biographical and anecdotal when it suits him. In his discussion of Freud's *Beyond the Pleasure Principle*, for example, he uses the fact that the child who plays the *fort/da* game is Freud's grandson, even though that is not made explicit in Freud's original text (see Derrida 1980: 313–40). As Chapter 3 suggested, when Deleuze puts writers and filmmakers (nearly) on a par with great philosophers, he regards them as prestigious individual thinkers with opinions and intentions. In other words

they are *authors* in a quite old-fashioned sense. Barthes's announcement of the death of the author is altogether too dogmatic for a committed overreader because it rules out a valuable source of speculation. The basic principle is: if it helps, use it; if it doesn't help, a discreet veil may be drawn over it.

2. *The potential of context to generate meaning is never exhausted.* The critique of context discussed in the previous section does not imply that contextual interpretation cannot be used. Historical, linguistic or biographical contexts should not be ruled out of order, but neither should they be invoked to close down interpretive endeavour. From a New Historicist perspective, a critic such as Stephen Greenblatt does not dispute the importance of Elizabethan England for understanding Shakespeare, but he opens up fresh ways of viewing that context by reading Shakespeare's plays alongside, for example, contemporary medical manuals; for Cavell the proper context for reading Shakespeare is philosophical skepticism, as it had been developed in the sixteenth century by Montaigne and would be refined a generation after Shakespeare by Descartes.[10] There are always new contexts to be found. The reverse side of this maxim is that reading *out of context* is also always legitimate because there is no fixed, determinate context for a work. As Žižek puts it, "Perhaps the most elementary hermeneutic test of the greatness of a work of art is its ability to survive being torn from its original context" (Žižek 2008: 129–30); we should "*decontextualize* the work, tear it out of the context in which it was originally embedded" (Žižek 2008: 130; emphasis in original). The overreaders release us from the tyranny of context by destabilising its boundaries. New contexts will unlock unexpected possibilities of meaning. To put it another way, contextual reading can never fix the meaning of a prestigious work because we do not have an agreed normative principle for deciding what a context is. Art maintains its hold on us because its significance is still to be discovered in future encounters.

3. *Nothing is only what it seems; anything is interpretable.* One of the interpretive gains of psychoanalysis has been to spread the insight that any apparently insignificant detail might bear unexpected sense, though this had in fact been long understood by the interpreters of sacred texts.[11] Levinas insists that in the Talmud more is always at stake than might

seem to be the case to a casual reader: "It is certain that, when discussing whether it is right to eat or not to eat 'an egg laid on a feast day' or the compensation due for damage caused by a 'mad bull,' the wise men of the Talmud are discussing neither an egg nor a bull but, without seeming to, they are questioning fundamental ideas" (Levinas 1968: 12). Overreaders apply this conviction to secular works. They are perpetually willing to transform a text by finding in it something which speaks to their concerns; so, Lacan could see in Poe's "The Purloined Letter" an allegory of psychoanalysis and Cavell could read it as an allegory of ordinary language philosophy. The overlooked detail, if viewed "awry" (as Žižek puts it in the title of one of his books), might always produce fresh signifying potential.

4. *The boundaries between the inside and the outside of a work are never certain.* In the nineteenth century Schleiermacher warned that it is an error to miss an allusion in a text when there is one, just as it is an error to see an allusion in a text when there isn't one (Schleiermacher 1985: 78–79). In principle we might readily agree with this, but deciding whether or not an allusion is actually present in a work may turn out to be difficult to ascertain. In specific instances it might not be possible to reach agreement on what is in the text and what is not. Does the ram in the Celan poem explored by Derrida in *Béliers* really allude to a battering ram, a sign of the zodiac and the ram sacrificed by Abraham, or not? One of the things that distinguishes cautious readers from speculative overreaders is their degree of certainty over what is "inside" the text or relevant to it. What is really there, and what is merely read in? Overreaders, typically, are unsure or unconcerned, and they prefer the interpretive gain of exploring possible resonances over the relative security of sticking to what is uncontroversially present.

5. *Mistakes don't matter too much.* This point follows on from the previous one. Taking interpretive risks means accepting that they will not always pay off. Cavell stoutly defends mistakes he might make in his account of films: "a few faulty memories will not themselves shake my conviction in what I've said, since I am as interested in how a memory went wrong as in why the memories that are right occur when they do" (Cavell 1979b: xxiv). Žižek approves of Cavell's self-defence: "Stanley Cavell was

right when, in a reply to his critics (who pointed out numerous mistakes in his retelling the story of films), he retorted that he fully stands by his mistakes" (Žižek 2004: 152). Žižek himself is highly mistake-prone,[12] whilst being quick to castigate others for their errors; but perhaps, he suggests, the worst blunders, such as locating Hitchcock's *Vertigo* in Los Angeles rather than San Francisco, should be taken as something positive, since they bear witness to the critic's "excessive subjective engagement" (Žižek 2004: 152) in the work being analysed. It is better to invest oneself without reserve in the work than to stand back from it with Kantian disinterest, even if our commitment risks blinding us to the glaringly obvious. And after all, in matters of cultural interpretation we do not actually risk much. Nobody dies, usually. The worst that is likely to happen to us is that we get ignored.

6. *There is no point in trying to persuade those who disagree with you.* Cavell's recourse to what he calls "a bunch of assertions" (discussed in Chapter 6) entails in part the acknowledgement that sometimes interpreters may be only too aware that they cannot offer watertight arguments in favour of their readings; they seek our assent, but acknowledge the likelihood of dissent. Sometimes, for theoretical or practical reasons, rather than being able to justify *why* we see things in a certain way, we may only be able to say, as Wittgenstein puts it simply, "*This is how it strikes me*" (Wittgenstein 1958: 85; emphasis in original). As noted in Chapter 3, Deleuze is more provocative in refusing to engage in any attempt at persuasion. He could accept that objections to his work might be correct without being willing to dwell on them any further: "Every time someone makes an objection to me, I want to say: 'Okay, okay, let's move on to something else.' Objections have never produced anything positive" (Deleuze and Parnet 1977: 7). (With regard to this and the previous maxim, one might object that it is easy enough for overreaders to be unconcerned about their mistakes and the opinions of others, speaking as they generally do from positions of relative institutional and financial security; it's a completely different matter if you are a student trying to pass an examination or a young academic applying for a job).

The final two maxims are the key items of faith in the hermeneutics of overreading:

7. *The work knows something; perhaps it knows everything.* The work rewards the devoted attention that is paid to it because there is in it a kernel of knowledge which only the most unstinting reader can discover. As the title of the book edited by Žižek suggests, Hitchcock knows everything you always wanted to know about Lacan; or as Žižek also tells us, "vulgar sentimental literature" may know what Kant did not (Žižek 1991: 160). Levinas's reverence for the Talmud comes from the unshakeable faith that in it everything has been thought; all views and positions are given voice within it, so that it speaks to us as much today as it ever did (see Levinas 1968: 16). For Levinas this can be explained by its combination of intellectual rigour and sacred inspiration. In secular contexts it is not so easy to understand how the work of art might come to acquire this commanding authority. Paul de Man describes his belief in the text's knowledge as a sort of enabling self-mystification: "I have a tendency to put upon texts an inherent authority, which is stronger, I think, than Derrida is willing to put on them. I assume, as a working hypothesis (as a working hypothesis, because I know better than that) that the text *knows* in an absolute way what it's doing. I know this is not the case, but it is a necessary working hypothesis that Rousseau knows at any time what he is doing and as such there is no need to deconstruct Rousseau" (De Man 1986: 118; emphasis in original). Cavell expresses a similar tension when proposing that one way to investigate the problem of interpretation is "to say that what you really want to know is what a text knows about itself, because you cannot know more than it does about itself; and then to ask what the fantasy is of the text's knowledge of itself" (Cavell 1984: 53). Cavell suggests that a text knows as much or more about itself than we can know about it; at the same time this conviction is held to be a fantasy. It is, however, no more dispensable for being a fantasy. Cavell's point seems to be that submission to the text is somehow necessary. We have no option but to believe that the work knows itself fully. This excessive belief or fantasy is a counter to the standing threat of skepticism; without it, too little might be knowable or worth knowing. The fundamental inner conviction of the overreaders is that the work knows something. The interpreter's activity consists in finding the appropriate caring attention or pressure or violence that must be applied to the work to persuade it to deliver its insight. The question of where its knowledge comes from leads to the final imperative in the hermeneutics of overreading.

8. *Believe!* Fredric Jameson's imperative, "Always historicize!" (Jameson 1981: 9), is replaced in overreading by "Always believe!" For Levinas, faced with the Talmud, there is evidently a religious aspect to this. Critical audacity is an act of devotion through which is achieved "the indispensable excess of research opening itself precisely onto an infinite reading with unexpected perspectives. A reading which is also, without metaphor, adoration" (Levinas 1987: 9). For others amongst the overreaders discussed here, the faith in the text is not so evidently religious; but it is faith nonetheless, and the acts of reading which it encourages are no less secular forms of adoration. This is why overreading is the precise opposite of the hermeneutics of suspicion. The aim of interpretation is to listen to the work rather than to demystify it. This willingness to submit to the text may be, of course, a further mystification. It is, however, the enabling self-delusion which makes possible the gains of overreading.

The work of what I am calling overreaders seems to me to be important for a number of reasons. It represents not a resolution of the ancient quarrel between philosophy and the arts so much as one of the modern forms of the fraught, loving and suspicious relation between them. For all their expressions of respect for art, the philosophers discussed here are not ready to renounce a distinctive and privileged place for their own discipline; but they are willing to attend with the utmost devotion to works in media and idioms very different from their own. They resist tying prestigious art to its historical epoch, so that they can explore ways in which a work may speak to us even if its originators could not have envisaged the terms in which it is made to resonate. These readers achieve a step beyond suspicion as they place their trust in works to which is now attributed the power to speak of what they know, rather than merely to hide what they could not conceive or openly state. Overreading must accept the risk that its results may be fatuous or silly, laughable or just plain dull. But on this matter Cavell makes what is for me the definitive statement in a passage which I have already quoted and which perfectly summarises the case for overreading. "In my experience," he writes, "people worried about reading in, or overinterpretation, or going too far, are, or were, typically afraid of getting started, or reading as such, as if afraid that texts—like people, like times and places—mean things and moreover mean more than you know. This is accordingly a fear of something real, and it may be a healthy fear, that is, a fear of something fearful. . . . Still, my experience is that most texts, like most lives, are underread, not overread" (Cavell 1981: 35).

The fear of overreading is a desire for containment, a longing for a stable, shareable world unspoiled by the taint of noumenal unknownness. This would be a world from which the possibility of skepticism had been forever banished. Overreading on the other hand dreams of a Promethean foray into uncharted territory, to steal or to recover some trace of a work's hitherto unspoken knowledge. It pushes at the limits of what can be said about the texts or films or people that matter to us, testing and refining our sensitivity to shards of meaning that risk going unheeded, extending the range of what might be known, heard or felt. In the end it is about learning to abide with the otherness of what is uncannily close, to recognise it as both intimately familiar and dizzyingly strange.

Notes

PREFACE

1. The exceptional position of Levinas in this list is explained later in this Preface and discussed in Chapter 4.

2. *Interpretation and Overinterpretation* also contains an essay by Christine Brooke-Rose, "Palimpsest History." I do not discuss it here because it does not deal directly with the issue of overinterpretation.

3. The readings of Derrida, Žižek and Cavell to which this paragraph refers are discussed in Chapters 2, 5 and 6 respectively.

4. Heidegger's phrase is quoted and discussed at the beginning of Chapter 1. Throughout this book, translations from French and German are my own except where reference is given to a published translation.

5. The key essay here is Levinas's "La Réalité et son ombre," first published in 1948. For further discussion, see Chapter 4.

CHAPTER 1

1. References to Plato's works follow the system of numbers and letters based on the 1578 edition of Henricus Stephanus. The edition used is given in the Bibliography.

2. For thorough discussion of this and further references, see Nehamas, "Plato on Imitation and Poetry in *Republic* 10," 47–78.

3. For careful discussion of contradictions between Books 2 and 3 and Book 10 of the *Republic*, see Annas, "Plato on the Triviality of Literature"; on the view that Book 10 is not an organic part of the *Republic* and for further references, see "Plato on the Triviality of Literature," 11, and Nehamas, "Plato on Imitation and Poetry in *Republic* 10," 53.

4. In these comments on *Phaedrus*, I follow Nussbaum, *The Fragility of Goodness*, 200–233.

5. Nussbaum characterises the Aristotelian ethics to which she acknowledges allegiance by four principal features: the noncommensurability of valuable things (so that there is no single measure by which to judge different things held to be

of value); the priority of the particular; the ethical value of the emotions; and the ethical relevance of uncontrolled happenings (Nussbaum 1990: 36–44).

6. How far Nussbaum actually achieves such an exchange in her literary criticism is a moot point; I discuss some misgivings in *Ethical Issues in Twentieth-Century French Fiction: Killing the Other*, 5–7.

7. In German, Heidegger distinguishes between *Dichtung*, poetry in the broader sense, i.e., as a fundamental opening onto the world-disclosing nature of language, and poetry in the narrower sense, *Poesie*, i.e., composing poems as we know them. For the distinction between the broader and narrower sense of poetry, see "The Origin of the Work of Art," 72. As we shall see, in the essay "Language in the Poem," Heidegger uses the term *Dichtung* differently.

8. See also Bowie's *From Romanticism to Critical Theory*, especially 164–92, for relevant discussion of Heidegger.

9. See Megill, *Prophets of Extremity*, 172; on Heidegger's "privileged texts," see 170–75.

10. Heidegger specifies that the essence of poetry is not something that would be present in every example of poetry; see *Elucidations*, 52. This insistence that what is essential to a medium is not to be found in most instances of it is repeated by Deleuze, who claims that the essence of cinema is thought, even if thought is not present in most films (Deleuze 1985: 219).

11. This is argued in detail in Young, *Heidegger's Philosophy of Art*.

12. This part of the preface reproduces a passage first used to introduce the lecture on Hölderlin's "Homecoming," which is included in the volume; see *Elucidations*, 222–23. The quoted variant on Hölderlin's sketch for the poem "Columbus" is not included in the cited edition.

13. This is discussed in Chapter 6.

14. For the designation of Derrida as a Heideggerian, see for example Rockmore, *Heidegger and French Philosophy*, 139–47, and Ferry and Renaut, *La Pensée 68*, chapter entitled "L'Heideggerianisme français (Derrida)," 197–236. Rockmore concludes that despite Derrida's questioning of Heidegger, "he remains mainly, perhaps even wholly within the Heideggerian fold. For if he occasionally rejects the letter of Heidegger's position, he invariably accepts his spirit as he understands it" (Rockmore 1995: 147). This conclusion seems to me to be wrong, but at least worth engaging with: what exactly is "the Heideggerian fold," what would it mean to be "wholly" within it, does the distinction between the "letter" and the "spirit" of Heidegger's position hold up to scrutiny? Much cruder, and not even worth treating with any intellectual seriousness, is Ferry and Renaut's assertion that "French Heideggerianism can be specified by the formula: *Derrida = Heidegger + Derrida's style*" (Ferry and Renaut 1988: 201; emphasis in original). From a position more sympathetic to Derrida, Critchley describes him as "the best and

most original philosophical reader of Heidegger," adding that "Heidegger informs just about everything Derrida writes" (Critchley 2008: 2).

CHAPTER 2

1. Rorty, for example, argues that Derrida is at his best when he breaks with traditional modes of doing philosophy; see *Contingency, Irony, and Solidarity*, 122–37, and *Essays on Heidegger and Others*, 119–28. Rorty makes explicit that he is arguing against works such as Gasché's *The Tain of the Mirror: Derrida and the Philosophy of Reflection* and Norris's "Philosophy as *Not* Just a 'Kind of Writing': Derrida and the Claim of Reason."

2. On the strange phenomenon of Derrida's work being dismissed by people who had not read it, see Critchley, "Derrida: The Reader," 6–8.

3. The point is made forcefully by Critchley, who describes Derrida as "a supreme reader of texts, particularly but by no means exclusively philosophical texts" (Critchley 2008: 1).

4. As Gasché's *The Tain of the Mirror* was published in 1986, it does not take account of texts by Derrida such as *Schibboleth pour Paul Celan* (1986) or *Ulysse gramophone: Deux mots pour Joyce* (1987). Whether they might have caused Gasché to moderate his formulation remains an open question.

5. On the question "What is literature?" and Derrida's treatment of literature in general, see Attridge, "Introduction: Derrida and the Questioning of Literature," 1–29; Maclachlan, "Introduction: Deconstruction, Critical Thought, Literature," in *Jacques Derrida: Critical Thought*, 1–13; Bass, "'Literature'/Literature," in *Jacques Derrida: Critical Thought*, 14–23; Gasché, *The Tain of the Mirror*, 255–70; Miller, "Derrida and Literature," in *Jacques Derrida and the Humanities: A Critical Reader*, 58–81; Clark, *Derrida, Heidegger, Blanchot* and *The Poetics of Singularity*; Glendinning and Eaglestone (eds.), *Derrida's Legacies: Literature and Philosophy*.

6. The claim that Derrida levels the distinction between philosophy and literature is made, for example, by Habermas in *The Philosophical Discourse of Modernity*, 185–210. In a spirited response, Derrida repeatedly points out that Habermas criticises him without quoting or referring to any of his work; see *Limited Inc.*, 244–47.

7. For the link between the law of the text and ethics, see Derrida, *Acts of Literature*, 66. On ethics and literature in Derrida's work, see Attridge, "Derrida's Singularity: Literature and Ethics."

8. On this point, see also Hoy, *Critical Resistance*, 37: "Derrida plays with the possibility of elevating this 'text' to the status of a paradigm, suggesting that the same conditions hold for all Nietzsche's (and Derrida's) texts, and perhaps for all writing as such."

9. On this point, see Madison, "Beyond Seriousness and Frivolity: A Gadamerian Response to Deconstruction," 127. This misuse of the term *hermeneutics* in French writing entirely overlooks the work done by Paul Ricoeur to maintain the vitality of the philosophy of interpretation in France; see Chapter 7 of this book for further discussion.

10. See for example Derrida, *La Dissémination*, 72, where Derrida asserts that anyone who thinks you can say "anything at all [*n'importe quoi*]" has understood nothing.

11. For the documents relating to the encounter, as well as a number of penetrating responses to it, see Michelfelder and Palmer (eds.), *Dialogue and Deconstruction: The Gadamer-Derrida Encounter.* On the Gadamer-Derrida debate and the links between hermeneutics and deconstruction, see also Madison, "Beyond Seriousness and Frivolity: A Gadamerian Response to Deconstruction"; Froman, "*L'Ecriture* and Philosophical Hermeneutics"; Bernstein, "The Constellation of Hermeneutics, Critical Theory and Deconstruction"; Dasenbrock, "Taking It Personally: Reading Derrida's Responses"; Behler, *Confrontations: Derrida/Heidegger/Nietzsche*; Risser, *Hermeneutics and the Voice of the Other: Re-Reading Gadamer's Philosophical Hermeneutics.*

12. The title of Philippe Forget's introduction to the original German publication of the papers by Derrida and Gadamer describes the debate as "improbable [*unwahrscheinlich*]"; see Forget, "Leitfäden einer unwahrscheinlichen Debatte."

13. See Emil Staiger et al., "A 1951 Dialogue on Interpretation: Emil Staiger, Martin Heidegger, Leo Spitzer."

14. In the original exchange with Heidegger, Staiger stressed that his reading of "scheint" as "seems" was not meant to imply that the lamp merely and deceptively *seems* to shine (see Staiger et al. 1990: 426).

15. Abrams concludes: "In brief, insofar as we set ourselves, in the old-fashioned way, to make out what the other means by what he says, I am confident that we shall come to a better mutual understanding. After all, without that confidence that we can use language to say what we mean and can interpret language so as to determine what was meant, there is no rationale for the dialogue in which we are now engaged" (Abrams 1988: 275).

16. Gadamer's reply to Derrida does contain one reference to Derrida's *La Voix et le phénomène* (1967) in parenthesis (see Gadamer 1991b: 56); it is unclear whether the reference was supplied by Gadamer himself or by the editors of the volume.

17. See Caputo, "Gadamer's Closet Essentialism: A Derridean Critique."

18. See for example Derrida, *Politiques de l'amitié* (1994) and *Chaque fois unique, la fin du monde* (2003).

19. This is the final line of Celan's poem which begins "Grosse, Glühende Wölbung," from the collection *Atemwende* (see Celan 1983: 97), quoted in full in *Béliers*, 26–27.

CHAPTER 3

1. Deleuze also had a wide interest in other art forms, as indicated for example by his study of the painter Francis Bacon, *Francis Bacon: Logique de la sensation* (1981). For a thorough account of Deleuze's work on the arts, see Ronald Bogue's trilogy of books, *Deleuze on Cinema*, *Deleuze on Literature*, and *Deleuze on Music, Painting, and the Arts*. On Deleuze and literature, and on the question of what a Deleuzian approach to literature might entail, see Bryden, *Gilles Deleuze: Travels in Literature*.

2. For discussion of Deleuze's reading of Proust, see the essays in Bryden and Topping (eds.), *Beckett's Proust/Deleuze's Proust*.

3. See for example Bogue, *Deleuze on Literature*, 38–39.

4. The second part of *Proust et les signes* makes a few more concessions to critical convention. Deleuze refers to works on Proust by Roland Barthes (147), Gérard Genette (147, 217), Georges Poulet (149) and Roger Kempf (163).

5. Although this tendency is less visible in part 2 of *Proust et les signes*, it does not entirely disappear. The stories of Charlus and Albertine, for example, are said to respond to "the same general law" even though there are important differences between them (Deleuze 1979: 213).

6. Deleuze and Guattari, *Qu'est-ce que la philosophie?*, 8: "philosophy is the art of forming, inventing, making concepts."

7. For this point, see Chateau, *Cinéma et philosophie*, 109.

8. For valuable studies of Deleuze's work on cinema, see also Bogue, *Deleuze on Cinema*; Rodowick, *Gilles Deleuze's Time Machine*; Kennedy, *Deleuze and Cinema*; and Buchanan and MacCormack (eds.), *Deleuze and the Schizoanalysis of Cinema*.

9. For further discussion, see my *Scenes of Love and Murder: Renoir, Film and Philosophy*.

10. See also Hallward, *Out of This World*, 181–82, where Hallward suggests that for Deleuze philosophy has no privileged status, but that its ontological precedence is nevertheless abundantly clear.

CHAPTER 4

1. Some of the material in this chapter first appeared in my article "Levinas and the Phenomenology of Reading," in *A Century with Levinas: Notes on the Margins of His Legacy, Studia Phaenomenologica* 6 (2006): 275–92.

2. Levinas would have been even more surprised, I suspect, to find his work discussed in the context of film studies. References to film in his work are virtually non-existent beyond a short discussion of Chaplin's *City Lights* in the early essay "De l'évasion" (1935); see Levinas 1982b: 87. There have nevertheless been some

attempts to bring Levinas into the world of film studies; see in particular Cooper (ed.), *The Occluded Relation: Levinas and Cinema*.

3. For a fuller version of this account of Levinas's treatment of the Talmud, see my *Levinas: An Introduction*, 106–19. There are two Talmuds, the Babylonian and the Jerusalem, containing texts which derive from separate Rabbinic academies. The passages which Levinas discusses are taken from the Babylonian Talmud.

4. An excellent introduction to Levinas's talmudic commentaries is given in Aronowicz's "Translator's Introduction," and her "The Little Man with the Burned Thighs: Levinas's Biblical Hermeneutic." Levinas presents the Talmud in the introduction to *Quatre lectures talmudiques*, 9–25. My discussion draws both on Levinas's texts and on a number of invaluable works: see in particular Banon, *La Lecture infinie*; Handelman, *The Slayers of Moses*; Hartman and Budick (eds.), *Midrash and Literature*.

5. On the consonantal nature of Hebrew and the possibilities of interpretation which it allows, see Banon, *La Lecture infinie*, 188–203.

6. Levinas discusses Spinoza in "Le Cas Spinoza" (*Difficile liberté*, 152–57), "Avez-vous relu Baruch?" (*Difficile liberté*, 158–69), and "L'Arrière-plan de Spinoza" (*L'Au-delà du verset*, 201–6).

7. See Spinoza, *Tractatus Theologico-Politicus*, chapter 7, "Of the Interpretation of Scripture."

8. In quotations from *L'Au-delà du verset* I have followed the excellent translation of Gary Mole.

9. On the presumption in Jewish hermeneutics that the sacred texts constitute a coherent whole, see Banon, *La Lecture infinie*, 89–90.

10. Hebrew letters have a numerical value, so words can also be read as numbers. See for example Levinas, *L'Au-delà du verset*, 132: the numerical value of the word *Thora* is 611; when this number is added to the two commandments heard directly from the voice of God, this makes 613, taken by one Rabbi to be the number of commandments given by God to Moses.

11. On the different levels of interpretation in Jewish hermeneutics, see Banon, *La Lecture infinie*, 205.

12. For discussion of this passage, see Aronowitz, "Translator's Introduction," xvii.

13. See also Levinas, *Du sacré au saint*, 15: "Obedience or audacity? Safety in proceeding or a taking of risks? In any case neither paraphrase nor paradox; neither philology nor arbitrariness."

14. On this issue in Jewish hermeneutics, see Goldin, "The Freedom and Restraint of Haggadah."

15. On this phrase, see Ricoeur, *Le Conflit des interprétations*, 284: "'The symbol gives rise to thought': this sentence which enchants me says two things; the symbol gives; I do not put meaning in it, it is the symbol which gives meaning;

but, what it gives is 'to think,' something to think about. . . . [S]o the sentence suggests both that everything is already said as an enigma, and yet that everything must be begun and begun again in the dimension of thinking." See also Ricoeur, *Finitude et culpabilité II: La Symbolique du mal*, especially 324–25.

16. Hirsch, for example, claims that Gadamer's hermeneutics provides no reliable means of distinguishing between competing interpretations; see Hirsch, *Validity in Interpretation*, 245–64.

17. There have in fact been numerous attempts to show the relevance of Levinas's work to a wide range of literary texts; see for example Astell and Jackson (eds.), *Levinas and Medieval Literature*; and New, Bernasconi and Cohen (eds.), *In Proximity: Emmanuel Levinas and the Eighteenth Century*. In the main, though, these attempts have been to apply Levinas's thought to literature rather than to extend his practice of reading, as exemplified in his talmudic commentaries, to secular texts.

18. On Levinas's views on art, in addition to Eaglestone's *Ethical Criticism: Reading After Levinas*, and Robbins's *Altered Reading: Levinas and Literature*, see my *After Poststructuralism: Reading, Stories and Theory*, 81–102; Hand, "Shadowing Ethics: Levinas's View of Art and Aesthetics"; and Bruns, "The Concepts of Art and Poetry in Emmanuel Levinas's Writings."

19. On ambiguities in Levinas's reading of Proust, see Robbins, *Altered Reading*, 80–82. Robbins concludes that "in short, in the Proust essay, Levinas seems to want to have it both ways. Poetry does and does not give access to the ethical" (Robbins 1999: 82).

20. See also *Du côté de chez Swann*, 419: "And Swann could feel close to his heart that Mohammad II whose portrait by Bellini he loved and who, having felt that he had fallen madly in love with one of his wives, stabbed her in order, as his Venetian biographer naively says, to recover his freedom of mind."

CHAPTER 5

1. There is now a growing body of work on Žižek, but relatively little of it specifically focuses on his treatment of literature and film; see for example Rex Butler, *Slavoj Žižek: Live Theory*; Tony Myers, *Slavoj Žižek*; Sarah Kay, *Žižek: A Critical Introduction*; Geoff Boucher, Jason Glynos and Matthew Sharpe (eds.), *Traversing the Fantasy: Critical Responses to Slavoj Žižek*.

2. In Poe's "The Purloined Letter," Minister D is able to steal a compromising letter under the eyes of its rightful owner, a woman, because she wishes to conceal it from the third person present at the scene, who is described as an "exalted personage" (Poe 1945: 442). Although it is not made explicit, it is hinted that the exalted personage and the woman are the King and Queen. The police fail to find the letter in the Minister's residence. Later, the amateur detective Dupin re-

trieves it when he realises that it was in fact hidden in full view of whomever had the guile to see it.

3. On the hostility between Derrida and Lacan, see Johnson, "The Frame of Reference: Poe, Lacan, Derrida," 117–18. My account of Lacan and Derrida here is heavily indebted to Johnson's essay.

4. It is to say the least interesting that Derrida's criticism of Lacan can be understood, for example, in the terms provided by E. D. Hirsch, who is usually considered to be one of the most conservative theorists of interpretation. In his *Validity in Interpretation* Hirsch offers four criteria for evaluating a reading: legitimacy, correspondence, generic appropriateness and coherence (Hirsch 1967: 236). Derrida does not dispute the legitimacy of Lacan's reading, but he suggests that it violates the principles of correspondence (details are misread), generic appropriateness (Lacan does not adequately account for the fictional status of the story) and coherence (the reading is unpersuasive).

CHAPTER 6

1. Cavell takes this lesson from Emerson; see *Emerson's Transcendental Etudes*, 95: "So the question Emerson's theory of reading and writing is designed to answer is not 'What does a text mean?' (and one may accordingly not wish to call it a theory of interpretation) but rather 'How is it that a text we care about in a certain way (expressed perhaps as our being drawn to read it with the obedience that masters) invariably says more than its writer knows, so that writers and readers write and read beyond themselves?' This might be summarized as 'What does a text know?' or, in Emerson's term, 'What is the genius of the text?'"

2. For a wide-ranging general study of Cavell's thought, see Mulhall, *Stanley Cavell: Philosophy's Recounting of the Ordinary*. Cavell's relevance to literary criticism is usefully examined in Fischer, *Stanley Cavell and Literary Skepticism*. On Cavell's reading of Shakespeare, see Bruns, "Stanley Cavell's Shakespeare," in *Tragic Thoughts at the End of Philosophy*, 181–97. For discussion of Cavell's work on film, see Mulhall, *On Film*; Rothman and Keane, *Reading Cavell's "The World Viewed": A Philosophical Perspective on Film*; Rothman's introduction to *Cavell on Film*; and Read and Goodenough (eds.), *Film as Philosophy: Essays on Cinema After Wittgenstein and Cavell*.

3. See Cavell, *In Quest of the Ordinary: Lines of Skepticism and Romanticism*.

4. On Thoreau, see Cavell's *The Senses of Walden*; Cavell's essays on Emerson have been collected in *Emerson's Transcendental Etudes*.

5. The first edition of the book had the title *Disowning Knowledge in Six Plays of Shakespeare* (1987), the updated edition being augmented by a later essay on *Macbeth*.

6. See also *Cavell on Film* (2005), which collects together many of Cavell's essays on film not contained in these books.

7. For discussion, see Chapter 5.

8. In a conversation with Andrew Klevan, Cavell suggests that he may have used the word *ontology* "in part to be somewhat provocative and mysterious," but also to serve the interest of asking "what makes film the specific thing it is" (Cavell 2005c: 194).

9. The following discussion is based on Cavell's chapter on *It Happened One Night* in *Pursuits of Happiness*. Cavell returns to the film in *Cities of Words*, 145–63.

10. In reference to Cavell's work, Rothman speaks of the "marriage" of film and philosophy; see for example the introduction to *Cavell on Film*, xiii.

11. On the resonance of the word *projection*, see Cavell, *Cavell on Film*, 285–6, commenting on the French translation of *The World Viewed* as *La Projection du monde*.

12. Cavell's "*North by Northwest*" was first published in *Critical Enquiry* (1981) and reprinted in *Themes out of School* and *Cavell on Film*. References here are to *Themes out of School*. Cavell's understanding of Hitchcock is informed by Rothman's *Hitchcock: The Murderous Gaze*, a book which is itself enlightened by Cavell's teaching. See also Rothman's essay "*North by Northwest*: Hitchcock's Monument to the Hitchcock Film," in *The "I" of the Camera*, 241–53.

13. Cavell attributes this sense to Hamlet, though in fact the line is spoken by Marcellus.

14. The example is one of Austin's to which Cavell refers on several occasions. See Austin, "A Plea for Excuses," 185. Austin comments: "'It was a mistake,' 'It was an accident'—how readily these can *appear* indifferent, and even be used together. Yet, a story or two, and everybody will not merely agree that they are completely different, but even discover for himself what the difference is and what each means" (184–85; emphasis in original).

15. On the Emersonian resonance of "partiality," see for example Cavell, *Emerson's Transcendental Etudes*, 149. Cavell quotes Emerson's statement that "thinking [not, as in Cavell's version, reading] is a partial act" and comments that "partial" implies both "not whole" and "favoring or biased toward." Cavell is quoting Emerson, "The American Scholar," 45.

16. Thoreau's "The mass of men lead lives of quiet desperation" is frequently cited by Cavell, for example as one of the epigraphs to *Cities of Words*, xiii; the original is from Thoreau's *Walden*, 9.

CHAPTER 7

1. The phrase is taken from Hirsch, *Validity in Interpretation*, heading to chapter 4, section A, 127.

2. For useful accounts of the development of hermeneutics, see Szondi, *Introduction to Literary Hermeneutics*; Mueller-Vollmer, "Introduction"; Weinsheimer, *Philosophical Hermeneutics and Literary Theory*, chapter 1, 1–23.

3. It may seem surprising to include Fish in this characterisation of the critical mainstream. Nevertheless, in *Is There a Text in This Class?* and later work, he provocatively concedes that there is something quite reassuring about what he says. The fact that texts have no inherent meaning or qualities does not mean that we can say anything we want about them. Our responses are constrained in advance by the norms and possibilities of the interpretive communities to which we belong.

4. In his reply to the comments of Rorty, Culler and Christine Brooke-Rose (whose paper is not discussed here because it raises different questions from the ones I am examining), Eco repeats Rorty and Culler's move of suggesting that, despite themselves, they must agree with him: "And I am sure that each of them thinks as I do. Otherwise they would not be here" (Eco 1992: 151). As we saw in Chapter 2, Gadamer does something similar in his debate with Derrida: "Even immoral beings try to understand one another. I cannot believe that Derrida would actually disagree with me about this" (Gadamer 1991: 55). The lesson is clear: when disagreeing with someone, insist that they in fact share your opinion even if they do not realise it.

5. Vattimo writes that "there is no experience of truth that is not interpretative," and that "this thesis is shared by all those who espouse hermeneutics, and is even widely accepted by the greater part of twentieth-century thought" (Vattimo 1997: 4).

6. For this account of the distinction between structuralist poetics and interpretation, see Todorov, *Qu'est-ce que le structuralisme? 2: Poétique*, 15–28.

7. As cited in Chapter 5, Žižek discusses a similar point with reference to Dostoevsky: he may have been an epileptic with an unresolved paternal authority complex, but not every epileptic with an unresolved paternal authority complex was Dostoevsky. As a reproach against the inability of psychoanalysis to explain the specificity of works of art, Žižek describes this argument as a "worn-out commonplace" (Žižek 1994: 176).

8. For criticism and discussion of this aspect of Gadamer's thought, see Hoy, *The Critical Circle*, 107–9.

9. Even Rorty, who seems to deny that there is anything in the text which was not put there by its readers, shares this aspiration for a transforming encounter with the work's otherness: "Unmethodical criticism of the sort which one occasionally wants to call 'inspired' is the result of an encounter with an author, character, plot, stanza, line or archaic torso which has made a difference to the critic's conception of who she is, what she is good for, what she wants to do with herself: an encounter which has rearranged her priorities and purposes" (Rorty 1992: 107).

10. See Greenblatt, *Shakespearean Negotiations*; Cavell, *Disowning Knowledge in Seven Plays of Shakespeare*.

11. On this aspect of Rabbinic interpretation, see for example Banon, *La Lecture infinie*. In *The Slayers of Moses*, Susan Handelmann makes a strong case for the persistence of Rabbinic modes of interpretation in poststructuralist critical practices.

12. See, for example, *The Plague of Fantasies*, in which Žižek refers to Steven Spielberg's *Star Wars* trilogy and relates the films to other works by the director (Žižek 1997: 75). Žižek seems, however, to be confusing Spielberg with George Lucas. Although Cavell defends his own mistakes in remembering and describing films, he can be highly critical of the mistakes of others; see for example *Philosophy the Day After Tomorrow*, 69–70.

Bibliography

Abrams, M. H. 1988. "The Deconstructive Angel." In *Modern Criticism and Theory: A Reader*, ed. David Lodge, 265–76. London and New York: Longman.

Agamben, Giorgio. 1999. *The Man Without Content.* Trans. Georgia Albert. Stanford: Stanford University Press.

Annas, Julia. 1982. "Plato on the Triviality of Literature." In *Plato on Beauty, Wisdom, and the Arts*, ed. Julius Moravcsik and Philip Temko, 1–28. Totowa: Rowman and Littlefield.

Aronowicz, Annette. 1990. "Translator's Introduction." In *Nine Talmudic Readings*, by Emmanuel Levinas, trans. Annette Aronowicz, ix–xxxix. Bloomington: Indiana University Press.

Aronowicz, Annette. 2003. "The Little Man with the Burned Thighs: Levinas's Biblical Hermeneutic." In *Levinas and Biblical Studies*, ed. Tamara Cohn Eskenazi, Gary Philips and David Jobling, 33–48. Atlanta: Society of Biblical Literature.

Astell, Ann W., and J. A. Jackson, eds. 2009. *Levinas and Medieval Literature: The "Difficult Reading" of English and Rabbinic Texts.* Pittsburgh: Duquesne University Press.

Attridge, Derek. 1992. "Introduction: Derrida and the Questioning of Literature." In *Acts of Literature*, by Jacques Derrida, 1–29. New York and London: Routledge.

Attridge, Derek. 2008. "Derrida's Singularity: Literature and Ethics." In *Derrida's Legacies: Literature and Philosophy*, ed. Simon Glendinning and Robert Eaglestone, 12–25. London and New York: Routledge.

Austin, J. L. 1962. *How to Do Things with Words.* Oxford: Oxford University Press.

Austin, J. L. 1979. "A Plea for Excuses." In *Philosophical Papers*. Third edition, 175–204. Oxford: Oxford University Press.

Badiou, Alain. 1997. *Deleuze: "La Clameur de l'être."* Paris: Hachette Littératures.

Badiou, Alain. 2009. *Second manifeste pour la philosophie.* Paris: Fayard.

Banon, David. 1987. *La Lecture infinie: Les Voies de l'interprétation midrachique.* Paris: Seuil.

Barthes, Roland. 1973. *Le Plaisir du texte*. Paris: Seuil.

Barthes, Roland. 1988. "The Death of the Author." Trans. Stephen Heath. In *Modern Criticism and Theory: A Reader*, ed. David Lodge, 167–72. London and New York: Longman.

Bass, Alan. 2004. "'Literature'/Literature." In *Jacques Derrida: Critical Thought*, ed. Ian Maclachlan, 14–23. Aldershot: Ashgate.

Baugh, Bruce. 2001. "How Deleuze Can Help Us Make Literature Work." In *Deleuze and Literature*, ed. Ian Buchanan and John Marks, 34–56. Edinburgh: Edinburgh University Press.

Beauvoir, Simone de. 1949. *Le Deuxième Sexe I: Les Faits et les mythes*. Folio edition. Paris: Gallimard.

Behler, Ernst. 1991. *Confrontations: Derrida/Heidegger/Nietzsche*. Stanford: Stanford University Press.

Bernasconi, Robert. 1991. "Seeing Double: *Destruktion* and Deconstruction." In *Dialogue and Deconstruction: The Gadamer-Derrida Encounter*, ed. Diane Michelfelder and Richard Palmer, 233–50. Albany: State University of New York Press.

Bernasconi, Robert. 1993. *Heidegger in Question: The Art of Existing*. Atlantic Highlands: Humanities Press.

Bernstein, Richard. 2002. "The Constellation of Hermeneutics, Critical Theory and Deconstruction." In *The Cambridge Companion to Gadamer*, ed. Robert Dostal, 267–82. Cambridge: Cambridge University Press.

Bloom, Harold. 1973. *The Anxiety of Influence: A Theory of Poetry*. London, Oxford and New York: Oxford University Press.

Bloom, Harold. 1975. *A Map of Misreading*. Oxford, New York, Toronto and Melbourne: Oxford University Press.

Bogue, Ronald. 2003a. *Deleuze on Cinema*. London and New York: Routledge.

Bogue, Ronald. 2003b. *Deleuze on Literature*. London and New York: Routledge.

Bogue, Ronald. 2003c. *Deleuze on Music, Painting, and the Arts*. London and New York: Routledge.

Boucher, Geoff, Jason Glynos and Matthew Sharpe, eds. 2005. *Traversing the Fantasy: Critical Responses to Slavoj Žižek*. Aldershot: Ashgate.

Bowie, Andrew. 1997. *From Romanticism to Critical Theory: The Philosophy of German Literary Theory*. London and New York: Routledge.

Bowie, Andrew. 2003. *Aesthetics and Subjectivity: From Kant to Nietzsche*. Second edition. Manchester and New York: Manchester University Press.

Brock, Werner. 1949. "Introduction." In *Existence and Being*, by Martin Heidegger, 13–248. Chicago: Henry Regnery Company.

Brooke-Rose, Christine. 1992. "Palimpsest History." In *Interpretation and Over-*

interpretation, by Umberto Eco, 125–38. Cambridge: Cambridge University Press.

Bruns, Gerald. 1999. *Tragic Thoughts at the End of Philosophy: Language, Literature, and Ethical Theory*. Evanston: Northwestern University Press.

Bruns, Gerald. 2002. "The Concepts of Art and Poetry in Emmanuel Levinas's Writings." In *The Cambridge Companion to Levinas*, ed. Simon Critchley and Robert Bernasconi, 206–33. Cambridge: Cambridge University Press.

Bryden, Mary. 2007. *Gilles Deleuze: Travels in Literature*. Houndmills: Palgrave Macmillan.

Bryden, Mary, and Margaret Topping, eds. 2009. *Beckett's Proust/Deleuze's Proust*. Houndmills: Palgrave Macmillan.

Buchanan, Ian, and Patricia MacCormack, eds. 2008. *Deleuze and the Schizoanalysis of Cinema*. London: Continuum.

Butler, Rex. 2005. *Slavoj Žižek: Live Theory*. New York: Continuum.

Caputo, John. 1991. "Gadamer's Closet Essentialism: A Derridean Critique." In *Dialogue and Deconstruction: The Gadamer-Derrida Encounter*, ed. Diane Michelfelder and Richard Palmer, 258–64. Albany: State University of New York Press.

Carroll, Noël. 2006. "Introduction to Part II." In *Philosophy of Film and Motion Pictures: An Anthology*, ed. Noël Carroll and Jinhee Choi, 51–65. Oxford: Blackwell.

Cavell, Stanley. 1972. *The Senses of Walden*. New York: Viking Press.

Cavell, Stanley. 1979a. *The Claim of Reason: Wittgenstein, Skepticism, Morality and Tragedy*. Oxford and New York: Oxford University Press.

Cavell, Stanley. 1979b. *The World Viewed*. Enlarged edition. Cambridge (Mass.) and London: Harvard University Press.

Cavell, Stanley. 1981. *Pursuits of Happiness: The Hollywood Comedy of Remarriage*. Cambridge (Mass.) and London: Harvard University Press.

Cavell, Stanley. 1984. *Themes out of School: Effects and Causes*. Chicago and London: University of Chicago Press.

Cavell, Stanley. 1988. *In Quest of the Ordinary: Lines of Skepticism and Romanticism*. Chicago and London: University of Chicago Press.

Cavell, Stanley. 1995. *Philosophical Passages: Wittgenstein, Emerson, Austin, Derrida*. Oxford: Blackwell.

Cavell, Stanley. 1996. *Contesting Tears: The Hollywood Melodrama of the Unknown Woman*. Chicago and London: University of Chicago Press.

Cavell, Stanley. 2003a. *Disowning Knowledge in Seven Plays of Shakespeare*. Updated edition. Cambridge: Cambridge University Press.

Cavell, Stanley. 2003b. *Emerson's Transcendental Etudes*. Stanford: Stanford University Press.

Cavell, Stanley. 2004. *Cities of Words: Pedagogical Letters on a Register of the Moral Life*. Cambridge (Mass.) and London: Harvard University Press.

Cavell, Stanley. 2005a. *Cavell on Film*. Ed. William Rothman. Albany: State University of New York Press.

Cavell, Stanley. 2005b. *Philosophy the Day After Tomorrow*. Cambridge (Mass.) and London: Harvard University Press.

Cavell, Stanley. 2005c. "What Becomes of Thinking on Film?" Conversation with Andrew Klevan. In *Film as Philosophy: Essays on Cinema After Wittgenstein and Cavell*, ed. Rupert Read and Jerry Goodenough, 167–209. Houndmills: Palgrave Macmillan.

Celan, Paul. 1983. *Gesammelte Werke. Zweiter Band: Gedichte II*. Frankfurt: Suhrkamp.

Chateau, Dominique. 2003. *Cinéma et philosophie*. Paris: Nathan.

Chladenius, Johann Martin. 1985. "On the Concept of Interpretation." In *The Hermeneutics Reader*, ed. Kurt Mueller-Vollmer, 55–64. Oxford: Blackwell.

Clark, Timothy. 1992. *Derrida, Heidegger, Blanchot: Sources of Derrida's Notion and Practice of Literature*. Cambridge: Cambridge University Press.

Clark, Timothy. 2005. *The Poetics of Singularity: The Counter-Culturalist Turn in Heidegger, Derrida, Blanchot and the Later Gadamer*. Edinburgh: Edinburgh University Press.

Cooper, Sarah, ed. 2007. *The Occluded Relation: Levinas and Cinema*. Special issue of *Film-Philosophy* 11: 2. http://www.film-philosophy.com/.

Costiucovich, Helena. 1982. "Umberto Eco: Imja Rosi." *Sovriemiennaja hudoziestviennaja litieratura za rubiezom* 5 (1982): 101–10.

Critchley, Simon. 2008. "Derrida: The Reader." In *Derrida's Legacies: Literature and Philosophy*, ed. Simon Glendinning and Robert Eaglestone, 1–11. London and New York: Routledge.

Culler, Jonathan. 1981. *The Pursuit of Signs: Semiotics, Literature, Deconstruction*. London and Henley: Routledge and Kegan Paul.

Culler, Jonathan. 1992. "In Defence of Interpretation." In *Interpretation and Overinterpretation*, by Umberto Eco, 109–23. Cambridge: Cambridge University Press.

Dasenbrock, Reed Way. 1994. "Taking It Personally: Reading Derrida's Responses." *College English* 56: 3: 261–79.

Davis, Colin. 1996. *Levinas: An Introduction*. Cambridge: Polity Press.

Davis, Colin. 2000. *Ethical Issues in Twentieth-Century French Fiction: Killing the Other*. Houndmills: Macmillan.

Davis, Colin. 2004. *After Poststructuralism: Reading, Stories and Theory*. London and New York: Routledge.

Davis, Colin. 2006. "Levinas and the Phenomenology of Reading." In *A Century With Levinas: Notes on the Margins of His Legacy*. *Studia Phaenomenologica* 6: 275–92.

Davis, Colin. 2009. *Scenes of Love and Murder: Renoir, Film and Philosophy*. London: Wallflower.

Deleuze, Gilles. 1968. *Différence et répétition*. Paris: Presses Universitaires de France.

Deleuze, Gilles. 1979. *Proust et les signes*. Fifth edition. Paris: Presses Universitaires de France.

Deleuze, Gilles. 1981. *Francis Bacon: Logique de la sensation*. Paris: Editions de la Différence.

Deleuze, Gilles. 1983. *Cinéma 1: L'Image-mouvement*. Paris: Minuit.

Deleuze, Gilles. 1985. *Cinéma 2: L'Image-temps*. Paris: Minuit.

Deleuze, Gilles. 1990. *Pourparlers*. Paris: Minuit.

Deleuze, Gilles. 1993. *Critique et clinique*. Paris: Minuit.

Deleuze, Gilles, and Félix Guattari. 1975. *Kafka: Pour une littérature mineure*. Paris: Minuit.

Deleuze, Gilles, and Félix Guattari. 1991. *Qu'est-ce que la philosophie?* Paris: Minuit.

Deleuze, Gilles, and Claire Parnet. 1977. *Dialogues*. Paris: Flammarion.

De Man, Paul. 1979. *Allegories of Reading: Figural Language in Rousseau, Nietzsche, Rilke and Proust*. New Haven and London: Yale University Press.

De Man, Paul. 1983. *Blindness and Insight: Essays in the Rhetoric of Contemporary Criticism*. Second edition. London: Methuen.

De Man, Paul. 1986. *The Resistance to Theory*. Manchester: Manchester University Press.

Derrida, Jacques. 1967a. *De la grammatologie*. Paris: Minuit.

Derrida, Jacques. 1967b. *La Voix et le phénomène*. Paris: Presses Universitaires de France.

Derrida, Jacques. 1972a. *La Dissémination*. Paris: Seuil.

Derrida, Jacques. 1972b. *Marges de la philosophie*. Paris: Minuit.

Derrida, Jacques. 1972c. *Positions*. Paris: Minuit.

Derrida, Jacques. 1978. *Eperons: Les Styles de Nietzsche*. Paris: Flammarion.

Derrida, Jacques. 1980. "Le Facteur de la vérité." In *La Carte postale: De Socrate à Freud et au-delà*, 439–524. Paris: Flammarion.

Derrida, Jacques. 1983. "The Time of a Thesis: Punctuations." Trans. Kathleen McLaughlin. In *Philosophy in France Today*, ed. Alan Montefiori, 34–50. Cambridge: Cambridge University Press.

Derrida, Jacques. 1986. *Schibboleth pour Paul Celan*. Paris: Galilée.

Derrida, Jacques. 1987. *Ulysse gramophone: Deux mots pour Joyce.* Paris: Galilée.

Derrida, Jacques. 1988. *Signéponge.* Paris: Seuil.

Derrida, Jacques. 1990. *Limited Inc.* Paris: Galilée.

Derrida, Jacques. 1991a. "Three Questions to Hans-Georg Gadamer." Trans. Diane Michelfelder and Richard Palmer. In *Dialogue and Deconstruction: The Gadamer-Derrida Encounter,* ed. Diane Michelfelder and Richard Palmer, 52–54. Albany: State University of New York Press.

Derrida, Jacques. 1991b. "Interpreting Signatures (Nietzsche/Heidegger): Two Questions." Trans. Diane Michelfelder and Richard Palmer. In *Dialogue and Deconstruction: The Gadamer-Derrida Encounter,* ed. Diane Michelfelder and Richard Palmer, 58–71. Albany: State University of New York Press.

Derrida, Jacques.1992. *Acts of Literature.* Ed. Derek Attridge. New York and London: Routledge.

Derrida, Jacques. 1994. *Politiques de l'amitié.* Paris: Galilée.

Derrida, Jacques. 2003a. *Béliers. Le Dialogue ininterrompu: entre deux infinis, le poème.* Paris: Galilée.

Derrida, Jacques. 2003b. *Chaque fois unique, la fin du monde.* Paris: Galilée.

Dostal, Robert, ed. 2002. *The Cambridge Companion to Gadamer.* Cambridge: Cambridge University Press.

Due, Reidar. 2007. *Deleuze.* Cambridge: Polity.

Eaglestone, Robert. 1997. *Ethical Criticism: Reading After Levinas.* Edinburgh: Edinburgh University Press.

Eagleton, Terry. 1983. *Literary Theory: An Introduction.* Oxford: Basil Blackwell.

Eco, Umberto. 1983. *The Name of the Rose.* Trans. William Weaver. London: Secker and Warburg.

Eco, Umberto. 1984. *Semiotics and the Philosophy of Language.* Houndmills: Macmillan.

Eco, Umberto. 1989. *Foucault's Pendulum.* Trans. William Weaver. London: Secker and Warburg.

Eco, Umberto. 1990. *The Limits of Interpretation.* Bloomington and Indianapolis: Indiana University Press.

Eco, Umberto. 1992. *Interpretation and Overinterpretation.* Cambridge: Cambridge University Press.

Eco, Umberto. 2006. *On Literature.* Trans. Martin McLaughlin. London: Vintage Books.

Emerson, Ralph Waldo. 1990. "The American Scholar." In *Ralph Waldo Emerson,* ed. Richard Poirier, 37–52. Oxford and New York: Oxford University Press.

Felman, Shoshana. 1987. *Jacques Lacan and the Adventure of Insight: Psychoanalysis in Contemporary Culture.* Cambridge (Mass.) and London: Harvard University Press.

Ferry, Luc, and Alain Renaut. 1988. *La Pensée 68: Essai sur l'anti-humanisme contemporain.* Folio essais edition. Paris: Gallimard.

Fischer, Michael. 1989. *Stanley Cavell and Literary Skepticism.* Chicago and London: University of Chicago Press.

Fish, Stanley. 1980. *Is There a Text in This Class? The Authority of Interpretive Communities.* Cambridge (Mass.) and London: Harvard University Press.

Fish, Stanley. 1989. *Doing What Comes Naturally: Change, Rhetoric, and the Practice of Theory in Literary and Legal Studies.* Oxford: Oxford University Press.

Forget, Philippe. 1984. "Leitfäden einer unwahrscheinlichen Debatte." In *Text und Interpretation,* ed. Philippe Forget, 7–23. Munich: Wilhelm Fink Verlag.

Forget, Philippe. 1991. "Argument(s)." Trans. Diane Michelfelder. In *Dialogue and Deconstruction: The Gadamer-Derrida Encounter,* ed. Diane Michelfelder and Richard Palmer, 129–49. Albany: State University of New York Press.

Freud, Sigmund. 1976. *Jokes and Their Relation to the Unconscious.* Trans. James Strachey. Pelican Freud Library, vol. 6. Harmondsworth: Penguin Books.

Freud, Sigmund. 1985. "Delusions and Dreams in Jensen's *Gradiva.*" In *Art and Literature,* trans. James Strachey, 27–118. Pelican Freud Library, vol. 14. Harmondsworth: Penguin Books.

Froman, Wayne. 1991. "*L'Ecriture* and Philosophical Hermeneutics." In *Gadamer and Hermeneutics,* ed. Hugh J. Silverman, 136–48. New York and London: Routledge.

Gadamer, Hans-Georg. 1986. *Wahrheit und Methode: Grundzüge einer philosophischen Hermeneutik.* Fifth edition. Tübingen: J.C.B. Mohr (Paul Siebeck).

Gadamer, Hans-Georg. 1991a. "Text and Interpretation." Trans. Dennis Schmidt and Richard Palmer. In *Dialogue and Deconstruction: The Gadamer-Derrida Encounter,* ed. Diane Michelfelder and Richard Palmer, 21–51. Albany: State University of New York Press.

Gadamer, Hans-Georg. 1991b. "Reply to Jacques Derrida." Trans. Diane Michelfelder and Richard Palmer. In *Dialogue and Deconstruction: The Gadamer-Derrida Encounter,* ed. Diane Michelfelder and Richard Palmer, 55–57. Albany: State University of New York Press.

Gadamer, Hans-Georg. 1991c. "Letter to Dallmayr." Trans. Diane Michelfelder and Richard Palmer. In *Dialogue and Deconstruction: The Gadamer-Derrida Encounter,* ed. Diane Michelfelder and Richard Palmer, 93–101. Albany: State University of New York Press.

Gadamer, Hans-Georg. 1991d. "*Destruktion* and Deconstruction." Trans. Geoff Waite and Richard Palmer. In *Dialogue and Deconstruction: The Gadamer-Derrida Encounter,* ed. Diane Michelfelder and Richard Palmer, 102–13. Albany: State University of New York Press.

Gadamer, Hans-Georg. 1991e. "Hermeneutics and Logocentrism." Trans. Diane Michelfelder and Richard Palmer. In *Dialogue and Deconstruction: The Gadamer-Derrida Encounter*, ed. Diane Michelfelder and Richard Palmer, 114–25. Albany: State University of New York Press.

Gadamer, Hans-Georg. 1997. *Gadamer on Celan: "Who Am I and Who Are You?" and Other Essays*. Trans. Richard Heinemann and Bruce Krajewski. Albany: State University of New York Press.

Gasché, Rodolphe. 1986. *The Tain of the Mirror: Derrida and the Philosophy of Reflection*. Cambridge (Mass.) and London: Harvard University Press.

Glendinning, Simon, and Robert Eaglestone, eds. 2008. *Derrida's Legacies: Literature and Philosophy*. London and New York: Routledge.

Goldin, Judah. 1986. "The Freedom and Restraint of Haggadah." In *Midrash and Literature*, ed. Geoffrey Hartman and Sanford Budick, 57–76. New Haven and London: Yale University Press.

Greenblatt, Stephen. 1988. *Shakespearean Negotiations: The Circulation of Social Energy in Renaissance England*. Oxford: Oxford University Press.

Grosz, Elizabeth. 2008. *Chaos, Territory, Art: Deleuze and the Framing of the Earth*. New York: Columbia University Press.

Habermas, Jürgen. 1987. *The Philosophical Discourse of Modernity*. Trans. Frederick Lawrence. Cambridge: Polity.

Hallward, Peter. 2006. *Out of This World: Deleuze and the Philosophy of Creation*. London and New York: Verso.

Hand, Seán. 1996. "Shadowing Ethics: Levinas's View of Art and Aesthetics." In *Facing the Other: The Ethics of Emmanuel Levinas*, ed. Seán Hand, 63–89. Richmond: Curzon Press.

Handelman, Susan. 1982. *The Slayers of Moses: The Emergence of Rabbinic Interpretation in Modern Literary Theory*. Albany: State University of New York Press.

Hartman, Geoffrey, and Sanford Budick, eds. 1986. *Midrash and Literature*. New Haven and London: Yale University Press.

Hegel, G.W.F. 1993. *Introductory Lectures on Aesthetics*. Trans. Bernard Bosanquet. Harmondsworth: Penguin.

Heidegger, Martin. 1949. *Existence and Being*. Trans. Douglas Scott, R.F.C. Hull and Alan Crick. Chicago: Henry Regnery Company.

Heidegger, Martin. 1959. *Unterwegs zur Sprache*. Tübingen: Neske.

Heidegger, Martin. 1961. *Nietzsche I*. Pfullingen: Neske.

Heidegger, Martin. 1971. *Poetry, Language, Thought*. Trans. Albert Hofstadter. Perennial Classics edition. New York: Harper and Row.

Heidegger, Martin. 1979. *Sein und Zeit*. Fifteenth edition. Tübingen: Max Niemeyer Verlag.

Heidegger, Martin. 1995. *The Fundamental Concepts of Metaphysics: World, Finitude, Solitude.* Trans. William McNeill and Nicholas Walker. Bloomington and Indianapolis: Indiana University Press.

Heidegger, Martin. 2000. *Elucidations of Hölderlin's Poetry.* Trans. Keith Hoeller. New York: Prometheus Books.

Hirsch, E. D., Jr. 1967. *Validity in Interpretation.* New Haven and London: Yale University Press.

Hoeller, Keith. 2000. "Translator's Introduction." In *Elucidations of Hölderlin's Poetry*, by Martin Heidegger, 7–19. Trans. Keith Hoeller. New York: Prometheus Books.

Hölderlin, Friedrich. 1965. *Sämtliche Werke.* Ed. Friedrich Beissner. Frankfurt: Insel-Verlag.

Hoy, David Couzens. 1982. *The Critical Circle: Literature, History, and Philosophical Hermeneutics.* Berkeley and Los Angeles: University of California Press.

Hoy, David Couzens. 2004. *Critical Resistance: From Poststructuralism to Post-Critique.* Cambridge (Mass.) and London: MIT Press.

Husserl, Edmund. 1977. *Cartesian Meditations: An Introduction to Phenomenology.* Trans. Dorion Cairns. The Hague: Martinus Nijhoff.

Iser, Wolfgang. 1988. "The Reading Process: A Phenomenological Approach." In *Modern Criticism and Theory: A Reader*, ed. David Lodge, 212–28. London and New York: Longman.

Jameson, Fredric. 1981. *The Political Unconscious: Narrative as a Socially Symbolic Act.* London: Methuen.

Johnson, Barbara. 1980. "The Frame of Reference: Poe, Lacan, Derrida." In *The Critical Difference: Essays in the Contemporary Rhetoric of Reading*, 110–46. Baltimore and London: Johns Hopkins University Press.

Jones, Ernest. 1949. *Hamlet and Oedipus.* London: V. Gollancz.

Kant, Immanuel. 1974. *Kritik der Urteilskraft.* Sixth edition. Hamburg: Felix Meiner.

Kay, Sarah. 2003. *Žižek: A Critical Introduction.* Cambridge: Polity.

Kennedy, Barbara. 2000. *Deleuze and Cinema: The Aesthetics of Sensation.* Edinburgh: Edinburgh University Press.

Lacan, Jacques. 1966a. "Présentation." In *Ecrits I*, 7–12. Points edition. Paris: Seuil.

Lacan, Jacques. 1966b. "Le Séminaire sur 'La Lettre volée.'" In *Ecrits I*, 19–75. Points edition. Paris: Seuil.

Lacan, Jacques. 1978. *Le Séminaire livre II: Le Moi dans la théorie de Freud et dans la technique de la psychanalyse, 1954–1955.* Paris: Seuil.

Lacoue-Labarthe, Philippe, and Jean-Luc Nancy, eds. 1978. *L'Absolu littéraire: Théorie de la littérature du romantisme allemand.* Paris: Seuil.

Levinas, Emmanuel. 1947. *De l'existence à l'existant.* Paris: Fontaine.

Levinas, Emmanuel. 1948. *Le Temps et l'autre.* Paris: Artaud.

Levinas, Emmanuel. 1949. *En découvrant l'existence avec Husserl et Heidegger.* Paris: Vrin.

Levinas, Emmanuel. 1961. *Totalité et infini: Essai sur l'extériorité.* Livre de Poche edition. The Hague: Martinus Nijhoff.

Levinas, Emmanuel. 1968. *Quatre lectures talmudiques.* Paris: Seuil.

Levinas, Emmanuel. 1976a. "L'Autre dans Proust." In *Noms propres,* 117–23. Livre de Poche edition. Montpellier: Fata Morgana.

Levinas, Emmanuel. 1976b. *Difficile liberté.* Livre de Poche edition. Paris: Albin Michel.

Levinas, Emmanuel. 1977. *Du sacré au saint: Cinq nouvelles lectures talmudiques.* Paris: Minuit.

Levinas, Emmanuel. 1982a. *L'Au-delà du verset: Lectures et discours talmudiques.* Paris: Minuit.

Levinas, Emmanuel. 1982b. *De l'évasion.* Montpellier: Fata Morgana.

Levinas, Emmanuel. 1987. "De l'écrit à l'oral." In *La Lecture infinie: Les Voies de l'interprétation midrachique,* by David Banon, 7–11. Paris: Seuil.

Levinas, Emmanuel. 1994a. *Beyond the Verse: Talmudic Readings and Lectures.* Trans. Gary D. Mole. London: Athlone Press.

Levinas, Emmanuel. 1994b. "La Réalité et son ombre." In *Les Imprévus de l'histoire,* 123–48. Montpellier: Fata Morgana.

Maclachlan, Ian. 2004. "Introduction: Deconstruction, Critical Thought, Literature." In *Jacques Derrida: Critical Thought,* ed. Ian Maclachlan, 1–13. Aldershot: Ashgate.

Madison, Gary. 1991a. "Beyond Seriousness and Frivolity: A Gadamerian Response to Deconstruction." In *Gadamer and Hermeneutics,* ed. Hugh J. Silverman, 119–35. New York and London: Routledge.

Madison, Gary. 1991b. "Gadamer/Derrida: The Hermeneutics of Irony and Power." In *Dialogue and Deconstruction: The Gadamer-Derrida Encounter,* ed. Diane Michelfelder and Richard Palmer, 192–98. Albany: State University of New York Press.

Marrati, Paola. 2003. *Gilles Deleuze: Cinéma et philosophie.* Paris: Presses Universitaires de Paris.

Marshall, Donald. 1991. "Dialogue and *Ecriture.*" In *Dialogue and Deconstruction: The Gadamer-Derrida Encounter,* ed. Diane Michelfelder and Richard Palmer, 206–14. Albany: State University of New York Press.

Megill, Allan. 1985. *Prophets of Extremity: Nietzsche, Heidegger, Foucault, Derrida.* Berkeley and Los Angeles: University of California Press.

Michelfelder, Diane, and Richard Palmer, eds. 1989. *Dialogue and Deconstruction: The Gadamer-Derrida Encounter.* Albany: State University of New York Press.

Miller, J. Hillis. 2001. "Derrida and Literature." In *Jacques Derrida and the Humanities: A Critical Reader,* ed. Tom Cohen, 58–81. Cambridge: Cambridge University Press.

Mueller-Vollmer, Kurt. 1985. "Introduction: Language, Mind, and Artefact: An Outline of Hermeneutic Theory Since the Enlightenment." In *The Hermeneutics Reader,* ed. Kurt Mueller-Vollmer, 1–53. Oxford: Blackwell.

Mulhall, Stephen. 1994. *Stanley Cavell: Philosophy's Recounting of the Ordinary.* Oxford: Clarendon Press.

Mulhall, Stephen. 2002. *On Film.* London: Routledge.

Murdoch, Iris. 1977. *The Fire and the Sun: Why Plato Banished the Artists.* Oxford: Oxford University Press.

Myers, Tony. 2003. *Slavoj Žižek.* London and New York: Routledge.

Nehamas, Alexander. 1982. "Plato on Imitation and Poetry in *Republic* 10." In *Plato on Beauty, Wisdom, and the Arts,* ed. Julius Moravcsik and Philip Temko, 47–78. Totowa: Rowman and Littlefield.

New, Melvyn, with Robert Bernasconi and Richard A. Cohen, eds. 2001. *In Proximity: Emmanuel Levinas and the Eighteenth Century.* Lubbock: Texas Tech University Press.

Norris, Christopher. 1987. *Derrida.* Cambridge (Mass.): Harvard University Press.

Norris, Christopher. 1989. "Philosophy as *Not* Just a 'Kind of Writing': Derrida and the Claim of Reason." In *Redressing the Lines: Analytic Philosophy, Deconstruction and Literary Theory,* ed. Reed Way Dasenbrock, 189–203. Minneapolis: University of Minnesota Press.

Nussbaum, Martha. 1990. *Love's Knowledge: Essays on Philosophy and Literature.* New York and Oxford: Oxford University Press.

Nussbaum, Martha. 2001. *The Fragility of Goodness: Luck and Ethics in Greek Tragedy and Philosophy.* Revised edition. Cambridge: Cambridge University Press.

Parr, Adrian. 2005. "Repetition." In *The Deleuze Dictionary,* ed. Adrian Parr, 223–25. Edinburgh: Edinburgh University Press.

Plato. 1961. *The Collected Dialogues.* Ed. Edith Hamilton and Huntington Cairns. Princeton: Princeton University Press.

Poe, Edgar Allan. 1945. "The Purloined Letter." In *The Portable Poe,* 439–62. Harmondsworth: Penguin Books.

Proust, Marcel. 1954. *Du côté de chez Swann.* Folio edition. Paris: Gallimard.

Rapaport, Herman. 1991. "All Ears: Derrida's Response to Gadamer." In *Dialogue and Deconstruction: The Gadamer-Derrida Encounter,* ed. Diane Michelfelder and Richard Palmer, 199–205. Albany: State University of New York Press.

Read, Rupert, and Jerry Goodenough, eds. 2005. *Film as Philosophy: Essays on Cinema After Wittgenstein and Cavell.* Houndmills: Palgrave Macmillan.

Ricoeur, Paul. 1960. *Finitude et culpabilité II: La Symbolique du mal.* Paris: Aubier-Montaigne.

Ricoeur, Paul. 1965. *De l'interprétation: Essai sur Freud.* Paris: Seuil.

Ricoeur, Paul. 1969. *Le Conflit des interprétations: Essais d'herméneutique.* Paris: Seuil.

Ricoeur, Paul. 1986. *Du texte à l'action: Essais d'herméneutique, II.* Paris: Seuil.

Risser, James. 1997. *Hermeneutics and the Voice of the Other: Re-Reading Gadamer's Philosophical Hermeneutics.* Albany: State University of New York Press.

Robbins, Jill. 1999. *Altered Reading: Levinas and Literature.* Chicago and London: University of Chicago Press.

Rockmore, Tom. 1995. *Heidegger and French Philosophy: Humanism, Antihumanism and Being.* London and New York: Routledge.

Rodowick, David. 1997. *Gilles Deleuze's Time Machine.* Durham: Duke University Press.

Rorty, Richard. 1989. *Contingency, Irony, and Solidarity.* Cambridge: Cambridge University Press.

Rorty, Richard. 1991. *Essays on Heidegger and Others: Philosophical Papers, Volume 2.* Cambridge: Cambridge University Press.

Rorty, Richard. 1992. "The Pragmatist's Progress." In *Interpretation and Overinterpretation,* by Umberto Eco, 89–108. Cambridge: Cambridge University Press.

Rothman, William. 1982. *Hitchcock: The Murderous Gaze.* Cambridge (Mass.) and London: Harvard University Press.

Rothman, William. 2004. *The "I" of the Camera: Essays in Film Criticism, History, and Aesthetics.* Second edition. Cambridge: Cambridge University Press.

Rothman, William. 2005. "Introduction." In *Cavell on Film,* by Stanley Cavell, xi–xxvii. Albany: State University of New York Press.

Rothman, William, and Marian Keane. 2000. *Reading Cavell's "The World Viewed": A Philosophical Perspective on Film.* Detroit: Wayne State University Press.

Sartre, Jean-Paul. 1960. *Critique de la raison dialectique.* Paris: Gallimard.

Schelling, Friedrich. 1978. "Philosophie de l'art (introduction)." Trans. Philippe Lacoue-Labarthe, Jean-Luc Nancy and Anne-Marie Lang. In *L'Absolu littéraire: Théorie de la littérature du romantisme allemand,* ed. Philippe Lacoue-Labarthe and Jean-Luc Nancy, 394–406. Paris: Seuil.

Schelling, Friedrich. 1988a. "Conclusion to *System of Transcendental Idealism.*" Trans. Albert Hofstadter. In *The Origins of Modern Critical Thought,* ed. David Simpson, 225–31. Cambridge: Cambridge University Press.

Schelling, Friedrich. 1988b. "On Dante in Relation to Philosophy." Trans. Elizabeth Rubenstein and David Simpson. In *The Origins of Modern Critical Thought*, ed. David Simpson, 239–47. Cambridge: Cambridge University Press.

Schlegel, Friedrich. 1988. "From *Critical Fragments*." Trans. Peter Firchow. In *The Origins of Modern Critical Thought*, ed. David Simpson, 188–91. Cambridge: Cambridge University Press.

Schleiermacher, Friedrich. 1985. "General Hermeneutics." Trans. J. Duke and J. Forstman. In *The Hermeneutics Reader*, ed. Kurt Mueller-Vollmer, 73–86. Oxford: Blackwell.

Simpson, David, ed. 1988. *The Origins of Modern Critical Thought*. Cambridge: Cambridge University Press.

Sontag, Susan. 1972. "Against Interpretation." In *20ᵗʰ Century Literary Criticism: A Reader*, ed. David Lodge, 652–60. London and New York: Longman.

Spinoza, Benedict de. 1987. *Tractatus Theologico-Politicus*. In *The Chief Works of Benedict de Spinoza*. Trans. R.H.M. Elwes. London: George Bell and Sons.

Staiger, Emil, Martin Heidegger and Leo Spitzer. 1990. "A 1951 Dialogue on Interpretation: Emil Staiger, Martin Heidegger, Leo Spitzer." *PMLA* 105: 3: 409–35.

Szondi, Peter. 1995. *Introduction to Literary Hermeneutics*. Trans. Martha Woodmansee. Cambridge: Cambridge University Press.

Thoreau, Henry David. 1997. *Walden: or, Life in the Woods*. Oxford: Oxford University Press.

Todorov, Tzvetan. 1968. *Qu'est-ce que le structuralisme? 2. Poétique*. Points edition. Paris: Seuil.

Vattimo, Gianni. 1997. *Beyond Interpretation: The Meaning of Hermeneutics for Philosophy*. Trans. David Webb. Cambridge: Polity Press.

Weinsheimer, Joel. 1991. *Philosophical Hermeneutics and Literary Theory*. New Haven and London: Yale University Press.

Wimsatt, W. K., Jr., and Monroe C. Beardsley. 1972. "The Intentional Fallacy." In *20ᵗʰ Century Literary Criticism: A Reader*, ed. David Lodge, 334–44. London and New York: Longman.

Wittgenstein, Ludwig. 1958. *Philosophical Investigations*. Trans. G.E.M. Anscombe. Oxford: Blackwell.

Young, Julian. 2001. *Heidegger's Philosophy of Art*. Cambridge: Cambridge University Press.

Žižek, Slavoj. 1991. *Looking Awry: An Introduction to Jacques Lacan Through Popular Culture*. Cambridge (Mass.) and London: MIT Press.

Žižek, Slavoj. 1992a. *Enjoy Your Symptom!: Jacques Lacan in Hollywood and Out*. New York and London: Routledge.

Žižek, Slavoj, ed. 1992b. *Everything You Always Wanted to Know About Lacan (But Were Afraid to Ask Hitchcock)*. London and New York: Routledge.

Žižek, Slavoj. 1994. *The Metastases of Enjoyment: Six Essays on Woman and Causality*. London and New York: Verso.

Žižek, Slavoj. 1997. *The Plague of Fantasies*. London and New York: Verso.

Žižek, Slavoj. 2000. *The Art of the Ridiculous Sublime: On David Lynch's Lost Highway*. Seattle: Walter Chapin Simpson Center for the Humanities.

Žižek, Slavoj. 2001. *The Fright of Real Tears: Krzysztof Kieślowski Between Theory and Post-theory*. London: British Film Institute.

Žižek, Slavoj. 2003. *The Puppet and the Dwarf: The Perverse Core of Christianity*. Cambridge (Mass.) and London: MIT Press.

Žižek, Slavoj. 2004. *Organs Without Bodies: On Deleuze and Consequences*. New York and London: Routledge.

Žižek, Slavoj. 2006. *The Parallax View*. Cambridge (Mass.) and London: MIT Press.

Žižek, Slavoj. 2008. *Violence: Six Sideways Reflections*. London: Profile Books.

Index

Lightning Source UK Ltd.
Milton Keynes UK
UKOW05f1611100717

305055UK00001B/288/P